Law in Society Series

Female Sexuality and the Law

Female Sexuality and the Law

A study of constructs of female sexuality as they inform statute and legal procedure

SUSAN S. M. EDWARDS

LAW IN SOCIETY SERIES

edited by

C. M. Campbell and Paul Wiles

Martin Robertson • Oxford

First published in 1981 by
Martin Robertson & Company Ltd.,
108 Cowley Road, Oxford OX4 1JF.

British Library Cataloguing in Publication Data

Edwards, Susan
    Female sexuality and the law.
    1. Rape — England
    I. Title
    364.1'532'0942   HV6569.G7

    ISBN 0-85520-382-X
    ISBN 0-85520-385-4 Pbk

Typeset in 10 on 12 pt English
by Pioneer Associates, Flimwell.

Printed on Publishers Antique Wove and bound in
Great Britain by Book Plan, Worcester.

Contents

Acknowledgements

This book arises largely out of research undertaken for a PhD thesis at the University of Manchester. Many people have in various ways provided enthusiasm and sustained my interest in the field of study. I would like to thank especially Dr D. H. J. Morgan whose support and advice were instrumental in the writing of this book. I would also like to thank Keith Soothill at the University of Lancaster who suggested that I write it. In this respect I would, of course, wish to acknowledge the series editors Paul Wiles and Colin Campbell for their continual assistance and Martin Robertson for its materialization.

The research itself would not have been made so pleasurable or the resources so readily accessible if it had not been for the kind and interested help of Ms Pat Cummings and Dr Alan Neville at the University of Manchester Medical Library who introduced me to the memorable Thomas Radford collection. To the librarians at the Manchester Public Library I owe a special debt of gratitude, and to Mrs Pat Hall who typed the manuscript with unfailing patience and precision I also extend many thanks.

Finally I would like to thank my friends, both interested and disinterested, for their love and generosity.

Susan Edwards
August 1980

To Abdul Redha

INTRODUCTION

The Social Control of
Female Sexuality

since a woman must wear chains [G. Farquhar]

INTRODUCTION

Female Sexuality and the Law proposes to examine the process by which the concepts of femininity, female sexuality, female criminality and female victimology come to influence and thereby inform the various negotiatory stages of the judicial process, and in turn to disclose the process of law as it reproduces these particular constructs, by studying the actual enactment of statute and the practice of law with regard to the processing of the complainant of a sexual assault. Since neither the theory nor the practice of law, nor the theory or the practice of medicine are truly impartial processes, an examination of the diverse sexual ideologies interposing in and thereby influencing the deployment of discretion in the decision-making process becomes a central concern. It seems particularly appropriate to begin this book with a preliminary statement of the extent of the social control of female expression as a topic of analysis in its own right before proceeding to investigate its particular connotation in the precise context of the legal management of sexual assault. The study then continues with an historical account of the intervention of specific constructs over the years as they are derived from medical, gynaecological, psychoanalytical and everyday discourses, and as these assumptions are assimilated and enshrined in statutes governing rape and indecent assault and as they are reproduced and perpetuated in the pre-trial, trial and post-trial procedures.

1

ORTHODOX APPROACHES

The diverse theoretical perspectives that have traditionally characterized sociological approaches to the problem of the oppression of women are conspicuous in their neglect of the role played by sexuality in this process. They have either displayed a tendency to evaluate women in their relation to the means of production, that is, their position in the productive process, or else have considered the question of female oppression as the consequence of reproduction of the division of labour by sex, which is again perceived within a materialist framework.

The rather more recent work on the position of women from a Marxist perspective has embarked on the inconsequential task of providing an account of the role played by domestic labour, i.e. housework, in the overall productive process. This is a consideration of only very tangential importance, which has rather surprisingly attracted a considerably more significant following than its relevance warrants.

Within the materialist framework, theoreticians attempted first and foremost to uncover the material bases of the subordination of women. Because capitalist society represents the most extreme form of exploitation and because of its peculiar system of exploitation, appropriation and distribution, it has been contended that the subordination of women, like that of the working classes, is at its severest under capitalism. Engels' formulation is most explicit: 'Here we see already that the emancipation of women and their equality with men are impossible and must remain so as long as women are excluded from socially productive work and restricted to housework, which is private' (1972, p. 152). But the view that the capitalist mode of production resulted in the bifurcation of the labour process along sex-gender lines — relegating women to the domestic sphere and men to the industrial sphere — is an oversimplification. The evidence suggests that the experience of women under capitalism has been characterized by diversity, not by uniformity. The class differences of women's experience were particularly sharp. For most women the experience of industrialization and emergent capitalism was made explicit in the exploitation of their labour in the mills, factories and sweated industries. They were to take on two roles — that of worker and that of houseworker. By contrast, their middle-class sisters experienced the oppression of isolation, boredom and imprisonment in domestic and family matters. During the 1850s, women and children constituted as much as 52 per cent of the total labour force. Female labour was a vital component of capitalism, ensuring that wages remained low and providing a reserve army of labour for seasonal and irregular employment. Engels predicted that this increasing participation of women in production would introduce substantive changes in the mode of reproduction. He also envisaged that with the 'passage of the means of production into common property' private housekeeping would become a social responsibility (1972, p. 83). Yet within this approach the role of the control over female sexuality goes unexplored in the overall oppression of women.

The other dimension from a materialist perspective that has been important in the evaluation of the position of women is the consideration of the fundamental division of labour by sex. This is expressed by Marx and Engels who write: 'The first division of labour is that between man and woman for child breeding' (Engels, 1972, p. 75). Disciples of this tradition have argued that the specific oppression of women arises from this biological division of the reproduction of the species for childbearing and childbirth. The result is that the cultural and ideological institutions of childcare and socialization of the young, together with the appropriate pattern of motherhood, relegate women to a subordinate role. In this context, childbirth and motherhood are perceived as atemporal phenomena in their specificity to women. By extension, female physiological and reproductive capacities determine the appropriate female role to the total exclusion of any alternative variables. Sexuality enters only as an appendage along with numerous other aspects important to the division of labour by sex. Sexuality is then not fully considered and Engels' attempt to account for it is only a token one.

In both these analyses the essential dimension of sexuality in female oppression has been obscured or else erroneously seen as wholly contingent on women's class position or else as the consequence of productive relations alone. These arguments are as confusing as they are unsatisfactory, providing only for an analysis of female sexuality as a 'superstructure'.

Since the regulation of female sexuality is a characteristic of

almost every social and economic formation, feminist anthro-
pologists in particular, in studying the general position of women in
pre-capitalist economies and the specific role played by female
sexuality in such formations, have started to provide an accom-
modation of this problem. It is perhaps something of a paradox that
the discipline of women's studies, whilst unorthodox in its subject,
has been orthodox in its methodology, which mistakenly extends
Marxist concepts to the analysis of female sexual status and thereby
overall position of women. The neglect of an adequate consideration
of this question has not arisen out of a disregard for the subject, but
rather is the result of an uncertainty and confusion concerning the
fundamental problems of analysis, and which particular theoretical
frameworks can best illuminate it.

Foucault (1978) identifies what is undoubtedly a central problem
encountered in any attempt to understand sexuality. He draws
attention to the tendency to patrol the boundaries of a discipline
and also points to the various strategies adopted for 'policing' and
delineating what may and what may not be thought (1978, p. 18).
The discipline of women's studies has been subject to this kind of
gatekeeping function of thought. However, the result in this instance
has been particularly devastating since many of the important
arguments 'can become silent for want of an appropriate structure'
(Rock, 1979, p. 76). The categories, taxonomies or units of analysis
used in the investigation of a certain problem tend to influence the
findings and also the conclusion of a given field of inquiry. Shanin
(1972, p. 351) has observed that the very conclusions that follow
from the investigation of a problem 'reflect both the phenomena
analysed *and* the applied scheme of analytical subdivision'. It is thus
not altogether surprising that if concepts are mistakenly deployed
the problem may be trivialized or totally misconceived, resulting in
the production of 'blind spots' in the field of knowledge. The
problem of the material basis and the reproduction of female sexual
control is such a 'blind spot' — a problem concealed by ignorance,
which can in part be explained by the persistent and rigid adherence
to orthodox methodologies. The result is that what is revealed in
these explorations is not *ipso facto* truth; similarly, what is concealed
is neither non-existent nor inconsequential. As Shanin again
maintains, 'The question is not which scheme of analysis is "right",
but what does each of them reveal'.

TOWARDS A THEORY OF FEMALE SEXUALITY

Certain more recent developments have shown great initiative in suggesting a more appropriate framework for the acquisition of female sexuality and the reproduction of a given system of sex-gender relations. The various developments in feminist anthropology, especially the attempt to locate sources of reproduction in non-capitalist formations, together with the efforts of various 'structuralist' enterprises to examine the mechanisms of psychic subordination, provide a springboard from which those issues central to female sexuality and its control might reasonably be considered.

Structuralist theory embraces a diverse yet interdisciplinary group of approaches (Marxist political economy, social anthropology, linguistics, psychoanalysis and the history of ideas) that, through their consistent emphasis on structure and on the *reality* of invisible underlying structures, to a certain degree achieve unification of the various and diverse traditions. Structuralism thus provides the most suitable framework within which to examine the control over female sexuality as it is structurally situated within the social fabric, since such an enquiry poses a number of questions relating to several disciplines. Structuralism is important for the disenchanted critic of Marxist thought, since it challenges the demonstration of the historicity of capitalism, and provides the opportunity for an independent analysis of pre-capitalist formations. Consider, for instance, the critique of capitalist economics advanced by Meillassoux (1972). In referring to Marxist economics, he asserts that the principal weakness is that the various concepts used to describe relations specific to capitalism are also used in the analysis of non-capitalist formations. 'Any kind of assets (tools, land, manure, etc.) are "capital" . . . ; any transfers of goods including stealing and giving, are "exchanges" . . .' (1972, p. 94). Meillassoux contends that these concepts are inadequate and inappropriate for the analysis of pre-capitalist formations. Following on from this, Godelier has similarly pointed out that whilst kinship relations are indeed economic relations it is not the case that all economic relations are based upon property (1977, p. 19). He further asserts that competition in a society should not necessarily be reduced to a 'mere market (of goods, power, values, etc.)'.

Structuralism also provides a potential link between theory and practice, a site in which particular problems might be resolved. Because of this, it is especially important in talking about the control over female sexuality as a general problem and also in eliciting its particular manifestations in law, medicine and everyday thought.

Despite the diversity of subject matter tackled by structuralists, Glucksmann, in a consideration of the work of both Levi-Strauss and Althusser, identifies five elements that might assist in providing a useful definition of structuralism more generally. Four of these five elements are especially important here. First, there is the epistemological dimension, which embraces the theory of the acquisition of knowledge and seems to characterize most elements of structuralism. Second, the philosophy of knowledge as a substantive world view is given some consideration. Third, the theory of knowledge provides a substantive hypothesis used to account for the object of study. Fourth, structuralism is characterized by a peculiar methodology concerned with essentially 'lower level prescriptions', either through experiment or the hypothetico-deductive method.[1] This methodology is particularly valuable for the study of sexuality in pre-capitalist and capitalist formations.

VIRGINITY – A COMMODITY?

At the very core of the control of female sexuality is the underlying structure of the virginity requirement. Engels approaches this question tangentially when he writes 'What for a woman is a crime entailing dire legal and social consequences, is regarded in the case of a man as being honourable or, at most, as a slight moral stain that one bears with pleasure' (1972, pp. 82-3). Moreover, Engels predicted that, with the passage of the means of production into common property, it might be accompanied amongst other things by a 'more lenient public opinion regarding virginal honour and feminine shame'.

The endeavour to protect virginity[2] or otherwise to control female sexuality is a feature of most societies ancient and modern, though the diverse efforts to achieve this particular end change form, depending on patterns of kinship, economic and power relationships (see Foucault, 1978, p. 122). The latent function of the virginity requirement discloses other processes at work. Virginity of women can be regarded in both economic and social terms. Godelier points out that, in primitive society, a woman is of crucial importance in the maintenance of communities 'through her reproductive and economic functions, and this importance makes access to women a necessary *social control'* (1977, p. 104; emphasis added). Meillassoux in *Femmes, Greniers et Capitaux* (1975) similarly maintains that '. . . power in this mode of production depends upon the control of the means of human reproduction: means of subsistence and women' (cited in Mackintosh, 1977, p. 120).

Taking the economic function, the concept of the 'exchange of women' recurrent in anthropological analyses of kinship and economic relations seems to be a basic point of departure from which control over female sexuality might be considered. This particular concept has been evoked in various ways to explain female subordination (see, for example, Levi-Strauss, Godelier, Meillassoux, Rubin, Aaby and O'Laughlin). In this process of exchange, women are treated as objects: sexuality is exchanged rather than labour power. In this way, we can talk of women as commodities, since their exchange generates wealth in the form of marriage presentations, bride wealth, bride price and dowry, and also produces a surplus in the form of 'a surplus destined for the functioning of the social structures (kinship, religion, etc.)' (Godelier, 1977, p. 110). At this point, a very useful analogy might be made between labour power as a commodity for exchange in an economic market and sexual celibacy as a commodity for exchange within a sexual market of kinship relations.

A commodity, strictly defined in Marxist terms, is characterized by its 'use' and 'exchange' value. It produces a surplus and a wage when labour power is exchanged, and it has a direct relation to capital. There are, however, some commodities that, although they do not bear a direct relation to capital, nevertheless have an economic function. In this sense the preservation of virginity and its exchange have certain similarities with the commodity form. Since use value is derived from the processes of production (either from the process itself or else from its properties), then virginity has a use value. Exchange value denotes the value relations established during the transfer of goods; it does not reflect the value of the commodity. The exchange value of virginity may not be represented in a wage form but it is represented by the individual possessions or presentations transferred to the father either directly or indirectly when his daughter is exchanged in marriage. This is recognized in most societies as dowry, bride price or bride wealth. (Dowry denotes the transfer of goods, usually from the parents to the daughter as pre-mortem inheritance to the bride, or else in the form of indirect dowry from the groom to the bride. In this latter instance, gifts are transferred first to the parents and ultimately to the bride. Bride price refers to the specific transfer of goods from the kin of the groom to the kin of the bride. This transfer is now also called bride wealth, since bride price tends to imply marriage by purchase — Goody, 1973, p. 2.)

Accepting this formulation, virginity might be expressed as a personal possession (rather than as strictly private property — Engels[3] makes this distinction clear when he explains that goods and resources with productive potential could be considered as property; whilst personal goods held by people individually are not property in the strict sense of the word). It has a precise economic function in that the practice of exchanging goods or gifts not only redistributes wealth, goods and possessions between families, but also implies the redistribution of wealth from the economic to the private sphere. In this way a woman is never in a direct relation with capital since transactions of this nature are made between men who 'own' and control female virginity and sexuality in their ownership of wives and daughters. Godelier recognizes this privileged position of men, although in merely stating 'But it is always *men* who exercise this control' (1977, p. 104) he fails to take up this question in a rigorous way. Goody observes that where wealth goes first to the father, in most cases he 'takes a cut' of the bride price (1973, p. 20). What the daughter then ultimately receives is substantially less than the value transmitted to her, and thus recognizes the appropriation of women as commodities.

Yet another issue crucial to the consideration of virginity as a commodity is the mystification of the process whereby virginity is ensured and appropriate behaviour reproduced. In this sense the *real* relations of male domination, female subordination and exploitation become hidden. Mystification is a particularly useful concept in the analysis of the control of female sexuality in capitalism. Within Marxist economics the concept of 'commodity fetishism' is used to denote objective reality that has the property of concealing the real essence of economic relations. Fetishism encapsulates two aspects: one considers the way in which the social objectivity of the forms of capitalist relations is reduced to natural objectivity, and another the way in which this social objectivity is reduced to social subjectivity. If the mystery of the commodity form entails mirroring for men a social character of their labour, also reflecting it as a natural property of things, then, in considering the emphasis placed on virginity of women and the related ideologies of female sexual passivity and the emphasis on ignorance in all sexual matters, virginity as a commodity mirrors the cultural character of sexuality. Sexual control is reduced to the 'natural property of things' and is thereby ascribed an immutable quality.

EXCHANGE OF WOMEN

The central characteristic accompanying most patriarchal structures and the virginity requirement is the 'exchange of women'. It is via this concept that a new consideration of women has been provided. Rubin (1975) focuses almost exclusively on the idea of the 'exchange of women' as an integral characteristic of pre-capitalist societies. In so doing she provides a theory of sex-gender relations, in that she separates the ideological relations of sex and gender from biological reproduction in a way Meillassoux and Godelier fail to do. Rubin abandons Marxist categories of analysis — like Meillassoux she considers them inappropriate. Instead, she favours the methodology of Levi-Strauss and Freud. The primary motivation for rejecting a Marxist type of analysis is consistent with the general stance adopted here, namely that the sexual control of women predates capitalism, and further, gender is a social product, acquired through language, that 'cannot always be explained in terms of economic forces' (p. 167). The basic unit of analysis in Rubin's account is kinship, which she stresses is 'the ostensible and empirical form of sex-gender systems'. The tendency to take kinship rather than the economy as the basic analytical unit has been also considered in various ways by Godelier and Meillassoux. Godelier, for instance, provides a trenchant critique of the erroneous tendency to regard kinship simply as a superstructure. He asserts that kinship and economics are not in fact separate. Indeed in some kinds of society kinship can function as 'relations of production, political relations, and as current ideologies' (1977, p. 123).

Rubin's main objective is to disclose the culturally specific forms of constructed sexual practices, and also the sexual division of labour. In this sense her analysis provides an important contribution towards the conceptual acquisition of sexuality and the construction of gender identity. She cryptically points out that 'Far from being the expression of natural differences, exclusive gender identity is the suppression of natural similarities' (Rubin, 1975, p. 177).

However, when she considers the usefulness of the 'exchange of women' she sees it as a problematic concept since these relations are culturally variable — in some cultures women are exchanged explicitly and overtly, whilst in others the exchange of women can be inferred. She uses the concept as 'a shorthand for expressing that the social relations of a kinship system specify that men have certain rights in their female kin'. The 'exchange of women' is by no means uniform and three types can be identified. First, there is the system wherein women are exchanged for one another: families exchange daughters for daughters-in-law. Second, there exists a commodity equivalent for the exchange of women, as in marriage. Third, there is the situation where women are exchanged as gifts, in the gift relation.

By locating the idea of 'exchange of women' at the centre of sex-gender rather than the definitive statement of kinship systems, Rubin provides an explanation of sexual asymmetry. This is extended in a study by O'Laughlin (1974), which goes some way towards providing what Godelier insisted was necessary — namely a scientific theory of 'kinship, politics and ideology'. In O'Laughlin's account we are directed to consider the various sexual ideologies that shore up sex-gender asymmetry, thereby contributing to the continual reproduction of sexual oppression. In focusing on the control over sexuality in pre-capitalist economies she does not, like Rubin, abandon Marxist categories and concepts. In fact, the methodology adopted involves a synthesis of both Marxist and anthropological categories by which an attempt is made to identify the process of sexual asymmetry in food prohibition. O'Laughlin analyses the 'sexual skewing' of food consumption of the M'bum Kpau in Tchad, Africa, where men only are permitted to eat surplus food (chicken and goats). She endeavours to show how a particular pattern of ideology might mediate contradictions such as this. She begins by locating the technical relations of production — namely the work process. Very little sex differentiation in agricultural practices can be observed. Yet in the actual social relations of production there is considerable differentiation and sexual inequality. For instance, it is the men who control the 'cash revenue of wives and unmarried sons'. Like Godelier, O'Laughlin stresses that men have the authority over resources and it is men who control bride wealth. Consequently, distribution is biased in their favour.

A contradiction is immediately apparent between the technical and the social relations of production. The structures of reproduction 'thus provide the link between economic infrastructure and politico-juridicial superstructure'. She distinguishes between three aspects of reproduction — of the means of production, the labour force and the relations of production. In the particular society under examination the material basis of male control is not the technically defined division of labour but instead is based on the control of women and surplus. Therefore there is a sexual asymmetry in the very appropriation of surplus labour.

The endeavours in the various arenas of structuralist anthropology to explore the problem of sex-gender relations has stimulated recent debate within the field of feminist anthropology (Young and Harris, 1976; Edholm, Young and Harris, 1977; Coward, 1980). The emphasis, however, has been on pre-capitalist structures. This may seem anachronistic in a study that sets out to consider the wider questions, means, mechanisms and forms of control since 1800 in particular. Their work is important because it proceeds from an examination of the acquisition of sexuality rather than defining the position of women as the product of the economic substructure. The central importance of sexuality has been recently stated thus: 'the control of sexuality must be regarded as a vital aspect of an analysis of women's subordination' (Bland *et al.*, 1978, p. 165). Some analyses have been more specific in their attempts to facilitate an understanding of the cultural acquisition of sexuality. Kinship increasingly becomes re-examined and relocated as the basic unit of analysis (Young and Harris, 1976; Aaby, 1977). Sex and gender are linked to the kinship, economic and ideological structures. The focus from here on is the continual reproduction of a given pattern of sexuality, such that

... the subordination of women in the reproductive sphere requires the massive dissemination of specific forms of sexual ideology (myths of masculinity, of motherhood, of maternal deprivation, of the primacy of heterosexual genital sex, etc.) in order to secure and maintain those unequal relations of reproduction. [Bland *et al.*, 1978, p. 171]

THE ACQUISITION OF SEXUALITY IN THOUGHT AND LANGUAGE

In considering how a system of sexual asymmetry and sex-gender relations is acquired and perpetuated, it is necessary to examine the way the continual reproduction of particular 'discourses' and institutional practices is secured. An important step in this direction is provided in the works of Foucault and Lacan. The emphasis in their exegesis is on the reproduction in ideas and in language of particular ways of perceiving and formulating social relations. Both authors provide an opportunity to examine the discursive and theoretical expressions as they define and thereby perpetuate a given system or pattern of sex-gender relations.

Foucault's work has been of a structuralist nature, since in his various studies on madness, knowledge and sexuality his principal endeavour has been the exposure of underlying mechanisms. However, in an interview in 1979, for reasons better known to himself, he totally abrogated any previous affinity he may have had with structuralism. This renunciation of a tradition that is inherent in his approach to all his works appeared to have arisen over the problem of power and his increasing emphasis on its importance. In a trenchant critique of structuralism, Foucault's main objection was that it tended to reduce every event and every structure to the same level (1979, p. 134).

One of Foucault's main concerns has been to examine the relation of knowledge to power. In *The Archaeology of Knowledge* (1972), knowledge is defined as being constituted by a whole set of practices, singularities and deviations, which may or may not acquire a scientific status. It is also taken to represent the space 'in which the subject may take up a position and speak of the objects' and is the field in which statements are defined and concepts appear. Lastly, knowledge is defined by the possibility of its use and appropriation. Foucault makes a crucial distinction between the use of knowledge and the formal rules by which it is governed. Thus he differentiates between the knowledge existing objectively in various disciplines about particular subjects or groups of subjects (*savoir*) and the knowledge that is subjective and is used to define those conditions by which a decision is reached about objects or subjects (*connaissance*). In examining the history of sexuality, the knowledge of sexuality constitutes both *savoir* and *connaissance* (1972, pp. 184, 15 n2).

This book provides a starting point for a consideration of underlying structure, particularly for the study of the knowledge of sexuality. Foucault explains how specific ideas are produced in discourses, which he defines as 'enigmatic groups of statements that are known as medicine, political economy or biology'. Dews[4] identifies *The Archaeology of Knowledge* as the middle period of Foucault's work, although it provides a basis for understanding his most recent work, *The History of Sexuality,* in which he is more specific: 'Indeed it is in discourse that power and knowledge are joined together' (1978, p. 100). In furnishing a theoretical basis, he writes

> instead of studying the sexual behaviour of men at a given period (by seeking its law in a social structure, in a collective unconscious, or in a certain moral attitude), instead of describing what men thought of sexuality (what religious interpretation they gave it, to what extent they approved or disapproved of it, what conflicts of opinion or morality it gave rise to), one would ask oneself whether, in this behaviour, as in these representations, a whole discursive practice is not at work; *whether sexuality,* quite apart from any orientation towards a scientific discourse, *is not a group of objects that can be talked about (or that it is forbidden to talk about),* a field of possible enunciations (whether in *lyrical, or legal language*). [Foucault, 1972, p. 193; emphasis added]

In this discussion Foucault maintains that such an archaeology would show how particular prohibitions, exclusions and limitations are linked to a particular discursive practice. This process of linkage is decisive, since it is through a specific location of prohibition and regulation of sexuality within discursive practices of law and medicine, for instance, that control over female sexual behaviour is secured. Foucault is not concerned with discovering the truth of sexuality but, more importantly, is attempting to reveal the way of speaking about it, and the way this is assimilated and integrated into a system of values and prohibitions.

In writing *The History of Sexuality,* Foucault moves to a position where sexuality is perceived not merely as a group of objects, enunciations, statements or prohibitions and regulations, but also as a question of power. In this work he systematically considers the diverse discursive practices in which past and present constructions of sexuality, and thereby prohibitions of sexual expression, have been contained. In so doing, the various underlying structures of thought and ideology are exposed. (The discursive practice refers to those things that may and may not be said, practised or spoken and that have a bearing on the same subjects, i.e. sexuality, or else represent similar levels of analysis or mechanisms of restriction.)

Following Godelier and Meillassoux, Foucault maintains that relations of sex gave rise 'in every society, to a *deployment of alliance*: a system of marriage, of fixation and development of kinship ties, of transmission of names and possessions' (1978, p. 106), thereby linking the cultural acquisition of sexuality to kinship structure. The specific question of the transmission of names and the symbolic order in its linkage to other structures is considered by Coward, Lipshitz and Cowie (1976), Kristeva (1977), Lacan (1977a) and Saadawi (1980). Foucault also points to the way in which sex is linked to the economy owing to the role it can play in the circulation or transmission of wealth, of which the body is the main relay since it produces and consumes.

However, the reproduction of sexuality is to be found in its 'privileged link with the law'. Here the laws that govern the *deployment of alliance* are built around a system of rules and regulations. The actual domain of control is directed towards women, children, procreative and perverse behaviour. Of particular relevance to our immediate concern is Foucault's thesis of the reproduction of sexuality in the discursive practices of medicine, psychology and psychiatry. (A consideration of these specific mechanisms of constraint is to be found in Chapter 3.)

The language of psychoanalysis in particular is a method by which the language and constructs of sexuality are effectively reproduced, thereby invidiously functioning as mechanisms of control over women. In his examination of the unconscious mind, Lacan (1977a) elaborates the role of language as the signifier in this process. His work is very much based on recent discoveries in structuralist anthropology and linguistics. Whilst Freud located fears, hopes and other unconscious experiences in basic biological differences, Lacan examines the social structuring and social acquisition of the unconscious through language. Within this analysis, the unconscious is articulated as the fundamental and most basic of structures hidden beneath an apparently conscious and lucid self-disposition. Language, writes Lacan, is the sign of the phallus; it is the 'symbolic order' of identifying with the father, writes Kristeva. If this is so, then language, rhetoric, signs and symbols within a culture are patriarchally ascribed and defined. The idea of the patriarchal word — or the paternal law in Lacan — is a new formulation whose originality lies in its presentation of the unconscious mind as an expression of language (Lacan, 1977b, p. 149) and in direct relation to a culture rather than to a biology of sexual differences.

There are, however, two aspects to the cultural acquisition of sexuality. The reproduction of the species occurs in the construction of sexual attitudes that place the woman as mother at the centre of a 'mystery of reproduction', whereby the family can function as the indispensable unit of production. Yet it is language in the name of the father that defines women, and it is this language that is hidden and mystified. Lacan provides the foundation of a materialist theory of the individual in the social process — the subject. The decisive contribution to the problem of analysis of sexuality is located in his attempt to accommodate sexual asymmetry via the construction of the unconscious attitudes in the reproduction of sex-gender relations. In this schematization, language is presented not merely as a means by which communication might be facilitated, but as a symbolic formulation that, inseparable from meaning itself, provides an elaboration of the subject in the socio-cultural formation. Hence, for Lacan, the essence of things becomes symbolized in the word itself and in its relation to other meanings, which ultimately are located in the unconscious.

In considering the category of the subject, some reconciliation is possible between psychoanalysis and Marxism through the concept of ideology, since in distinguishing between concrete individuals and concrete subjects, Althusser maintains that ideology transforms the individual into a subject (1971, p. 272). Although Lacan avoids the reduction of language to ideology, he asserts that language is not to be separated from it or to be conceived as in some way existing before it. Although not entirely clear, the distinction suggests that Althusser's formulation contains certain similarities with Lacan's treatment of the subject (men), the signifier (phallus), or symbol (figurative representation of male desire) (see Lacan, 1977a, pp. 280-91). Kristeva (1977) somewhat more lucidly explicates this relationship of sign to symbol: the phallus is the symbolic word and the subject is man or woman. Barthes has explained this formula in similar terms: the penis represents the sign, the phallus the signifier and the male the signified.[5] Hence it becomes clear that 'one may, simply by reference to the function of the phallus, indicate the structures that will govern the relations between the sexes' (Lacan, 1977a, p. 289).

Lacan's work is not merely restricted to a consideration of the individual (subject) in the symbolic system, but also examines the law of the 'Other', which delineates how the 'I' subject can function. In this way Lacan provides a means for examining both the way the subject is constructed, and also the process whereby the subject 'I' constructs other individual subjects in and through language. If the entry of the individual subject into language is sex-specific, so too is the symbolic construction of the conscious and unconscious of other subjects. It is this latter respect — especially the socio-cultural construction of the symbolic image of the female sexual unconscious and the application of the signifier to the individual subjects — that is particularly important for a consideration of the acquisition of female sexuality.

Kristeva points to the particular dilemma facing women's entry into language: 'In a symbolic productive/reproductive economy centered on the Paternal Word (the Phallus, if you like), one can make a woman believe that she *is* (the Phallus, if you like) even if she doesn't have it (the serpent—the penis) (Kristeva, 1977, p. 22). The Lacanian position then implies that there is an inbuilt structural necessity for paternal law and paternal power to be maintained. This is achieved via the structure of language itself whereby unconscious and conscious desires are structured and situated in language. Thus the phallus represents the paternal law where motherhood is subordinate and narcissistic.

And so sexuality is acquired via a vast and complicated array of structural mechanisms — of social organization, of kinship, of knowledge, of discourse, of language and of symbols — in which sex-gender asymmetry is inbuilt. These diverse theoretical approaches provide a basis from which the control of female sexual behaviour and identity might be interpreted. At this point it is time to examine the central concern of this book — a consideration of the assimilation and reproduction of sexual constructs in a specific legal context. Everyday legal practice provides a setting for an elaboration of the control over female sexuality through language, discourse and cultural organization.

THE LEGAL REGULATION OF FEMALE SEXUAL BEHAVIOUR

The regulation of female sexual behaviour finds one of its more resolute expressions in the law as it governs sexual relations (Foucault, 1978). This is particularly the case in the trial procedure for certain sexual offences where the burden of proof is on the prosecutrix. The system of classification of sex crimes reflects and enshrines certain widely held beliefs and assumptions about the nature of sex-gender asymmetry and appropriate styles of sex-gender conduct. However, the wide diversity of statutes governing sexual expression thwarts any provision of a general theory on the nature of the specific relationship of sex legislation to social or economic forces, although certain particular trends may be observed and their linkages clearly elucidated.

The range of sexual behaviour being regulated has resulted in a series of sex laws that are often contradictory and anomalous. Consider, for instance, the ten-year penalty in cases of homosexual assault as compared with the penalty of up to two years for indecent assault upon a female. This particular disparity finds further expression in the proposals of the Advisory Council on the Penal System for a reduction in certain sentences, for instance that homosexual assault should be punishable with up to five years whilst indecent assault on a woman remains a lesser offence punishable with two years. There are numerous other anomalies too, the most glaring being the definition of certain sex crimes such that a particular sex-gender bias is often institutionalized. The legal definition of rape provides one such example, since it encompasses exclusively the forcible penetration of the vagina by the penis, whilst the forcible insertion of objects and instruments into the vagina, such as curling tongs and broomhandles, is considered not nearly so heinous, being processed either as indecent assault or else as grievous bodily harm.[6]

The most productive way of examining sex laws is to observe the principal criteria behind the system of classification. The criterion of consent appears as the key factor, and results in a major division between activities that are illegal although the parties consent and activities that are illegal where the parties do not consent. In the first category there are three sub-divisions: certain kinds of sexual activity between men and women; sexual activity of a heterosexual nature with minors; and ritualistic whipping and related activity. The principle that has guided legal practice in this last context was expressed by Chief Justice Coleridge in the case of *R v Coney* 1882: '. . . The consent of the person who sustains the injury is no defence to the person who inflicts the injury'. He continued, 'An individual cannot by such consent destroy the right of the Crown to protect the public and keep the peace'.[7] However, providing that no serious physical harm is done, consent may be offered as a defence in such cases. The distinction between serious and non-serious physical harm has proved a very difficult line to draw, especially since in sexual matters the actual extent of the injury sustained often exceeds that which is initially agreed upon or anticipated. This particular problem lay at the crux of the decision in the *Donovan* case in 1934, where a girl of 12 received a severe beating with a cane, which exceeded that which she had initially consented to. Donovan was convicted of common and indecent assault, though this decision was reversed at an appeal hearing since the girl in question had consented.[8]

The second principal category of sex law statutes covers activities where consent is not a feature either in law or in fact. This category enshrines a specific sex-gender bias since it is sex-specific — regulating acts of sexual violence perpetrated against women almost exclusively, as in rape and indecent assault. In the definition and especially the legal management of these crimes are institutionalized certain assumptions about the sexual predilections of women. In this way the negotiation and processing of female victims of rape and indecent assault reveal a particular expression of the control over female sexuality within the legal system, and the linkage between law and the deployment of female sexuality.

PART 1

The Female Paradox

CHAPTER 1

Female Sexual Passivity
in Sexual Offences Statutes

It is generally true, that the males are more active, energetic, eager, passionate, and variable; the females more passive, conservative, sluggish . . . [Patrick Geddes]

INTRODUCTION

Since there is an approximate correspondence between sexual offence statutes and the accepted and appropriate pattern of male and female sexuality, it becomes imperative first and foremost to expose the underlying pattern of sexual typifications that inform the law. In focusing exclusively on female sexuality as it is socially constructed and as it is reproduced in sex laws, two pursuits are central. The immediate endeavour is to explain the recent developments in statutory law as it prescribes appropriate and inappropriate sexual behaviour. It is also necessary to provide some account for the way a given pattern of sex-gender relations and sexual asymmetry becomes institutionalized within the legal process.

From within the boundaries of statutory law, it is the sexual behaviour of men that immediately appears as the primary object of control. By contrast, the sexual behaviour of women seems to have been systematically excluded thereby contributing to the erroneous belief that men rather than women are the objects of legal control. In so excluding women, the law has done no more than to absorb and assimilate particular prevailing constructs of sexuality. Since the notions of male and female sexuality existing at any given time are, more often than not, contradictory and dissenting, the scenario is more complex than is immediately supposed. It is perhaps curious that most, if not all, laws prescribing the appropriate expression of the sexual impulse and sexual behaviour disclose a belief in the sexual passivity and ignorance of women, which sharply contrasts with the belief in the sexual activity of men.

The selection of the early nineteenth century as the decisive point of departure for the analysis of sex regulation in relation to society is by no means arbitrary. For two reasons in particular this historical moment marks a decisive juncture in the development of law and in the constructs of sexuality that inform it. First, from the beginning of the nineteenth century onwards, the definition, expression and proliferation of sexual offence statutes extended to incorporate a greater variety of sexual diversity than ever before encountered. Second, the procedural rules in trials for rape and related offences subjected the complainant to an increasingly detailed and onerous cross-examination as to sexual and moral character. Indeed, far from repressing sexual behaviour, the nineteenth century exposed and smoked sexuality out like a witchhunt at every available opportunity.

With regard to both statutory and procedural aspects of law, two conflicting beliefs are at work. By the very exclusion of women from the statutory definition, legislation upheld and enshrined the belief in female passivity. However, case law and procedural rules reflected a very different construct of female sexuality. My immediate concern is the extent to which statutes relating to sexual offences have been formulated and predisposed by an adherence to the doctrine of female sexual passivity. Women were excluded from offences involving no 'consent in fact' — as in rape and indecent assault — as well as from offences providing no 'consent in law' — as in homosexual offences (Brazier, 1975, p. 422) — since they were considered incapable of perpetrating any form of sexual activity, and by extension incapable of committing any sexual offence. Some consideration is given to historical analysis of this formulation, since the development and elaboration of law cannot be considered as a seamless and unchanging web throughout time. For instance, at some periods the influence of the doctrine of passive female sexuality is more marked than at others. The emergence of new statutes often marks certain significant transformations in social attitudes to female sexuality, or else suggests that certain beliefs have been called into question.

Three separate phases of development can be identified,

demarcated by certain legal watersheds that very often represent a change in emphasis within the law. In the first phase, 1800–61, sexual behaviour was regulated by several Vagrancy and Police Clauses Acts. The passing of the Offences Against the Person Act 1861, although little more than an exercise in the consolidation of previous laws, nevertheless represented an important legal juncture since, until 1921, the statutes that followed reflected certain changes in attitudes and opinions about the definition of female sexuality. By 1921, and indeed from 1921 to 1976, legislation and its interpretation within the courts reflected the emerging and rapidly growing ambiguities regarding the passivity of women, and also the various shortcomings of the legislature in its ability to reprimand women who had committed, for all intents and purposes, a sexual offence that the law was deemed incapable of recognizing since women were excluded from the statute.

PASSIVE FEMALE SEXUALITY IN EVERYDAY THOUGHT

To the nineteenth-century mind in particular, women were typically considered to be totally devoid of sexual feelings, desires or needs. William Acton remarked that women were not troubled by sexual feelings of any kind whatsoever. And the various schools within the medical and psychological disciplines, in their own particular ways, echoed this belief. During the latter part of the century, Cesaere Lombroso wrote that women were 'naturally and organically frigid'. Ellis summed up the mood of this period when he remarked '. . . it seems to have been reserved for the nineteenth century to state that women are apt to be congenitally incapable of experiencing complete sexual satisfaction, and peculiarly liable to sexual anesthesia' (1930, Vol. 3, p. 193-4). This deep-seated conviction in female passivity was extended to a consideration of femininity. This view is nowhere more strongly reinforced than by the medical profession. Clouston declared:

> The woman has developed more on the lines of sympathy, emotion, of wanting to please those she loves, yielding to a man's wishes, delighting in being mistress of a household, and loving children

passionately. She is the centre of the home-life, and revels in the knowledge that she is so. [1906, p. 198]

Women were even discouraged from obtaining knowledge about the structure and function of their own bodies and, even more so, about matters related to the sexual union. So the very heart of the paradox is contained here: female sexual expression was denied, whilst male sexual expression was increasingly and apparently articulated and regulated.

A possible explanation for the belief in female sexual passivity may be located in the fundamental biological distinction between the sexes. The structure of the genitalia resulted in a particular social construction of female and male sexuality being propounded by various institutions. The inversion of the vagina and the orthodox position adopted by the female during the act of coitus contributed to a conceptualization of women as essentially passive. The obvious protrusion of the penis resulted in male sexuality being construed as active. Female sexuality was not defined in its own right but was instead regarded as a response to male sexuality. Sexual asymmetry in social, medical and legal relations emanated from these fundamental dissimilarities in genitalia. Indeed, Geddes and Thomson, two eminent behaviourists writing in 1899, stated that the difference between the sexes depended on the greater sexual activity of the male, implying at the same time that the female sex was biologically incapable of an active sexual life. Whilst Engels insisted that sexual asymmetry arises from a fundamental division of labour by sex and the relegation of women to childbreeding, Geddes and Thomson offered a different explanation: 'Here, at the very first, is the contrast between male and female . . . The same antithesis is seen when we contrast, as we shall afterwards do in detail, the active motile, minute, male element of most animals and many plants, with the larger passively quiescent female-cell or ovum' (1899, pp. 18-19).

In fact, women who displayed anything other than total and complete sexual passivity and ignorance of related matters were often considered 'sick'. The working-class prostitute was regarded as suffering from an overproduction of male hormones and sometimes from chromosomatic imbalance. As for the aberrant ladies of the middle classes, their behaviour was frequently explained as resulting from gynaecological malfunction or else some form of mental abnormality. Such women were typically explained by Greg:

'In the other sex, the desire is dormant, if not non-existent, till excited; always till excited by undue familiarities; almost always till excited by actual intercourse'.[1]

The passive standard of sexual behaviour was predominantly a middle-class vision. The well-known and often quoted adage 'Polite ladies musn't move' meant just that. Middle-class ladies found themselves trapped in sexually passive and suffocating roles by discursive practices of appropriateness that emphasized polite and decorous behaviour and especially stressed virginity and chastity. This essentially bourgeois idea of female sexual passivity was enshrined in a belief in the superior moral behaviour of the middle class. The proclaimed passivity of women was important in upholding and maintaining a class system, and was revealed at each and every level of the superstructure — in education and the media, in art, literature, medicine and law, in both formal institutions and discursive practices.

The statutes regulating sexual behaviour represent an explicit statement of notions of passivity. Indeed, the processes involved in the formation of statutes are particularly illuminating. The various Criminal Law Amendment Bills of the 1880s, for example, disclose very clearly indeed the extent to which models of sexuality inform law in the making. The debates of the second half of the nineteenth century in particular expose the dual-pronged attack of a parliamentary monopolistic patriarchy in imposing sexual passivity and appropriate gender roles, especially where women of their own class were concerned.

Femininity was also derived essentially from a model of passivity. This produced a discourse that provided for a passive construction of gender and social role. A corresponding and justificatory rationale and accompanying discourse were generated that upheld as virtuous the feminine traits of meekness, helplessness and innocence. A good woman was devoted to her family, to domesticity and to the adoration of her husband. She was to recognize and acknowledge his supreme position and, by the same token, she was expected to be obedient and subservient. Correspondingly, the law demanded the complete complicity of the wife with the wishes and desires of the husband. In marriage she was the servant, and he the master. Marx wrote: 'The modern family contains in embryo not only slavery (*servitus*) but serfdom also . . .' (Engels, 1972, p. 68).

The image of the socially passive and goodly wife was made

explicit in literature. It was personified in Coventry Patmore's portrayal of the domestic saint 'The Angel in the House' in the early nineteenth century. By 1860, this passive vision of femininity had undergone little real change. John Ruskin, in 'Lilies. Of Queens' Gardens', eloquently reiterated the adoration of female passivity. During this time, growing feminist criticism of the subordination of women and their lack of social and political status resulted in various male writers extolling passivity almost as a palliative, such that passivity was from thereon defined as woman's power and strength. Ruskin, in particular, praised the power and strength of women although it was really little more than a ploy to encourage women to accept their inferior status. He spoke of the power of a woman over her children and her husband. She was presented as the centre of order and the balm of distress: 'the woman's power is for rule, not for battle — and her intellect is not for invention or creation, but for sweet ordering arrangement, and decision'.[2] In 1876, in a Letter to Young Girls, he stresses the importance of female subservience to men. He asserts that women should be doubly submissive, first to God and second to those whom God has 'given you for superiors'. He continues, 'And you are not to submit to them sullenly but joyfully and heartily'.[3] In literature, as in science, within the everyday workings of institutions and within discursive practices, women were thought to be socially as well as sexually passive.

The passivity of feminity also found expression in law. Consider, for instance, Mr Beresford Hope's opposition to the second reading of the Women's Disabilities Removal Bill in 1872. He commented that a woman's heart ruled her head, and whilst he praised her for such sensitivity it would be disastrous in politics, leading to reckless expenditure on philanthropic schemes.[4] The reproduction of this construct of passivity in both social and domestic affairs, together with the fundamental conviction that female passivity was natural, led inevitably to the reification of an 'order of things', which resulted in a fierce resistance to change of any kind. Few people were of the mind of J. S. Mill who argued that woman's position was the product of 'a given system of cultivation'.[5]

MECHANISMS OF DESEXUALIZATION

The passivity of women in outward appearances and behaviour, if not in inner impulses and desires, was achieved via an overwhelming emphasis on the desexualization of all things animate and inanimate. Desexualization of women in particular was regarded as a virtue. In women the desexualized image became part of the concept of the good wife and mother, frequently portrayed as innocent and immature. The desirability of innocence and immaturity of women is aptly expressed in Dickens' character Dora Copperfield, whose innocence was seen as both goodly and saintly. Deborah Gorham in her study of white slave traffic (1978) observed that many of the young moral reformers considered the young prostitutes to be sexually innocent and essentially passive victims.

Thus ignorance in all matters relating to sexual union, the structure of the genitalia and the functions of the reproductive organs and childbirth was considered both honourable and virtuous. Writing in the early nineteenth century, Jeremy Taylor stressed this: 'Virgins must contend for a singular modesty; whose first part must be an ignorance in the distinction of the sexes of their proper instruments' (quoted in G. R. Taylor, 1958, p. 101). Sir James Paget, a physician of some eminence, remarked that ignorance of such matters was not only an asset but also a characteristic of 'civilized society'. Throughout the nineteenth century there was an emphasis on ignorance in sexual matters in both literature and Parliament. In 1883, Lord Mount-Temple, like many other 'noble' lords and parliamentary members, considered it his duty to save women from moral pollution. He referred to a particular criminal trial heard at Winchester where the judge advised the women present to leave the courtroom. In spite of this advice, 'some well dressed women seemed to have made up their minds to remain'. The judge then retorted: 'Now that all the respectable women have left the Court, the case may proceed.' Lord Mount-Temple said that the women left, not wishing to appear lacking in respectability.[6]

Indeed, throughout the nineteenth century any public discussion of sexual matters was considered indecent. Various agencies reflected this prohibition, from medical education to the media. The middle-class press for the most part refrained from any discussion of prostitution or other matters of a sexual nature, such as sexual offences. For the readers of the *Illustrated London News* and *Punch*, for instance, such evils did not exist. Most sex crimes were under-reported in the media, and the real details were often obscured by the frequently used phrase: 'the details of the case were unfit for publication'. Instances of rape, attempted rape, indecent assault and — towards the end of the nineteenth century — 'gross indecency between males' were rarely, if ever, reported. The press preferred to describe such events with polite euphemisms, such as 'gross outrage', or 'aggravated assault'. Yet since these terms were not always confined to sex crime reportage, their use led to a great deal of ambiguity.

This preoccupation with desexualization and the specification of ignorance in all matters had its backlash too. Women knew little about their own bodies and were totally uneducated in matters relating to reproduction and childbirth. In fact, surprising as it may seem, it was not uncommon for a woman to give birth without any prior knowledge of her own pregnancy.[7] However, ignorance in matters related to reproduction was not confined to women themselves. Midwives and so-called obstetricians and gynaecologists were also insufficiently versed in the physiology of the reproductive life-cycle and childbirth. It was not until 1902 that legislation was introduced that required the appropriate training and regulation of midwives, while the study of gynaecology was withheld from medical schools. Matilda Blake, a nineteenth-century feminist, alluded to this appalling anachronism in English law. In 1878 dentists were required to register by Act of Parliament, followed in 1883 by veterinary surgeons; the health of women and children was to follow and not to lead.

F. W. Newman remarked that young men in the public hospitals and medical schools should not study female disease and female anatomy (quoted in Cominos, 1963, p. 46). Dr E. J. Tilt, in a paper on the diagnosis of sub-acute ovaritis, actually proposed that the examination of unmarried women should be delayed as long as possible to avoid wounding the feelings of the patient.[8] Dr Reid stated that in 1870 a medical student could take his clinical midwifery by simply paying his fee: 'He could attend his cases all through without ever having seen another confinement or knowing anything whatever about the matter'.[9]

Shame and humiliation accompanied ignorance, especially regarding those 'private areas'. Women endured, suffered and often eventually died as a result of some gynaecological disorder. Physical discomfort was usually infinitely preferable to the shame incurred by an examination by a male practitioner. Female patients were even further deterred from disclosing details of their gynaecological problems to male practitioners since disorders of a gynaecological nature were often considered the consequence of sexual impropriety. Indeed, the resolute and steadfast determinedness of Elizabeth Blackwell in her strivings to become a medical practitioner was in part the result of her own disaffection with the male-dominated medical enclave, and also the death from cancer of a close friend, who had said: 'If I had been treated by a lady doctor, my worst sufferings would have been spared me'.[10]

The desexualization of women together with their lack of legal, social or political standing resulted in their exclusion from medical schools. The vociferous resistance to the admission of women was voiced in the *Lancet* of 1871 where the campaign to permit women to enter the profession was considered as 'morbid agitation'. Bennett, writing in *The British Medical Journal* (16 February 1878), asserted that the admission of women would result in the immediate deterioration of the profession (p. 244) — a view that was widely supported. John Stuart Mill, a decade earlier, had anticipated this barring of doors to women when mentioning (in a debate in Parliament to extend the franchise of women) the experience of Miss Garrett, who was accepted only by The Society of Apothecaries — though they thought it 'objectionable . . . that women should be the medical attendants even of women'.[11]

Women were similarly excluded from participation in almost all other forms of public life. Their necessary confinement to the appropriate social tasks of their sex was given repeated emphasis. Many statutes passed during the nineteenth century affecting the lives and liberties of women denied them entrée into spheres of public life by exploiting those arguments that laid stress on the passivity and weakness of the female sex.

The various parliamentary debates preceding the passage of particular statutes illuminate how certain important decisions were actually made. Interestingly, even those members who were active in supporting the campaign for the extension of rights for women adhered to the belief in the essential passivity of women, although they devised very different solutions for the problem of female weakness than did the opponents of such measures. Most of the reform movements of the nineteenth century reflect a commitment on both sides of the House to the ultimate goal of the protection of women. Consider, for example, The Married Women's Property Bill. This was first moved by Sir Erskine Perry, who said in the

House: 'If there must be any difference between the rights of husband and wife, the woman ought to be the favoured party, for she was the weaker, and assuredly stood more in need of the protection of the law'.[12] By contrast, honourable members opposing the Bill to extend property rights to women agreed with the opinion that women were weaker than men but did not regard it as appropriate to extend rights to them independently. In fact, they thought independence would lead to gross irresponsibility. Mr Butler feared that financial independence would result in women investing large sums of money in worthless railway shares or else finding themselves in debt or, worse still, being bailed out of prison (*The Times,* 16 July 1856). Mr Lopes, in his objection to such measures, was more concerned with the disruption to family life such economic independence would bring. Moreover, it would lead to immorality, since Karslake conceded that it would enable women to say: 'I have my own property, and if you don't like me I can go and live with someone who does'.[13]

The movement for the extension of the franchise to women was opposed and supported by the self-same rationales. Supporters maintained that the female sex was in need of protection, whilst opposers declared that, as women were already protected by men, no reform was necessary. The opponents of women's emancipation considered that it would debase and degrade women. Mr Karslake remarked: 'She would be in danger of losing those admirable attributes of her sex — namely, her gentleness, her affection, and her domesticity'.[14]

Yet the various legislative measures (both those proposed and those passed) claiming to protect passive women are contradictory and reveal the paradoxical status of women in society. The measures relating to provisions regarding the guardianship of infants are a classic example. Throughout the nineteenth century, and even after the passage of the Guardianship Acts of 1883-4, mothers were denied legal status or recognition as guardians of their own children in their own right. In art, in literature, in medical discourse and in everyday practice, the virtues of the wife and mother were extolled. But the law granted these beliefs no validation whatsoever. On the other hand, so long as the appropriate role for women was seen to be within the enclave of the family and the household, the various efforts by women to enter the professions were persistently challenged.

The experiences of working-class mothers were similar; they too were denied guardianship rights, yet they competed alongside men in appalling working conditions. Their participation in the workforce, in sweated industries, mills and agricultural work went unchallenged. Sachs explains:

> The fact that millions of women, both married and single, worked in paid employment outside the home, showed that there was no overwhelming biological or cultural aversion to women working for cash. There was nothing intrinsic to the female condition, no special frailty, that the male legislators and judges were bent on respecting. [Sachs and Wilson, 1978, p. 59]

The patriarchal claim to protect female sexuality and femininity, because women were after all passive and weak, had little foundation in reality.

'MALE PROTECTIVENESS' IN MARRIAGE

The worship of the passivity of women, in sexual as in other matters, and the desire to protect women, which was so repeatedly and fervently expressed throughout the nineteenth century, came into full flower in the laws regulating marriage. Here, perhaps more consistently than anywhere else, is revealed the desire to protect; and yet the law enshrines the husband's right to batter, abuse, intimidate and rape at will. Since women were defined as passive, they were afforded few, if any, legal rights. Far from being protected by men, they were appropriated.

In marriage a wife was owned by a husband and had a monetary value as any other goods or services. Prior to the royal assent of the Matrimonial Causes Act 1857, s59, a husband could bring an action for damages against his wife's seducer, adulterer or rapist, even if the wife had previously deserted him. Such civil actions were known as *crim cons* (criminal conversation) and enabled the husband to issue a 'writ of ravishment or trespass *vi et armis de uxore rapta et abducta*' under which he could obtain damages against a defendant who had taken his wife away (Bromley, 1976, p. 123). Compensation for the loss of a wife's services provided a form of monetary redress for a husband's wounded honour. No such action or similar redress was available to the wife. In the case of *Macfadzen v Olivant* (1805), a plea of trespass was proposed wherein the defendant with 'force and arms made an *assault* upon

G. the plaintiff's wife, and then and there seduced her, *whereby* the plaintiff during all the time aforesaid lost and was deprived of the comfort, society, and fellowship . . .'. In summing up, Lord Chief Justice Ellenborough declared that, since the body and mind of the wife had been corrupted, the wife was 'less qualified to perform the duties of the marriage state'.[15] In 1825, in *Cox v Kean,* Cox brought an action for damages against Kean, his wife's paramour. This particular case became a *cause célèbre* since at that time Kean was at the pinnacle of his career as a professional actor. Kean was entitled to a verdict in his favour if he could prove that the plaintiff had condoned his wife's behaviour. Moreover, if he could show that the plaintiff's wife had lapsed from virtue before their liaison, then he would only be required to pay nominal damages (Playfair, 1969, pp. 12-44).

Under the 1857 Act, *crim cons* were abolished, being replaced by a statutory claim for damages (s33), which provided for the following: the husband had power of control; the wife was his child; the wife's earnings were seized by the husband; and the wife was subjected to physical punishment. In such instances, the 'value' of a wife was assessed on two grounds: pecuniary 'value', which was assessed according to her moral character, and injury to a husband's feelings. In *Lynch v Knight* (1861), Lord Wensleydale declared that the loss of a wife's consortium (sexual congress and household duties appropriate to the female role) 'is of material value, capable of being estimated in money'.[16] In certain consortium actions the 'reputation for chastity' of a wife would affect the amount awarded for damages. In consequence, the loss of the consortium of an immoral wife, even though she may well have been good, kind and gentle, was considered far less important than the loss of a moral wife, even though she may have been aggressive and slovenly and cruel. In such actions, a clear distinction emerges between the wife who encourages or precipitates such behaviour to take place and the wife who is seduced. Thus two categories of the immoral woman were created. In *Keyse v Keyse and Maxwell* (1886), Sir James Hannen said to the jury: '. . . you are not here to punish at all. Any observations directed to that end are improperly addressed to you'. He then explained the principle of loss: 'If he did not seduce her away from her husband that makes a very material difference in considering the damages to be given'.[17] This principle was reiterated in *Butterworth v Butterworth* (1920), where Judge McCardie declared: 'If the wife be of wanton disposition or disloyal instincts, it is obvious that her general value to the husband is so much the less'.[18] Again in *Comyn v Comyn and Hump* (1860), Mr Justice Cresswell declared, 'If a woman surrenders herself very readily to a man, who takes no pains to obtain her affections, or if you have reason to suppose that she has made the first advances, you are to estimate, as far as you can form an estimate in money, the loss the husband has sustained'.[19] In *Darbishire v Darbishire* (1890), Sir James Hannen declared: 'Now, remember, there is a particular distinction between the value of different wives . . . if she has led a loose life before marriage, her value is not the same as that of a virtuous woman . . . If a man's wife goes and walks the streets, the husband is not entitled to come here and recover damages against any man who goes and consorts with that woman'.[20]

The general consortium action was not confined to a husband's rights to the consortium of a wife, but also embraced fathers' rights over daughters. The Offences Against the Person Act of 1861, s53, provided that, in the event of the abduction of a daughter 'against the will of the father', a father could bring an action for the loss of services of his daughter. A similar action could be brought against a person who enticed away a servant (Puxon, 1967, p. 34). In *Smith v Kaye* (1904), where a married woman was enticed away from her husband, Mr Justice Wright reiterated this principle in summing up, ruling that the husband has the right to the service and society of his wife, just as a father has the right to the service of his children. Again, the question that had to be decided was under what circumstances she left her husband. Only if she was persuaded, induced, incited or procured to leave should damages be awarded.[21] These principles applied similarly in cases of seduction of daughters.

So much for the protection afforded to women in law. It appears from the consortium action that they were not protected but owned as property — their worth being estimated according to their chastity value. The right to consortium of a wife extended beyond the award of damages to a wounded husband in the event of his wife's adulterous behaviour; it encompassed the 'right to rape'. In *The History of the Pleas of the Crown* first published in 1736, Hale asserted,

> But the husband cannot be guilty of a rape committed by himself upon his lawful wife, for by their mutual matrimonial consent and

contract the wife hath given up herself in this kind unto her husband, which she cannot retract. [Hale, 1971, p. 629]

It is worth noting the remarks of the judge in *Smith v Kaye* disclosing the double standard: 'Apparently the law takes the view that the wife has no such right of control or claim to a husband's services as is possessed by the husband with regard to the wife'.[22] He continued by saying that the wife had made a contract that she could not retract. The principle of the 'right to rape' was enshrined in *R v Clarence* (1888), which stands as a test of the Hale doctrine. Mr Justice Hawkins, the presiding judge, declared:

> The sexual communion between them is by virtue of the *irrevocable privilege conferred once for all on the husband* at the time of the marriage, and not at all by virtue of a consent given upon each act of communion, as is the case between unmarried persons.[23]

Thereby firmly establishing as a precedent the husband—wife rule (see Mitra, 1979).

During the nineteenth and twentieth centuries several actions for rape by a husband were brought by the wife. In *R v Jackson* (1891), in a case where the husband enforced his conjugal rights, Halsbury held that a husband could be convicted of assault in this case, but could not be convicted of enforcing his conjugal rights.[24] During the twentieth century, certain technical exceptions to this rule have evolved. Consider, for instance, the case of *R v Clarke* (1949) where Mr Justice Byrne decided that a husband could be found guilty of raping his wife if a separation order had been granted, since such an order would automatically revoke her consent to intercourse.[25] In *R v Miller* (1954), Mr Justice Lynskey decided that a husband could be found guilty of rape if he and his wife had entered into a separation agreement containing a non-molestation clause. In this particular case there was no separation order or agreement in force. The judge held that the husband could not be guilty since there was no evidence in law that the wife's consent had been revoked.[26] The principle in *Clarke* was extended to *R v O'Brien* (1974).[27] The judge declared that where a *decree nisi* brings the marriage to an end, a husband could be found guilty of rape. And, more recently, a husband can be guilty of rape after his wife has obtained a non-molestation injunction.[28] The real extent of this prodigious desire to protect women can be summed up in the words of Lord Dunedin when he talks about the exercise of gentle violence:

If the wife is adamant in her refusal the husband must choose between letting his wife's will prevail, thus wrecking the marriage, and acting without her consent. It would be intolerable if he were to be conditioned in his course of action by the threat of criminal proceedings. [Smith and Hogan, 1973, p. 325]

The absence of the consent to intercourse on the part of a wife 'wrecks' the marriage, whilst the rape and violence against a wife that the law institutionalizes apparently do not, but by force hold it together. On the whole, the exemption of husbands from charges of rape brought by a wife has remained (see Maidment, 1978).

The desexualization of women, the denial of rights and the ascription of passivity to all women were assisted by their effective incorporation into the wider social and moral system of goodness. This provided yet another mechanism in the control of women. The sexually passive woman was perceived as a good mother, daughter or wife, whilst the woman who was not passive was altogether bad and sinful. Dostoevsky's portrayal of Sonia Semenovna as an 'innocent prostitute' and Sonia Andreievna as a 'saintly adulteress' satirizes the orthodox conception of the relationship of chastity to morality. In sociological parlance, the process of stereotyping describes the components at work. The most significant point to be made is that when a woman is thought to behave in a way that contravenes the appropriate sexual stereotype of female behaviour, then all other undesirable traits are attributed on the basis of this one activity.

The image of female sexual passivity and femininity was largely confined to bourgeois idealist views of women. Passivity came to symbolize the chaste middle-class lady. Working-class women were not seen as chaste or as ladies and the *deployment of sexuality* had little influence over their behaviour (Foucault, 1978, p. 121). Working-class women were therefore considered aberrant, but the middle and upper classes had their deviants too, who kicked against the stupefying system of female passivity.

Two disparate types of deviant emerged who were unified in their deliberate attempts to defy the convention of passivity. From 1860 onwards an increasing number of women voiced their opposition to the socially constraining role expected of women. Their defiance was political. The hostility, ostracism and derision experienced by Josephine Butler, Millicent Fawcett and Lydia Becker was due to their public rejection of the passive role considered appropriate for women. Josephine Butler railed against patriarchal laws in launching a vociferous campaign against the contagious diseases legislation of 1864 and 1866 in an effort to repeal the Acts. Millicent Fawcett's opposition was marked by her organizing the Women's Social and Political Union, whilst Lydia Becker edited the *Women's Suffrage Journal,* which exposed patriarchal asymmetry and male domination at each and every level.

At this time there was growing pressure from certain groups endeavouring to educate women in matters of birth control. Such efforts encountered fierce opposition. In 1876-77 Parliament decided to prosecute the English publisher of Knowlton's *Fruits of Philosophy*, a book that discussed the advantages of birth control. The response of Charles Bradlaugh and Annie Besant was to organize The Free Thought Publishing Company, which produced a new edition of this prohibited book. Their defiant action resulted in criminal prosecution being brought against them. This type of legal repression also followed the publication of Dr H. A. Allbutt's *Wife's Handbook*, which like Knowlton's treatise addressed the very taboo subject of birth control. As a result of the persistent agitation and pressure of the Leeds Vigilance Association, Allbutt was removed from the Medical Register. The repression or prohibition of discussions of sexual matters and especially concerns related to female sexuality persisted into the twentieth century. The tremendous and courageous efforts of Marie Stopes's birth control programme for the education of working-class women met with fierce opposition and hostility. Despite the constant reiteration of the appropriate image of female sexuality and feminine passivity, the real lives of certain women denied such an image.

The greatest enshrinement of passivity, especially female sexual passivity, is observed in the legal institutions through the statutory definition of sexual offences legislation. Although the challenge to the doctrine of passivity had already begun, in law it was to persist for some considerable time longer.

FEMALE SEXUAL PASSIVITY
IN STATUTE

The social construction of the sexual passivity of women as it relates to sexual offences has not only provided the predominant model influencing the formulation of the various sexual offences' statutes during the nineteenth and the twentieth centuries. It has also informed the interpretation of statute by the judiciary. Although the doctrine of passivity has been the subject of recent dissension, it has nevertheless had a considerable impact within popular culture and the law since the early nineteenth century.

In statute, only men were considered capable of actively committing a sexual offence, although a woman may passively permit an offence to be perpetrated against her. This belief has only recently been challenged. The ability or inability to commit a sexual offence is a judgement derived essentially from the doctrine of sex-gender asymmetry in sexual relations, where the male advances whilst the female acquiesces. Hence the predilection to commit a sexual offence arises essentially as the result of the symbolic power ascribed to the phallus. By contrast, the hidden structure of the vagina contributes to its passive ascription. The consequence of this is that men become defined as capable of committing sexual offences whilst women are seen only in the role of victims. This view has informed statutes from the definition of heterosexual activity where non-consent is in evidence, to homosexual acts, to crimes against the family and also to instances of sexual diversity. In each instance the role of women is defined as passive. Women may, however, permit, submit or consent to certain heterosexual or homosexual acts. Thus most crimes of a sexual nature are considered sex specific since they may be committed by men only.

However, there is another aspect to be considered here. Not only were women considered both physically and morally incapable of committing a sexual act but if on one occasion it came to light that a woman had indeed committed a sexual act, it was thought that no moral harm was done. In consequence, it has generally been the rule that woman cannot commit a rape, an indecent assault or a homosexual act. This remained the case until the 1930s when the statute relating to indecent assault was interpreted in a significantly new way. Taylor, commenting on nineteenth-century attitudes, remarked of the law:

> It would seem to be the Victorian assumption that women are devoid of sexual desire which is responsible for the fact that several of these regulations, passed in the last century, apply only to men. Thus the law does not provide for the contingency, by no means impossible, that a woman should abduct a boy, or that she should seduce a male imbecile. [1953, p. 311]

In 1948, commenting on the sexual offences statutes, Sir Norwood East similarly alluded to what he regarded as sex bias in the law. He claimed that the law had been more concerned with protecting women and girls from men than men and boys from women.[29]

The statutes relating to certain sexual offences held the protection of the virtue of women as their primary aim. Consider, for instance, the key objectives of the Criminal Law Amendment Act of 1885, which provided for the protection of women and girls, including the suppression of brothels. From 1800 to the present, sociological constructs of sexual passivity have influenced the formation of laws regulating sexual conduct. Disagreement over the social constructs of female sexuality, together with the redundancy of laws unable to prosecute women, have resulted in a growing awareness of the inaccuracy of the image of female passivity. Nevertheless, in general, women are still seen as passive within the statutory formulation. The history of the influence of this formulation is presented next.

RAPE AND RELATED OFFENCES

Historically and cross-culturally rape has been defined as an exclusively heterosexual crime involving the penetration of the vagina by the penis through force, fraud or fear, although the role of a woman as an accomplice has been recognized for some time. The Offences Against the Person Act of 1861, s48, stated: 'Whosoever shall be convicted of the crime of rape shall be guilty of a felony and being convicted thereof shall be liable . . . to be kept in penal servitude for life.' It was not until the late nineteenth century that the categories of force and fear were incorporated into the statutory definition. Previously it had been considered impossible to rape a woman who was an unwilling party, unless a great amount of violence accompanied the offence. In case law, the trial of *R v Camplin* (1845) established that evidence of force was not necessary to prove that rape had occurred. The judge decided that it was possible for a woman to be raped 'without her consent' as opposed to 'against her will', since in this case the complainant had been drugged with alcohol. Patteson J. delivered this judgment: '. . . a great majority of judges are of the opinion that the evidence that the rape was committed without the consent and against the will of the prosecutrix was sufficient'.[30] Impersonation or trickery was recognized in the trial of *R v Case* (1850) where a medical man fraudulently had intercourse with a 14-year-old girl by saying 'Then I must try further means with you' on the pretext that it would cure her of her complaint. Lord C. J. Wilde said 'Children who go to a dentist make no resistance; but they are not consenting parties'.[31] The recognition of fraud was central to the ruling in *R v Flattery* (1877) where a medical practitioner had told a female patient that a simple operation (carnal connection) would cure her of her complaint. He fraudulently told the prosecutrix, in the presence of her mother, that 'it was nature's string wanted breaking'.[32] There was still much dispute over consent since the decision in *R v Barrow* (1868) — 'where consent is obtained by fraud, the act done does not amount to rape' — was never overruled.[33] Nevertheless, it was decided that consent must be to sexual connection and nothing else if it was to amount to rape.

By 1884 the legal definition of rape, together with the various categories of force, fraud and fear, was discussed in the Committee stage of the Criminal Law Amendment Bill. Lord Bramwell moved an amendment that allowed for the possibility of rape by threats and intimidation, by false pretences and by fraud. The amendment resulted in a lengthy and prolonged debate in the House. The main point of conjecture was whether or not the commission of rape by false pretences was to be regarded as a misdemeanour. Mr Stanley proposed that any attempt to procure by threats or intimidation was indeed rape. The product of these various deliberations emerged in section 3 of the 1885 Criminal Law Amendment Act:

> Any person . . . By threats or intimidation procures or attempts to procure any woman or girl to have any unlawful carnal connection . . .
> or
> Any person . . . By false pretences or false representation procures any woman or girl, not being a common prostitute or of known immoral character, to have any unlawful carnal connection.
> or
> Any person . . . Applies administers to or causes to be taken by any woman or girl . . . anything . . . with intent to stupefy her . . . shall be guilty of a misdemeanour only.

Thus the contention proposed by Mr Hopwood and his supporters that rape by fraud constituted a misdemeanour only was given royal assent, and the decision of *Flattery* appeared overruled. Section 4 of the 1885 Act gave statutory credence to the vexed distinction between acts 'against her will' and acts 'without her consent'. However *R v O'Shay* (1898) established that if the consent of a

woman was obtained by fraud then the prisoner may be convicted
of indecent assault and not merely misdeameanour as laid down in
the 1885 Act.[34]

During the twentieth century, case law continued to make
judgments that influenced the decisions in future rape cases. In
1923, *R v Williams* involved the rape of a pupil by a choirmaster.
The choirmaster had successfully persuaded his pupil that a simple
operation might assist her in reaching the required notes. He said 'I
am going to make an air passage', and was charged and found guilty
under the 1885 Act of rape, since it was decided that consent and
submission obtained by fraud did not diminish the fact it was rape.[35]
Finally, by 1956, the Sexual Offences Act incorporated both
categories of fraud and fear. Section 3 asserted: 'It is an offence for
a person to procure a woman, by false pretences or false
representations to have unlawful sexual intercourse . . .'.

The history of the statutory law since 1800 as it relates to rape
reveals a concern to control the inappropriate sexual activity of
men. It is based on the belief that the ultimate threat to women is
the penetration of the vagina by the penis, which excludes the
possibility of the rape of men by women. (The possibility of rape
also excluded young boys, since males under 14 were considered
incapable of sexual intercourse. However, even if statute did not
accommodate this possibility, when it in fact occurred it was dealt
with as indecent assault.)

INDECENT ASSAULT

The interpretation of the legislation regulating indecent assault
committed by men on women, children and other men provides
particularly illuminating evidence of the instrumentality of sexual
asymmetry. For instance, the commission of an indecent assault on
a male child by a woman was particularly unthinkable to the
nineteenth- and early twentieth-century public mind and legal
profession, so statute declared that the crime of indecent assault
could be committed by a man only. In the Offences Against the
Person Act 1861, indecent assault on a woman is provided for in this
way: 'Whosoever shall be convicted of any indecent assault upon a
female . . . shall be liable at the discretion of the court to be
imprisoned for any term not exceeding two years.'

However, it is interesting that by the early decades of the twentieth century both the judiciary and Parliament alike expressed growing objection to many of the earlier interpretations of the 1861 statute, which had consistently excluded women from the definition of sexual assault. By the twentieth century the 1861 Act was given a far wider interpretation.

The case of *R v Hare* (1934) signifies a decisive turning point in both the interpretation and application of statute. In this case, the defendant Ms Hare was indicted on a charge of having sexual intercourse with a boy of 12, whereby he contracted venereal disease. As the boy had fully consented and participated in sexual activity, it was decided that a guilty verdict could not be returned since the defendant had passively permitted sexual intercourse to take place. As a result of the decision in *Hare,* the Court of Criminal Appeal allowed for a new interpretation of sections 61 and 62 of the 1861 Act. Mr Justice Avory delivered judgment:

> Having regard to the fact that the word 'Whosoever' in s.61 admittedly includes a woman and that the first part of s.62 admittedly includes a woman, there is no reason for saying that the phrase: 'Whosoever . . . shall be guilty . . . of any indecent assault,' does not include a woman.[36]

Given this new ruling, the concept of 'passive indecent assault' arose. It was from that moment onwards recognized that women could initiate sexual activity; nevertheless the legal conception still remained informed by a belief in the activity of male genitalia and passivity of female genitalia.

The question of the nature of female sexuality arose again in the judicial deliberations surrounding the decision in *Fairclough v Whipp* (1951). In this case, a girl of 9 alleged indecent assault by a man when she had been invited to touch his exposed penis. Lord Chief Justice Goddard remarked: 'It seems to me there must be an act done to a person'.[37] The possibility of indecent assault by a woman on a man was provided for in the Sexual Offences Act 1956, s15, whereby 'It is an offence for a person to make an indecent assault on a man', but it is material and necessary to prove that the woman did something to him or that she handled him indecently. The 1960 Indecency with Children Act created a new offence of committing an act of indecency towards a child under 14 or inciting a child. Hence in 1977 a court convicted a man for allowing a child to hold his penis. However, this Act made no provision for a woman indecently assaulting a young male child. The conception of female sexuality even then remained ambiguous in law. This was reflected in *R v Mason* (1968), in which a woman was indicted on a charge of indecent assault under section 15 of the 1956 Act. Her alleged crime was that she, with several boys aged 14–16, had participated in the act of sexual intercourse. The judge advised the jury that 'a woman who passively permits sexual intercourse at the suggestion of a boy of fifteen is not assaulting the boy. I have equally no doubt that, if the original suggestion came from her, it is still not an assault on the part of a woman'.[38] In consequence, the jury returned a 'not guilty' verdict. According to the judge's interpretation, it must be proved that she committed an indecent act and, although she handled the private parts of the boys before intercourse, it was considered that this could not be indecent assault. Nevertheless, the judge, in summing up, expressed his personal disapproval: '. . . she has behaved in a wholly disgraceful way and in a way which many imagine many harlots would be ashamed'.

This case clearly shows the difficulty of sustaining a charge of indecent assault by a woman on a boy, since consenting sexual relations have developed a pattern where the woman submits. Consider the Rt Honourable Mr Justice Wien's comments in *R v Upward* (1976). The female defendant had participated in intercourse with several boys under 16 and was indicted on a charge of indecent assault. The presiding judge ruled that a woman could not commit a sexual offence simply by having intercourse with the boys: 'It has never been an offence for a woman to have sexual intercourse with a boy, perhaps for the simple reason that Parliament has never thought it fit to legislate for it, or alternatively it may be that Parliament, which passes these Acts, takes the view that no great moral harm is done' (*The Guardian* 8 October 1976). However, a case in 1979 clearly heralded a change in the attitude of the court to such women, since the defendant was found guilty of indecent assault after having intercourse with a 14-year-old boy. However, in giving her a two-year probation order, the court reflected its reluctance to punish the offence (*Daily Mail*, 24 July 1979).

These particular cases, which follow the ruling in *Hare* (1934), reflect the tremendous ambiguity with which female sexuality can be held before the law and the changes in the legal conception of female sexuality during the last 50 years, which are confusing and difficult to unravel. If a woman engages in an act of sexual intercourse with a boy under 16, she cannot as a rule be found guilty of indecent assault because her role is the passive one. A boy under 14 cannot be guilty of rape because he is deemed mentally and presumably physically incapable, and yet he is capable of intercourse in the case of indecent assault. The notion of female sexual passivity persists in the law unless the prosecution can prove that the woman actually did something to the male — verbal suggestions by the defendant are not enough.

INDECENCY BETWEEN FEMALES

The nineteenth century was particularly characterized by a belief in the sexual passivity of women. Since sexual activity in women in heterosexual relations was not recognized, it is not altogether surprising that homosexuality between women appeared as an anachronism. Lesbianism was recognized by the medical profession, which understood it as a dysfunction of chromosomatic or physiological origin, but the law did not recognize, even less make provisions for, its regulation. The denial of such activity in society and law reflects the complete abnegation and abrogation of female sexuality.

By contrast, homosexuality between men was rigorously dealt with. The Offences Against the Person Act, 1861, explicitly provided for a wife to obtain a divorce from her husband if he were a homosexual. (Lesbian activity, on the other hand, was not identified as constituting grounds for a divorce action until the 1940s, when it was accepted as material evidence of cruelty to a husband.) By 1885, the Criminal Law Amendment Act regulated acts of 'gross indecency' between males, extending the law to all homosexual activity other than buggery. The widely held rumour that lesbianism was not introduced because Queen Victoria thought it impossible has little or no foundation (see Pearsall, 1969, p. 576; Cohen *et al.*, 1978, p. 95). However, the existence of lesbianism was acknowledged by Mr Justice Lopes in 1885, even though he may have stood alone in this matter. In presiding in the Armstrong case he concluded that indecent assault could be committed by a woman, since striking or touching of another person, without his or her consent, was an assault. If the assault were to be accompanied by indecent circumstances, then it was indecent assault.[39] Some years later, in 1913, an MP tried to bring the existence of sexual activity between females to the attention of the House. The Home Secretary refused to consider any amendment incorporating sexual acts between women and so turned down the proposal even before it appeared on the Order Paper.

Although sexual activity between women was not a concern of the statute, it was by the early twentieth century punishable by law to some extent. The Pemberton-Billing libel case of 1918 is especially interesting and significant. Pemberton-Billing was sued for criminal libel by Maud Allan, whom Billing's *Vigilante* paper had implied was a lesbian and a sadist.[40]

In the parliamentary discussion of the Criminal Law Amendment Bill of 4 August 1921 a clause was introduced by Mr Macquisten that presented the topic of indecency between females for discussion before the House for the very first time. The subject created quite a furore and the views expressed by parliamentary members reflected disgust, disdain and often disbelief in the existence of such activity. However, its very introduction revealed a growing climate of opinion that recognized that women were not entirely sexually passive. The clause read: 'Any act of gross indecency between female persons shall be a misdemeanour and punishable in the same manner as any such act committed by male persons under section eleven of the Criminal Law Amendment Act, 1885.' Mr Macquisten, in his opening speech to the House, stressed, 'there is in modern social life an undercurrent of dreadful degradation, unchecked and uninterfered with'. He furnished details of homes and family life that had been wrecked by this form of sexual activity.[41] In the discussion generated in the House, Colonel Wedgwood agreed that it was an objectionable vice but added 'How on earth are people to get convictions in a case of this kind?'. Opposing the clause, Colonel Webb and Sir Ernest Wild declared that it was a beastly subject and they did not wish to 'pollute' the House with knowledge of it.[42] Nevertheless, Sir Ernest Wild maintained that lesbianism 'saps the fundamental institutions of society', 'stops childbirth', 'debauches young girls', and 'produces neurasthenia and insanity' and 'causes our race to decline'.[43]

Although no legislation was passed that directly prohibited indecency between females during the early decades of the twentieth century, the law did signify its acknowledgement and disapproval indirectly in that indecency between females came to represent both immorality and unchastity. Consider, for instance, *Kerr v Kennedy* (1942), an action for slander where the defendant had accused the complainant (plaintiff) of being a lesbian. The defendant was charged under section 1 of the Slander of Women Act of 1891. Mr Justice Asquith decided:

> The false imputation of unchastity, in whatever sense of the term, to a woman . . . is calculated both to bring her into social disfavour and, as the phrase runs, to damage her prospects in the marriage market and thereby her finances.[44]

In the opinion of the judge, an imputation of lesbianism was an imputation of unchastity.

Evidence of indecency between females has also constituted evidence of cruelty to a husband in a divorce action. In *Gardner v Gardner* (1947) the wife's 'unnatural sexual relations' with another woman provided grounds for divorce. The 'unnatural' relations referred to evidence that the wife 'was and is a lesbian'.[45] In the divorce action of *Spicer v Spicer* (1953), evidence of the wife's lesbianism also provided grounds for divorce.[46]

Public opinion had for some time been outraged by lesbianism, but it was not until 1956 that sexual activity between women was recognized in law and made a criminal offence in the Sexual Offences Act, ss 14 and 15. From thereon a woman could be prosecuted for the indecent assault of another female, although no such case appears to have been brought before the courts. In 1957, the Royal Commission on Homosexual Offences and Prostitution (s103) reported that it 'found no case in which a female has been convicted of an act with another female which exhibits the libidinous features that characterise sexual acts between males'.

The reluctance of the legislature to regulate female homosexuality was based not just on the difficulty of enforcing such a law, but on the refusal of the legislature to acknowledge that such behaviour existed. The belief in the passivity of femininity arose from the view that women were biologically and physically incapable of committing an offence. By extension, it seemed incongruous to suggest that women were capable of actively making sexual advances towards other equally passive women.

INCEST

In the statutory provisions governing incest, once again the legislature has been informed by the doctrine of passive female sexuality. Women have been, up until the present, defined as capable of 'permitting', 'submitting' or 'consenting' to sexual relations, but never construed as capable of 'committing' incest. This may appear to the male eye as a piece of gross injustice. It illustrates perfectly the tendency to assume *a priori* the passivity of women in every conceivable sphere involving sexual activity.

Incest came under criminal jurisdiction in the Punishment of Incest Act of 1908, where it was stated that a man commits incest if he has, or attempts to have, sexual intercourse with a daughter, sister, granddaughter or mother. A woman who 'permits', 'submits' or 'consents' to sexual relations was to be regarded as an accomplice in the crime. In *R v Stone* (1910), where a brother had sexual intercourse with a sister, it was decided that the sister's evidence must be corroborated[47] since it was crucial to distinguish between 'submission' and 'consent'. In *R v Dimes* (1911), the defendant was charged with the rape of a sister. He was found not guilty of rape, but guilty of incest. The charge of rape arose since it was decided that the sister had in fact 'submitted'. The presiding judge asserted: 'There is a distinction between submission and permission'.[48] This very fine distinction was further elaborated in the case of *R v King* (1920), where it was decided that a woman could be punished for 'permitting' incest and not just charged with being an accomplice. It was stated: 'Any female person of or above the age of sixteen years who with consent permits her grandfather, father, brother, or son to have carnal knowledge of her . . . shall be guilty of a misdemeanour'.[49] The Sexual Offences Act, 1956, s11, stated that a woman of 16 or over who permits a man to have intercourse with her whom she knows is her grandfather, father or brother is guilty of an offence.

The law relating to incest most explicitly reveals the doctrine of female sexual passivity, since a woman can never actually 'commit' incest but only 'permit' it. Again, such a conception is informed by the basic biological distinction of sexual asymmetry. It further discloses the contradictions in the law relating to sexual offences with regard to the precise role adopted by women.

EXPOSURE, EXHIBITIONISM OR OUTRAGING
PUBLIC DECENCY

The statutory provisions relating to indecent exposure and exhibitionism illustrate what is considered perverse and offensive.

A woman may take off her clothes in public but cannot be charged with indecent exposure, though she may be charged with outraging public decency under section 5 of the Public Order Act, 1936. Since the nineteenth century, partial or complete male nudity has been governed by the Vagrancy Acts of 1824 and 1838 and the Town Police Clauses Act of 1847, s28, where it was stated: 'Every person . . . who wilfully and indecently exposes his person . . .' commits an offence under this law. The distinction arises essentially because of the way the exposure of the 'person' is perceived. The interpretation of 'person' as the phallus is demonstrated in several early nineteenth-century cases. In *R v Webb* (1848), the presiding judge explained that the defendant 'did expose his private parts'.[50] The exposure of the female genitalia was not regarded to be as threatening to social morals as the exposure of the penis. Throughout the nineteenth and twentieth centuries there were many convictions for such behaviour. On this issue of 'person' as the phallus, it might be interesting to consider the remarks of a nineteenth-century judge, which suggest that he at least did not interpret the word 'person' exclusively to mean penis. Mr J. Hawkins, in pronouncing a decision in *R v Clarence* (1888), suggested that the meaning of 'person' might be negotiable: 'The wife submits to her husband's embraces because at the time of marriage she gave him an irrevocable right to her person'.[51] Mr Justice Bramwell in *R v Wood* (1877) reiterated the more typical meaning of the word when in a trial for rape he said that the defendant '. . . had committed this assault upon her by the insertion of his person'.[52]

This sexual asymmetry still persists. In the case of *Evans v Ewels* (1972), where a man had exposed his stomach, the judge had to decide the scope of the word 'person': 'The word "person" means penis and not any other part of the body not withstanding that there may be an intention to insult a female'.[53] The Report of the Working Party on Vagrancy and Street Offences (1976) proposed that female nudity should like male nudity be subject to sanctions and prohibitions (p. 44). Nevertheless, the committee also alluded to the difficulties involved in treating these two instances in a similar manner because of the basic biological differences between the sexes.

In this Pandora's box of misdemeanour, as embodied in and regulated by statutory law, an inbuilt structure is apparent that has sustained a belief in the sexual passivity of women and the sexual activity of men. This sexual asymmetry has dominated parliamentary thinking and influenced and informed the various statutes relating to sexual expression. The justification for the reproduction of this passive/active distinction in a legal form is the professed desire to protect women and to control virile male sexuality. But the systematic exclusion of women from legislation in the ways I have suggested has not been liberating. In denying female sexuality, the basic element in self-identity, the very existence of women is denied. Statutory law relating to sexual offences has in several invisible ways served to shore up a patriarchal system that proclaims the absolute hegemony of male sexuality.

The statutory definitions of sex crimes as we recognize them today have evolved over the past 180 years. During the nineteenth century, women were excluded from statutes regulating sexual activity. From 1900 onwards the law began slowly to assimilate and reflect the changes in social attitudes towards the sexuality of women. By the mid-twentieth century the doctrine of female sexual passivity was being challenged in both social and legal spheres.

CHAPTER 2

Female Sexual Precipitation in the Legal Process

Out in the desert, half-submerged, a sphinx.
Gazed at her awful mirrored loveliness. [Ellice Hopkins]

INTRODUCTION

Just as there is an approximate correspondence between the law as it regulates sexual behaviour and the accepted pattern of male and female sexuality, there is a similar correspondence between legal procedure and appropriate patterns of sexuality. The development of case law relating to evidence and procedure in trials for rape and related offences provides a testing ground for this relationship. In these cases the belief that the woman might have encouraged the activity and precipitated the assault is a view not uncommonly held. Whilst the statutory provisions relating to rape have evolved to protect women, procedural rules have evolved with the protection of the (male) defendant in mind. The development of these rules since 1800 reveals a growing preoccupation with the moral character of the complainant (Wigmore, 1940, p. 457). It is in the rules of evidence and procedure that we find the reproduction of the precipitating construction of female sexual behaviour that makes a charge of assault by the complainant difficult to sustain.

The model of female sexuality that informs procedural rules and judicial precedent stands in sharp contrast to the model of female sexual passivity that has consistently informed legislation. In the development of case law is enshrined a belief in female precipitation. The chaste/unchaste, good/bad, virgin/whore and madonna/magdalene distinction is well understood in nineteenth- and twentieth-century accounts of femininity. In talking about female sexuality, however, the dualism is somewhat different and more

49

specific. In law as it relates to sexual offences, and as it relates to rape more especially, the passive/precipitating distinction is particularly appropriate. In a rape trial, it is invariably the case that a model of female sexuality as *agent provocateur,* temptress or seductress is set in motion. From Hale to Hailsham this view is apparent from observing judicial utterances in court.

Why this sharp dichotomy arises is uncertain. It is perhaps of some significance that a statute is the product of many long deliberations in Parliament, whilst the evolution of case law comprises a series of judicial decisions arrived at in particular cases. And so, in rape especially, we are left with a complex and often very confusing legal picture. Whilst women were considered by statute to be quite incapable of committing a sexual offence, as victims of sexual assault they have been seen as 'precipitating' or in some way contributing to its commission.

In examining the extent and persistence of this interrelation, only the procedures applicable to the trial for rape and related offences need concern us. By elaborating how this relationship works at each and every level of the legal system, we are also concerned with the far broader consideration of the role played by procedural rules in the reproduction of sexual typifications and sexual asymmetry that are decisive to the control over female sexuality. Consider, for instance, the particular image of female sexuality conjured up in a recent rape trial. In summing up the case for the defence, defending counsel drew the attention of the jurors to the need for corroboration in such cases. He resorted to an image firmly belonging in the 1880s when he reminded the court of the tendency for women to make false allegations of this nature against men whilst travelling in railway carriages.[1] At the same time, in the actual process of a rape trial, considerable partiality seems to be exercised regarding legal protection for a particular victim. For instance, case law announces its preparedness to protect women who are 'true' victims of sexual assault. But the complainant is much more likely to qualify if her behaviour is congruous with the appropriate female sexual and social role. If it is not, her testimony is far less likely to be regarded with credulity. As has been already suggested elsewhere, the claim to 'male protectiveness' within the law is more correctly seen as the control of the sexual behaviour of women via defining ideologies.

SOME NOTES ON PRECEDENT

Prior to discussing procedures in rape trials, a few comments must be made regarding the nature of judicial decision-making. The common law developed historically by judges making and following or adding to the accumulated body of individual decisions. Of course judges are bound by Acts of Parliament, but equally they make crucial decisions in interpreting or applying the provisions of Acts. Judges have the power to make particular decisions according to the merits of the individual cases brought before them. However, the doctrine of judicial precedent announces that prior decisions are binding on later courts faced with similar issues. Thus counsel cite past decisions as authority for the point or argument they are seeking to establish. Some aspects of the doctrine are clear, for example that the decisions of higher courts are binding on lower courts, but there is a complex and technical literature concerning the exact weight and authority to be given to judicial decisions in different circumstances. It is the *ratio decidendi* that is binding on later courts and not *obiter dicta* — the observations or comments made by judges that were not strictly necessary to determination of the case. Judicial decisions can develop an identity and impetus of their own. Statute law and case law can thus represent independent aspects of law that are not always complementary. The result can be that judicial precedent does not assist in the pursuit of justice, since following earlier decisions may entail following an erroneous decision (because it is binding) for some considerable time.

The decisions made in rape trials in 1812 and 1817 constituted precedents that were to remain for 150 years, although not all judges dealing with rape and related offences necessarily followed former rulings slavishly. Certain nineteenth-century judges were reluctant to follow the *ratio decidendi* of earlier cases. In *R v Barker* (1829), for example, the *Hodgson* decision to disallow admissibility of particular facts was not rigorously followed, despite some considerable conjecture. Although the judge in considering the precedent in *Hodgson* said 'I have great doubt whether, since the case of *R v Hodgson,* I can admit you to prove particular acts of criminality in the prosecutrix', he nevertheless allowed details relating to particular and general character and held that she could be contradicted.[2] But, in general, the doctrine of judicial precedent declares that relevant prior rulings must be observed and followed and this has resulted in the continuous application of some rules of evidence and procedure in rape trials that are truly obsolescent. Remarking on the recent status of the doctrine of judicial precedent, Blom-Cooper and Drewry write,

> At the heart of the British appellate system — or, perhaps, hovering over it — like a 'brooding omnipresence' is *stare decisis*: a doctrine which compels judges to synthesize present decisions (or at least articulate the reasons for such decisions) out of the accumulated wisdom (or folly) of their judicial forebears.[3]

The doctrine of judicial precedent may not be as rigid now as it was in the nineteenth century but it is still of overwhelming importance. Precedents that are out of date or anachronistic may have such authority that they can only be overruled by statute. In other instances, only if a particular case goes to the Court of Appeal or House of Lords — an exceptional circumstance — is there even an opportunity for judges, should they be willing, to amend or reverse a prior decision.

In observing the way case law has evolved over time to deal with rape, my objective is to examine how the court process has assimilated and reproduced constructs of female sexuality. The first step in this direction is to investigate the breadth and depth of the typifications of female precipitation, participation and contributory fault in everyday thought and popular culture.

FEMALE PRECIPITATION IN EVERYDAY THOUGHT

In sharp contrast to the idealized nineteenth-century bourgeois image of the sexually passive and innocent women, stands the woman of sexual experience, who might vary from the unmarried woman with a lover, to the woman of varied sexual experience, to the prostitute. The various degrees of unchastity were regarded with greater or lesser social hostility, and were also differentiated in the legal process and in legal interpretation. This particular type of woman has more often than not been described as 'unchaste' or 'fallen', and for the purpose of the social construction of female sexuality was regarded as 'bad' and, towards the end of the nineteenth century, invariably as 'mad'. Such women were continually portrayed in medical literature and popular culture as temptresses, as the evil seducers of men and young boys, and were often considered responsible for the moral pollution of the nation.

The unchaste woman was not simply different from the passive woman; she was instead explained as if something were functionally wrong. A biological dysfunction or else circumstances of social deprivation were said to have resulted in her plight. Since the desire for sex in women was supposedly non-existent, those women who showed any interest in that direction were considered grossly abnormal. It was frequently said that such women had an overproduction of male hormones or else were suffering from either a mental or gynaecological disorder. Therefore, desire for sex in women was still desexualized, by being defined as an innate malfunction or disease. For instance, in the Minutes of Evidence submitted to the Royal Commission upon the Administration and Operation of the Contagious Diseases Acts (1871), the Reverend Dr Hannah asserted that a fallen girl would be likely to have fallen from 'a sort of innate want of virtue'.[4] This particular view was common until the end of the nineteenth century. For instance, Mercier (1899) described chastity as an instinct, thereby defining prostitution as the absence of this instinct. Routh and Magnan maintained that the sexual behaviour or appetite of the prostitute was the result of a reflex action in the posterior cerebral cortex (Routh, 1886).

Yet another explanation for the behaviour of unchaste women was provided in the social and economic conditions of the poor. It is perfectly true that the social conditions in which working-class women were compelled to live contributed to a pattern of living that placed little if any importance on sexual morality. The moral code of the middle and upper classes made very little impact on working women, since their very squalid living and working conditions and perpetual sexual harrassment at work militated against any attempt to aspire to this standard. Thompson's evidence supports this view; he reveals just how deplorable conditions really were, where factories were 'immoral places of sexual licence, where foul manners and cruelly violent incidents took place' (1970, p. 339). Women working in the industries often had to leave children completely unsupervised. The Factory Commissioners Report of 1837 disclosed the desperate economic plight of working women, who because of dire need and force of circumstance returned immediately to the workplace after childbirth without any period of confinement (Engels, 1974, p. 34). In 1899, Booth, of Salvation Army fame, remarked that the living conditions of the poor, even by that time, were no better. Overcrowding compelled children to witness every aspect of life, and was considered one of the main contributory factors in cases of incest. Austin, an Assistant Poor Law Commissioner, said that the sleeping of boys, girls, young men and women together in one bed inevitably had the effect of breaking down the barriers, such as 'to create early and illicit familiarity between the sexes'; and according to Professor Peckham incest was an integral part of a Victorian culture of poverty.[5] One of the paradox's characterizing the position of women is that their apparent economic independence brought them no other independence — whether political, legal or social — as Engels had prophesied. In law especially, they remained and were to remain subservient to men.

The stereotype that portrayed working-class women as unchaste, as lacking in morals and as adulteresses was greatly assisted by legislation that discriminated against this class. First, institutionalized forms of marriage amongst the working classes in general, and especially amongst rural workers, were not considered fashionable. Very often the expense entailed in a licence and formal wedding militated against a legal ceremony.[6] Amongst the people of rural areas, custom did not demand any official state legitimation of marriage; jumping over a broom, or similar rural customs, marked the status passage and validated the union. Industrial workers were also very reluctant to engage in a legal marriage ceremony. Harrison maintains that the 'demand for cheap labour caused marriage to be forbidden in certain working-class occupations' (1967, p. 257). So it is not altogether surprising that middle-class opinion defined the working classes as living in sin.

Adulterous behaviour was also thought to characterize the working-class. This arose from differences in police detection, cautioning and conviction. Moreover, the apparent tendency of the working class to commit adultery was also the product of a legislature that made divorce a possibility only for those who could pay. It was even more difficult for working-class women, since women in general had to prove that a husband was guilty of rape, sodomy, bestiality or incest — the simple evidence of adultery was not in itself sufficient. The result of this was that working-class men and women were often tried and convicted for bigamy. The practice of wife selling became very common for the working class in certain locales.

Whilst working-class behaviour in general was considered immoral, it was the sexual behaviour of working-class women that was the most criticized. The image of the working-class woman as immoral, promiscuous and precipitating was constantly promoted by the media and in popular culture. A report in the *Illustrated Police News* of 27 June 1896 reproduced this typification of working-class female sexuality in a story headed 'Women act like wild beasts':

> A man who had been living in the neighbourhood for forty years said that the women acted like wild beasts. This was now getting very common — it was impossible for a respectable person to go about in the day or night without being insulted and probably assaulted by gangs of lecherous and disorderly women who infect the neighbourhood.

MECHANISMS OF CONTROL OF FEMALE UNCHASTITY

Throughout the nineteenth and twentieth centuries, the sexual behaviour of all women was the object of control, both direct and indirect, and not of protection. Male control extended throughout all patriarchal institutions, though the degree and form of control varied according to the social class of the women concerned. Ladies of the middle classes were as a general rule considered passive and therefore were to be protected. So the myth of 'male protectiveness' provided the primary excuse for the passage of certain laws and policies. It was control under another guise nevertheless. The social and sexual behaviour of middle- and upper-class wives and daughters was also controlled via the father's and husband's right to consortium, which was determined in part by the 'value' of the wife or daughter with regard to her chastity. The behaviour of working-class women was regulated and rigorously controlled via the laws relating to vagrancy and prostitution. Unchaste victims of sexual assault were controlled through legal procedures that permitted cross-examination as to moral character. Moreover, unchaste women were further controlled and punished in their effort to gain access to employment.

The sharp division between moral and immoral women performed a powerful role in circumscribing appropriate behaviour. However slight or unintended a woman's indiscretion might be, she was defined as fallen. The duality of moral and immoral behaviour was very closely paralleled in the construction of the behaviour of middle-class and working-class women. Furthermore, the indiscretions of working-class women were flagrantly exposed by the media, whose latent function in this instance was to reaffirm the widely held belief in the immorality of the working class. The indiscretions of the middle and upper classes, on the other hand, were carefully concealed. This concealment was made possible through the power and economic resources of this class. The daughter of an upper-class family would not be forced to resort to ridding herself of an unwanted child by self-inducement or the services of a quack. Ladies of the middle classes so 'caught' discreetly went on a long journey abroad.

The unchaste woman especially, then, was subject to legal and ideological controls. On the legal front she was the object of direct legislation, as in the regulation of prostitution, and of indirect informal ideologies, as in the experience of rape trial procedures.

The state regulation of prostitution

The prostitute was the ultimate in unchastity and immorality. She was controlled by the Vagrancy Act of 1824 and the Metropolitan Police Act of 1829, s7, which read:

> It shall be lawful for any man belonging to the said police force, during the time of his being on duty, to apprehend all loose, idle, and disorderly persons whom he shall find disturbing the public peace, or whom, he shall have just cause to suspect of any evil design . . .

This provision was followed by the Metropolitan Police Act, 1839, which greatly extended the powers of the police to apprehend anyone disturbing the peace or acting suspiciously. This inevitably left police with enormous room to interpret and negotiate the wording 'acting suspiciously'. This Act gave the police powers to: 'take into custody . . . all persons whom he shall find between sunset and the hour of eight in the morning, lying or loitering in any highway, yard, or other place, and not giving a satisfactory account of themselves'. The 'sus' provisions in the early nineteenth century discriminated exclusively against the poor and especially against working-class women.

The regulation of the prostitute was for the first time made explicit in the Town Police Clauses Act, 1847, s28, which legislated against 'Every common prostitute or nightwalker loitering and importuning passengers for the purpose of prostitution'. It also, for the first time, said of the interpretation of the Act that 'wordings importuning of the masculine gender shall include females'. From this point onwards, the law relating to the regulation of prostitutes provides the most lucid expression of a legal attempt to control and victimize the unchaste woman.

The Contagious Diseases Acts of 1864 and 1866 are explicit legal statements of the belief in the precipitating sexuality of certain women. The 1864 Act was designed 'to Prevent the Spreading of Contagious Diseases to certain Naval and Military Stations'. It gave JPs, inspectors, magistrates and medical practitioners the power to apprehend a woman and 'convey her with all practical Speed to the Hospital' for an examination — a policeman, peace officer, owner occupier or manager had only to report to a magistrate that 'he had reasonable cause to believe any common Prostitute to have a Contagious Disease' (ss14, 18). The 1866 Act gave police even greater power to detain and also to examine such suspected women. Moreover, women so suspected could be issued with a notice requiring them to be examined, and be detained in hospital against their will and without their consent; if they refused to be medically examined they could be imprisoned (ss15, 16, 25, 29, 35).

The Acts were quite clearly devised and instituted to protect men by subjecting a certain class of woman to periodic, and if necessary forcible, medical examination and registration with the police as prostitutes. This legislation was founded on an erroneous principle, namely that unchaste women carried and transmitted venereal disease whilst the men who consorted with them only contracted it. They were therefore not subject to any form of control. Surgeon Major, Mr J. Wyatt maintained that there was a value in examining men in the interest of their health and the health of their children,[7] thus revealing that the sole endeavour was to protect men. This conviction is illustrated in the Memorial to the Lord President of the Council from the President of the Royal College of Physicians and others respecting the extension of the Contagious Diseases Act 1866. They were of the opinion that the Act should be extended to the civil population because women were likely to spread disease.

Control over female unchastity in employment

The sexual behaviour of women was also a consideration of
employers. A woman's reputation not only influenced marriage
prospects but also job opportunities. On 21 May 1890, the Midwives
Registration Bill was given its second reading. Female midwives
who wished to register were required to produce a certificate of
good character that had to be signed by a magistrate or a clergyman.
In 1902, the Midwives Act institutionalized this type of discrimination. Section 2 gave a woman permission to enter the profession, if
'she bears a good character'. It also provided the Board with the
power to remove her 'for other misconduct'. *Stock v Central
Midwives Board* (1915) reveals the power of the Board to
discriminate against women.[8] Mrs Stock had been struck off the
midwives roll on the ground that she had been guilty of misconduct
under section 3 of the 1902 Act (her husband had left her some
years previously and she had been cohabiting with a particular man,
a child being born from this liaison). Mrs Stock appealed against the
decision of the Central Midwives Board. The comments of Lord
Robert Cecil showed the bias and discrimination with which women
had to contend in employment. He said that there were two good
reasons for the action taken by the Board. First, a midwife of bad
character, if called upon to attend a married woman, might corrupt
the husband. Second, a midwife of bad character might also
influence the wife. It was decided that a certificate should not be
given to women of bad repute. Clearly, the Central Midwives Board
had firmly decided that Mrs Stock was just that kind of woman!
However, sexual relations for women seemed at this time to be
negotiable; Lord Reading at the Court of Criminal Appeal argued
that cohabiting was not misconduct and the appeal was allowed.

THE CONTROL OF FEMALE SEXUALITY
IN THE RAPE LAW

The precise relationship of sexuality to sex law is to be treated with
some considerable caution since there is not always a correspondence between social and legal changes in attitudes to sexuality.
For example, the social attitudes that have restricted the sexual

behaviour of women have undergone considerable change since 1800, but the implications of such changes were not incorporated in law until 1976. Three particular aspects of legal importance illustrate the unique way in which rape is handled. First, the 'burden of proof' lies with the complainant in cases of larceny, rape and assault. Second, in cases of rape, attempted rape, indecent assault and gross indecency between males, it is for the prosecution to prove that the complainant did not consent and that the defendant intended to have intercourse with the complainant even if she/he refused or resisted. Third, in cases of rape, attempted rape and indecent assault a corroboration warning is given to the jury with the precise intention of protecting the defendant from the possibility of a false allegation. The requirement of corroboration was first expressed by Bracton in the twelfth century and reiterated by Hale in the seventeenth century. The need for such a warning was stressed in case law and then given statutory force in the Sexual Offences Act 1956, ss2, 3 and 4.

A woman bringing a charge of sexual assault is also in a unique position regarding the social construction of sexuality as it informs the legal process. First, it is much more likely that the unchaste woman will be thought to have consented than a virgin. Second, there is a belief that much more harm is done in the case of rape on a virgin than a rape on an unchaste woman. Whilst women are thought to be physically incapable of instigating sexual advances, they are thought to be capable of inviting them. This belief originally related to working-class female behaviour, but over time it has come to be seen as a generalized characteristic of female sexuality existing in varying degrees in all classes. This image has informed the legal process at several levels in the criminal justice system from 1800 onwards. For instance, in the nineteenth century 'want of chastity' led to the complainant being cross-examined on questions relating to previous criminal record and whether the victim had been in the workhouse or in a house of correction. The complainant would be questioned about work relationships with men and about various aspects of her social life, for instance whether she frequented public houses, drank beer or whether she talked to men. During the twentieth century, it appears that the courtroom inquisition has accelerated. There has been an emphasis on criminal record, and more recently on probation and psychiatric orders. Intimate details of the sex life and activities of the complainant have been revealed, especially regarding type of contraceptive used and the number of boyfriends, abortions and children the woman has had; details of any psychiatric care or treatment are also considered relevant.

THE TRIAL PROCESS

The trial for rape and related offences begins with the submission of evidence-in-chief. It is at this juncture that evidence relating to criminal convictions and convictions for prostitution may be admitted. The complainant may be cross-examined by the defence on specific details and she can be contradicted if she denies the evidence brought before the court. The object of examination-in-chief is to obtain testimonials in support of the version of the facts in issue (sometimes called 'principal facts') or relevant to that issue. The second line of inquiry concerns cross-examination regarding circumstantial evidence, *factum probans* or facts relating to the issue in chief. Cross (1967, p. 5) explains the purpose of such evidence as being that the judge or jury may infer from it the existence of a fact in issue. The complainant may not be cross-examined if she denies the matter nor can witnesses be brought to contradict her.

But the rules of procedure relating to the offence of rape or indecent assault on a woman disclose an anomaly within the legal process, as Nokes remarks:

> A prosecutrix is in the same position as a prosecutor, except that a woman supporting a charge of sexual crime against herself is peculiarly liable to an attack on her moral character by the defence, and some special rules apply . . . In cases of rape, however, it is impossible to set up a defence of consent without imputing immorality to the prosecutrix . . . [1962, pp. 145-51]

Over the years, the law has both restricted and admitted evidence as to moral character in certain specific ways. The actual imputation of immorality to the prosecutrix arises from the conceptual organization of the presentation of evidence and the facts themselves and also from the way legal precedents have been instituted and followed.

In discussing the first point, Cross takes up Wigmore's (1940) classification of prospectant, concomitant and retrospective evidence, which provide the main types of argument by which one fact is related to another. Prospectant evidence is particularly important in the imputation of immorality since it provides for the idea that an act, a state of mind or a state of affairs in the past justifies an inference that an act, a state of mind or a state of affairs existed at the moment of time into which the court is enquiring (Cross, 1967, p. 28). In this specific context 'The fact that someone was in the habit of acting in a given way is relevant to the question whether he acted in that way on the occasion into which the court is enquiring' (p. 30).

The use of this kind of reasoning is powerfully exploited in the cross-examination of the rape complainant, which almost invariably results in the imputation of immorality to the prosecutrix. The process by which this occurs comes under consideration in sociological theory, which explains how present behaviour is interpreted and ascribed in the light of past conduct. We can take Tannenbaum as our point of departure:

> The process of making the criminal is a process of tagging, defining, identifying, segregating, describing, emphasizing, making conscious and self conscious; it becomes a way of stimulating, suggesting, emphasizing, and evoking the very traits that are complained of.[9]

Interactionism is especially significant in so far as it considers social reaction as a process in the social construction of the victim or offender. It provides a framework within which the 'moral career' of the rape victim can be constructed, and enables us to examine how a present predicament is interpreted in the light of past behaviour. For instance, if the defence can produce evidence of the sexual experiences of the complainant prior to the rape, then the fact of the rape may be interpreted as sexual intercourse by consent. Consider how one might interpret the behaviour of an acquaintance who has spent some time in a mental hospital. Consider also the infinite ways in which that behaviour might be interpreted if onlookers had no prior knowledge of her/his incarceration.

What I am suggesting here is that the process of social construction in the courtroom is a reflection of the process by which facts are organized in everyday life. It has been discussed more fully in the context of mental illness (Smith, 1978). In prospectant evidence, for instance, it is assumed that 'What he is now is "after all" what he was all along'.[10] Goffman's *Stigma* illustrates the way in which people are analysed in the light of previous events. He presents us with the case of the thief who said 'they're always expecting me to do it again'.[11] Ray's study provides insights into society's reaction to drug addicts who have kicked the habit. One addict explained: 'Finally, I just got disgusted because nobody wanted to believe me and I went back on'.[12]

The organization of the facts in the courtroom is rule-bound by three major constraints of precedent that have martialled evidence as to moral character along three lines of cross-examination — whether a prostitute, past relation with the accused and want of chastity. Each of these three categories has been informed by particular assumptions regarding sexuality. Although the first two lines of inquiry stand on a different legal footing regarding the legal right to cross-examine and contradict, all three play a part in providing evidence for the argument that 'what she was she still is'.

Whether a prostitute

On the one hand, history has shown that a prostitute is no more or less immune from sexual attack than a virgin, although opinion on this matter has been conflicting. Judges have recognized that a prostitute can also be the victim of rape. In *R v Hallett* (1841) the presiding judge, Justice Coleridge, upheld the view that a charge of rape will lie notwithstanding that the woman concerned is a prostitute. Later, in *R v Holmes and Furness* (1871), Justice Byles remarked 'that the prosecutrix, on an indictment for rape could not be contradicted by men called to speak to connection with her, since rape may be committed on a prostitute; and the evidence was therefore declared to be immaterial'.[13]

Yet, despite these various judicial utterances, the fact that a woman is a prostitute has been taken, in the trial process, as material to whether she consented to sexual intercourse or not. Since consent is determined by both material evidence and circumstantial evidence, it is very unlikely that a man would be convicted of rape on a woman known to be a prostitute. In theory, of course, all women come under the auspices and protection of the law; however, in legal practice only certain women actually receive this legal protection. When a prostitute alleges that she has been raped, the social construction of promiscuity is set in motion. The development of case law reflects the various ways in which the prostitute as complainant has been considered over time. The very paucity of judicial decision, reported in the law reports or not, gives some indication of the reluctance of prostitutes to bring a criminal charge and, should they so do, of the tendency for police to dismiss such allegations as false.

Judicial rulings on the admissibility of evidence relating to prostitution and moral character begin with *R v Hodgson* (1811-12) in so far as the prosecuting counsel attempted to introduce facts related to her general moral character and sexual experiences with other men.[14] The decision to disallow cross-examination as to character was not followed in *R v Barker* (1829), where the defending counsel, with a view to contradicting her, asked the complainant: 'Were you not, on Friday last, walking the High Street of Oxford, to look out for men?' and 'Were you not, on Friday last, walking in the High Street with a woman reputed to be a common prostitute?'[15] The details admitted in *Hallett* (1841) disclose the extent to which evidence relating to prostitution can be admitted, and the way it works to the discredit of the complainant, despite the utterances of Justice Coleridge. In this case, eight men raped the complainant who was known to be a prostitute. The prisoners were indicted for feloniously ravishing the woman in question. In cross-examination, the complainant admitted she had 'been on the town' since the time of the alleged offence. She denied, however, that she had been so before, although she admitted it was not the first time she had experienced intercourse. The significance of circumstantial evidence is provided in the remarks of Justice Coleridge who, when addressing the jury, had this to say:

> . . . it is well worthy of your consideration whether, although she at first objected, she might not afterwards (on finding that the prisoners were determined) have yielded to them, and in some degree consented; and this question is the more deserving of your attention when you come to consider what sort of person she was, what sort of house she lodged in, and that she herself told them that she would make no objection if they came one at a time.[16]

The jury returned a verdict of guilty of assault but not of rape. This was followed in 1843 by *R v Tissington* where it was ruled that evidence relating to the general indecency of the prosecutrix (although she was under 12) could be given.[17] In *R v Clay* (1851) police evidence was introduced relating to the complainant's moral character some 20 years prior to the offence at issue. The police constable stated that he had seen the prosecutrix on the streets of Shrewsbury, and knew her to be a reputed prostitute.[18]

During the nineteenth century, the legal treatment of the prostitute as complainant reflected very much the belief that such a kind of woman had received her just deserts in rape or sexual assault and also that no moral harm was done. The twentieth-century treatment of the prostitute as complainant was not to change. Despite certain improvements in social attitudes to the prostitute in law, her allegation of sexual assault continued to be treated with great caution. Consider, for instance, the treatment of the raped prostitute as disclosed in the following cases. In *R v Greenberg* (1923), the Court of Appeal considered an appeal against conviction for indecent assault where the complainant's evidence concerning an allegation of intercourse by force was not corroborated. The prosecution had cross-examined the complainant as to moral character and said she had brought the charge against the defendant in order to extract money. Justice Avory remarked 'People do not always ask for what they expect'.[19] This comment is not atypical of the types of remarks made concerning what women want, etc., which will be exposed in detail later. In *R v Greatbanks* (1959) the defending counsel wanted to introduce evidence to disclose that the complainant was of notoriously bad character, wanting in chastity and common decency.[20] However, evidence of her connection with other men was held not to be admissible, although evidence that she was a prostitute and of loose character in fact was. More recently, in *R v Bashir and Manzur* (1969), where the defendants claimed that the complainant had invited sex for money and had actually accosted the defendants, it was submitted in evidence that she had remarked 'Lumb Lane, Bradford, was a good place for business'.[21] Mr Justice Veale permitted the defending counsel to introduce evidence to establish that she was a prostitute. The judge held that in a case other than rape such evidence would not be admissible, but reiterated that in rape cases 'special rules apply' relating to past moral character and general evidence. In this respect, the case of *R v Krausz* (1973) is especially interesting since it established that evidence that a woman is in the habit of submitting her body is relevant. However, the evidence submitted in this case amounted to the bad reputation of the particular public house, from which it was inferred that the girl went there to get picked up to have sexual intercourse for money.[22] The extent to which this type of evidence is irrevocably damaging to the credibility of a complainant's story was revealed in a case at Manchester Crown

Court in 1975. The defence counsel introduced evidence to the effect that the complainant had a conviction for prostitution of fifteen years before. At that point the complainant broke down in the witness box and the court adjourned.[23] The slur on her character and credibility had been cast.

The 1976 Act did nothing at all to affect the status or treatment of the prostitute as a rape victim, or to change the nature of evidence-in-chief. The result is that despite non-partisan claims that prostitutes receive equal treatment under the law, as a group they remain unprotected and stigmatized. The discrepancy between theory and practice remains.

Prior relation with the accused

In the nineteenth and twentieth centuries, 'prior relation with the accused' constituted evidence that was material to consent. As this stands as evidence-in-chief, this means that in law such matters are considered of direct relevance to the facts in issue. In technical terms the complainant may be asked specific questions about her relationship with the accused and her answers may be contradicted. The assumption behind this particular ruling is that 'acts of voluntary intercourse between the same two people are liable to be repeated' (Cross, 1967, p. 218). This particular assumption relates very much to the view expressed in the law as it applies to sexual consortium, where the husband has absolute right over his wife. This seems, at least in court practice, to extend to the rights to consortium of a common law husband and also, in this case, apparently to the rights of a past lover over a girlfriend.

In legal history the point of departure is probably *R v Martin* (1834), in which it was held that 'On the trial of an indictment for a rape the prosecutrix may be asked, whether previously to the commission of the alleged offence, the prisoner has not had intercourse with her by her own consent'.[24] However, in this case, as in others, the prisoner is not asked, nor *can* he be asked, whether he was taking liberties with her, or whether this past behaviour proved his intent. Such evidence of a past relationship between the accused and the complainant only goes to show *her consent* and not his intent. The precedent was stated yet again in *R v Cockcroft* (1870), in which questions were put to the complainant about her previous relation with the defendant. Justice Willes asserted that the witness may be examined with respect to particular acts of connection with the prisoner, but if she denies it then it is permissible to call witnesses to contradict her.[25] This principle was further enshrined in *R v Riley* (1887). In this case the defendant was charged on an indictment of assault with intent to commit a rape, and two other counts of indecent and common assault. In cross-examination it was disclosed that the complainant had had previous voluntary connection with the accused. The defending counsel proposed to call witnesses to prove this fact, but the judge intervened and disallowed this. The decision in this case was subsequently reversed on appeal on the ground that evidence of the relation between the woman and the man prior to the alleged criminal attempt is admissible as affecting her credibility on a matter directly pertinent to the issue.[26]

It is interesting to note that, in the case of rape, there was no immediate readiness to entertain the remarks of Judge Hamilton on consortium, uttered in *R v Clarence* (1888): 'In the case of unmarried persons, however, consent is necessary previous to every act of communion, . . .'[27]

Throughout the twentieth century, evidence relating to a prior relationship between the defendant and complainant continued to be admissible. In *R v Bradley* (1910) an appeal against a conviction for rape introduced evidence to show that they were previously acquainted.[28] In *R v Horn* (1912) there was an appeal against conviction of indecent assault, since there was no corroboration of the girl's story. Since the girl was 'respectable', there was no reason, said the Deputy Chairman, why she should concoct such a story.[29] In a more recent case of rape where the defendant and complainant had been sexually acquainted, *R v Gardner* (1973), the defendant was acquitted.[30]

The law thus leaves a woman unprotected against the unwanted harassment of previous lovers. The view of sexuality that has informed the legal process since 1800 is founded on a belief that a woman who once consents to a man's advances will do so again, and by the same token it is believed that it is a man's right to sexual consortium *ad infinitum* with a woman he has 'won'. In addition, her credibility is immediately affected and it becomes difficult to 'organize the text' in any other way except to believe that she consented.

Want of chastity

The admissibility of past moral character stands on a very different legal footing to whether the complainant was a prostitute or whether she had a prior relationship with the accused. Evidence relating to moral character is regarded as circumstantial evidence and not evidence-in-chief. As such, any evidence admitted or withheld cannot be contradicted, and only matters relating to general and not particular character may be disclosed. However, despite the apparent secondary legal significance of evidence as to character, circumstantial evidence has a profound and powerful influence on the way the facts of the matter may be organized and interpreted. Consider, for instance, material evidence of marks of bruising. These facts corroborate a complainant's allegation, but it is the jury that is left to decide the meaning of such marks and how they were sustained. In this context, if circumstantial evidence is introduced concerning the sexual character of the complainant, it may result in the jury concluding that such marks are not evidence of force but evidence of consent. It is this aspect that has been most exploited by the defence; it has also been the subject of persistent disagreement and heated controversy over the last 150 years. Certain nineteenth- and twentieth-century judges have recognized that the admissibility of details relating to the moral character of the complainant has put women at a considerable disadvantage. However this view has been overtly expressed by only a very small handful of judges since 1800. Lord Coleridge, CJ, had this to say in 1887:

> It has been held that evidence to shew that the woman has previously had connection with persons other than the accused, when she has denied that fact, must be rejected, and there are very good reasons for rejecting it. It should in my view be rejected, not only upon the ground that to admit it would be unfair and a hardship to the woman, but also upon the general principle that it is not evidence which goes directly to the point at issue at the trial. . . . It is obvious, too, that the result of admitting such evidence would be to deprive an unchaste woman of any protection against assaults of this nature.[31]

More recently, Justice Veale in *Bashir and Manzur* (1969) also expressed this view.[32]

Past moral character has been very widely interpreted by counsel since 1800. It has included details of sexual, moral, criminal and social history, and of mental and social disposition. In *R v Hodgson*

(1811-12), Harriet Halliday (a spinster) accused Hodgson of rape. The significance of this case lies in the fact that it established a precedent that was to remain for many decades, although a number of judges departed from it.[33] In cross-examination, Halliday was asked by counsel whether she had had connection with men other than the defendant, and one particular man was named. The prosecuting counsel objected to the admission of any evidence relating to particular facts. The presiding judge, Mr Baron Wood, disallowed the question on the ground that there was no exception to the rule in the case of rape: 'Upon an indictment for rape, the woman is not compellable to answer whether she has had connection with any other men or with a particular person named, nor is evidence of her having such a connection admissible'.[34]

It was *R v Clarke* (1817) that established a precedent in cases of attempted rape permitting the cross-examination of the prosecutrix as to chastity. The indictment was one of assault with intent to commit rape. Mr Justice Holroyd asserted: 'The defendant in such case may *impeach her character for chastity* by general, but not by particular evidence' (emphasis added) thereby allowing cross-examination as to general facts.[35] In this case, Mrs Webb, the complainant, had been sent to the House of Correction for stealing money from her domestic employee. She was also asked if she had been admitted to the Refuge for the Destitute — so as to discredit her. It was also established in *Clarke* that evidence 'may be adduced to shew that her character has since been good' and also that the speed with which she makes the complaint is to be taken as evidence to her credit.

This precedent was referred to in *R v Holmes and Furness* (1871) where the prisoners were indicted on two charges, one of indecent assault, the other of attempted rape. During cross-examination, the complainant was asked if she had previously had connection with a particular man. The man was then called and asked if she had had connection with him. The prosecuting counsel objected and the judge, in allowing his objection, said:

> If such evidence . . . were admitted, the whole history of the prosecutrix's life might be gone into, if a charge might be made as to one man, it might be made as to fifty, and that without notice to the prosecutrix. It would not only involve a multitude of collateral issues but an inquiry into matters as to which the prosecutrix might be wholly unprepared and so work great injustice.[36]

The nature of the cross-examination in this case illuminates those issues that were considered relevant to female moral character in the nineteenth century. Facts relating to general evidence were allowed but particular evidence was not. If in *Krausz* (1973) it was said that the complainant had consumed three gin and tonics, in *Holmes* it was revealed of the complainant that she had consumed a large quantity of beer.

In *R v Lillyman* (1896) the prisoner was indicted on three counts — attempt to have carnal knowledge with a girl aged 13—16, attempt to ravish and indecent assault. The cross-examination contains some interesting parallels with the approach adopted by counsel in recent times in that the social, sexual and drinking habits of the complainant became the main cause for concern.[37] However, past moral character has apparently been given a far wider interpretation. The focus in the twentieth century has been concerned with details of pre-marital and extra-marital relations, illegitimate children, divorce, occupation, abortion, mental and psychological state of mind, and, much more recently, whether a permanent form of contraception is used. Social attitudes to female sexual freedom might have changed — the girl next door can sleep with her boyfriend without too much criticism — but if she is raped then the social construction of promiscuity is set in motion.

In *R v Jones* (1909) evidence was introduced to show that the complainant was immoral.[38] In *R v Cargill* (1913) the defendant was convicted for having unlawful carnal knowledge of a girl aged 13—16. Cargill appealed since he claimed that she was then already a loose and abandoned girl who had previously had connection with other men.[39] In *R v Winfield* (1939) the defendant was found guilty of indecent assault on a woman.[40] He appealed on the grounds that evidence relating to his moral character was improperly admitted. In this case, the indecent assault, according to the court, was committed 'on a perfectly respectable married woman in her house'. The conviction was quashed for want of corroboration. In *R v Parks* (1961) the defendant was indicted on a count of indecent assault. Great emphasis was placed upon the complainant's seven convictions for dishonesty (the last being in 1954). Yet Lord Parker, CJ, conceded that she was, nevertheless, in his words 'grievously assaulted'. The indecent assault conviction was quashed on a point of identification.[41] Finally, want of chastity was exploited to the full in *R v Buttolph* (1974), where the complainant was asked if she was on the pill and why she chose to live alone.

The past moral character or want of decency of the complainant have little to do with the actual commission of crime and are unlikely to have any influence on the motivation of the accused, although defending counsels often claim that the defendant thought she was easy, or else had heard she was and therefore behaved in that way to her. Where rape is concerned the traditional methods of criminological analysis, criminal motivation and criminal behaviour are superseded by a preoccupation with the victim, her motivation, her proclivity for sexual experience and her moral behaviour. And yet it is not the sexual experience of the complainant that is on trial, but a man who it is alleged has had intercourse with her by force.

By contrast with statute law, case law has tended almost exclusively to mirror a belief in precipitating sexuality. This is not to say that female sexuality was acknowledged; it was thought to occur only in a perverse form in the unchaste or promiscuous woman. Trial procedures in rape cases turned on its head the orthodox concern with motivation or intent, i.e. whether the defendant was the type to commit such an offence, etc. The only time such evidence was admitted was in *Winfield* (1939), and then it was declared improperly admitted and the conviction quashed. Yet when a female complainant stands in the witness box, the logic of the prospectant construction of events is mobilized and her character is exposed in almost every conceivable detail.

There is a double edge to the law relating to rape: it may exist to protect women, but trial procedures disclose multifarious ways of controlling women through public attempts to disgrace a woman of sexual experience, as a warning to all women to behave 'congruously'. In courts, any and every possible moral and sexual detail that might be incompatible with the ideal image of sexuality is smoked out, with the unwitting consequence that sex-gender relations are reproduced in the way a trial is exercised.

PART II

Scientia Gynaecologia et Sexualis

CHAPTER 3

The Gynaecology of Offenders and Victims

The gynaecologist besides inserting his two fingers into the vagina must very delicately insert his two fingers also into the soul of the woman. [Dr A. G. Gabrielianz]

INTRODUCTION

From the mid-nineteenth century in particular, there has been an increasing medicalization of all varieties of sexual expression — normal, deviant and criminal. Foucault identifies this particular deployment of medical science as the *'scientia sexualis'* (1978, p. 53). This discourse intervened, both in the public and private sphere of sexual expression, through either the legitimation or else prohibition of particular forms of sexual activity. One of Foucault's central contentions is that the medical discourse, rather than evolving towards the uncovering of a deeper understanding of sexuality, produced instead a wealth of misunderstandings (*méconnaissance*) (1978, p. 56). In approaching female sexuality he identifies the 'hysterization of women's bodies' as the key strategic unity of knowledge and power by which women are controlled. Foucault's interpretation of this specific feature is that '. . . the feminine body was analyzed — qualified and disqualified — as being thoroughly saturated with sexuality; whereby it was integrated into the sphere of medical practices, by reason of a pathology intrinsic to it' (1978, p. 104).

The way in which particular gynaecological constructs have informed an understanding of female sexuality, female criminality and female victimology provides the crucial point of departure in this chapter. Thus, it is not simply a scientification or medicalization of female sexuality *per se*, or even 'a hysterization of women's bodies', that provides the focal concern, but the *scientia gynaecologia* of female sexuality whereby female sexual and social expressions and manifestations are almost exclusively comprehended on a gynaecological basis. Indeed, nineteenth- and early twentieth-century medical literature reveals the extent and pervasiveness of this preoccupation. Otto Weininger captured this particular obsession when he wrote, 'Man possesses sexual organs; her sexual organs possess women'.[1] The role gynaecological constructions have played in shaping past and present knowledge of female sexuality is particularly important in the assimilation of certain ideas within the legal process.

The specific purpose of this chapter is to disclose the origin and the reproduction of the various notions of the female offender and victim of sexual assault. In so doing, it is hoped to contribute to an understanding of femininity as it is constructed and assimilated in the criminal justice process, since it has pervaded and influenced the interpretation of all kinds of behaviour. During the nineteenth century, legal practice for instance was increasingly influenced by medical and especially gynaecological precepts of sexuality, which came to inform the various stages, at each and every level, of the criminal justice system. As law breakers, women were rarely, if ever, recognized as criminals, though they may well have committed crimes equal to those committed by male counterparts. Instead, the female law breaker was defined as 'sick', and the origin of her sickness was located in her gynaecology. Similarly, when women alleged that they were the victims of sexual assault, a model of gynaecology and psychology was set in motion. Victims of sexual assault were thought to bring false accusations against innocent men, for a variety of motives — accounted for by recourse to the gynaecology of women.

THE GYNAECOLOGICAL BASIS
OF FEMININITY

From the nineteenth century onwards, medical practitioners, gynaecologists and obstetricians, mental health physicians and asylum attendants, in their various ways inhibited, prohibited and regulated female behaviour by defining the discourse of appropriate sexual and social behaviour. A particular understanding of female sexuality was achieved through the reproduction of knowledge within the medical profession, and also through the dissemination of medical constructs of sexuality in everyday consciousness. The medical discourse provided an extremely powerful and effective rationale for the prohibition of a variety of forms of social and sexual activity. As the dominant ideology, it legitimated the subordination of women in various significant ways. This was achieved variously by asserting their physical limitations and physiological weakness, and also by perpetuating the belief in their psychological instability. This model became the dominant discursive practice informing decisions and resolutions affecting the lives and liberties of women in legal and everyday life.

The medical theories functioned as a 'surveillance' system whose object was to ensure the social control of appropriate gender behaviour of women. Certain things women said or did were frequently identified as symptomatic of mental illness, either the result of the natural cyclical process of reproductive life, or else the consequence of a particular gynaecological disorder. This construct embodied an inherent contradiction. Whilst reproduction and related functions were features of the natural life process, they were, at the same moment, regarded as 'pathological', and thereby frequently considered a cause of mental instability.

As a general statement, any woman suffering from a gynaecological, as opposed to a reproductive, disorder was treated punitively because such dysfunctions were assumed to be in some way related to sexual activity and abuses. For the single or married unchaste woman, the medical discourse repeatedly warned of the multiplicity of diseases, illnesses and gynaecological complaints that would follow after sexual activity or inappropriate behaviour. So it was not the wrath of God that women came to fear, but retribution through the infliction of a horrible disease, madness or surgical intervention. (It was not until the end of the nineteenth century that this belief was challenged. Dr Allbutt remarked 'It is not to be assumed that all these patients who complain of discomforts about the genital organs are masturbators or debauched . . .' (1899, p. 149).)

During the nineteenth century, the medico-gynaecological model was invoked in order to explain, diagnose, and treat various aberrant expressions of behaviour, where in fact, in the majority of cases, no evidence of organic disease or disorder was present. As a result, behaviour that at other historical moments was regarded as an expression of rebellion or simply a contravention of prevailing social norms was identified in medical rhetoric. This had the effect of introjecting expressions of behaviour onto problems of personal pathology, which supported the status quo, since 'pathologists typically see problems in terms of an individual'[2] and do not focus on problems of social structures or more pertinently, in this case, on problems of definitions, rhetoric or language.

If, as Coulter suggests, perceptual categories concerning the various definitions of mental illness are closely tied to both membership and conceptual categories,[3] then a consideration of these two categories is crucial to an analysis of the entire process of negotiation whereby women, rather than men, are defined as mentally unstable. Such an inquiry necessitates a consideration of how definitions of mental illness arose and appeared to conform and align themselves to conceptions of femininity. It is certainly curious that the conceptual categories of mental illness, crime and alcoholism, for instance, included predominantly the members of one sex. In this task of examining how others perceive, define and ascribe mental illness, an analysis of 'second order constructs' (that is, the way a shared understanding of common definitions is arrived at) is necessary. A consideration of the sequencing and organization of events as integral to such an analysis has been expressed rather more recently by Smith (1978) who describes the process by which mental illness is recognized and ascribed: 'It is not just a record of events as they happened, but of events as they were seen as relevant to reaching a decision about the character of these events' (p. 24). Smith analyses the structure of the conceptual scheme of mental illness — how it is recognized as such and how the text is organized. These two features are important in approaching gynaecological constructions of female behaviour in the nineteenth- and twentieth-century medico-legal practice.

PHYSIOLOGICAL 'CRISIS' STAGES

The gynaecology of women, that is, the structure and function of the ovaries and uterine appendages in the process of female physiology, was frequently perceived by the gynaecologist in particular, but also by the mental health physician and the asylum attendant, as the precipitating factor in derangement and aberrant behaviour. The normal stages in the reproductive life cycle were paradoxically regarded as 'crisis' stages by medical practitioners and the Lunacy Commissioners. The onset of menstruation and the subsequent experiences of pregnancy, childbirth, post parturition, lactation and the climacteric were all regarded as marking critical neurological and physiological episodes in a woman's life, functioning as the predisposing causes of instability. Savage adhered most rigidly to this view: 'There are special conditions, both physical and moral, which dispose to insanity; in women, menstruation with its irregularities, childbirth, and the change of life are potent influences' (in Allbutt, 1899, p. 184).

Menstruation

The first 'crisis' stage is marked by the onset of menstruation. Fantasies, delusions, epilepsy and hysteria were all considered to be possible consequences of this crisis. Maudsley, remarking on puberty in the female sex, said that it frequently resulted in a 'mental revolution' where young girls experienced 'fanciful quasi-hysterical feelings', and where 'although there were no fixed delusions, there are unfounded suspicions or fears . . .' (1870, p. 84). During this time it was thought that delusions of a sexual kind occurred, and that girls often imagined that they were pregnant. Mercier described this stage in similar rhetoric as a 'tumultuous revolution' and also 'a time of danger' (1890, p. 213). He maintained that the instances of rage, temper and hysteria accompanying this phase are the result of an 'indirect stress of an internal origin'. The common attitude to menstruation, despite the development of the medical discourse, was unenlightened, pristine and often based on mythology. Dr Milne wrote 'Oh menstruation thou art a fiend' (quoted in Pearsall, 1969, p. 267). In 1878, the *British Medical Journal* published certain correspondence on the subject of menstruation. One British Medical Association member reported that in his own experience women who cured hams during menstruation caused the meat to go bad. A number of letters in subsequent issues tended to confirm this view (2 March 1878, p. 324). Consider also the report of Dr Porteous to the *Obstetrical Transactions of Edinburgh* in 1877, who reported witnessing a case of vicarious menstruation where bleeding occurred from the nose and the ears.[4] Menstruation was also seen to precipitate derangement of various kinds. Mr Christopher Martin maintained in 1893 that menstruation caused increased instability and excitability, often resulting in menstrual epilepsy, where the patient is the subject of seizures. He claimed that there was a relationship between the ebb and flow of the menstrual tide and a 'menstrual nerve centre'.[5] Similarly Lawson Tait, the gynaecologist and police surgeon, argued that menstruation frequently led to derangements.

Menstruation was regarded, above all other phases, as both normal and pathological. The 'monthlies' were seen as a natural process that might precipitate a 'crisis'. Geddes and Thomson were more explicit in that they considered the phenomenon of menstruation as pathological but normal in so far as it is a normal physiological process that lies on the borders of pathological change (1899, p. 244). Marshall had this to say: 'The phenomenon of menstruation must be looked upon as belonging to the borderland of pathology' (1910, p. 112). This belief in the pathology of menstruation was made most explicit by certain medical practitioners throughout the nineteenth and twentieth century. Curiously, this view was shared by theorists in a wide variety of disciplines. Durkheim wrote: '. . . one is obliged to place menstruation among the morbid phenomena for the disturbances it causes increase female susceptibility to disease' (1964a, p. 51). There was clearly a consensus of opinion regarding the role of menstruation as a contributory factor in various forms of mental illness or aberrant behaviour.

Pregnancy and childbirth

The woman who was pregnant was considered 'sick' and in a very delicate condition. Indeed, the various stages in the childbearing process were considered a contributory factor in what the medical profession defined as mental illness. Clouston's interpretation of clinical findings of pregnant women confirmed this belief. He found that 10 per cent of insanity in women was precipitated by the reproductive phase leading up to childbirth.[6] Indeed, the Lunacy Commissioners' reports reveal the extent to which insanity in women was attributed to pregnancy. The interpretation and understanding of women during childbirth was influenced by fear and superstition. Maudsley contended that insanities during and after pregnancy occur most frequently in illegitimate pregnancies or else in women who have married late in life. He argued that melancholia was the most common form of insanity associated with this phase although, as he indicated, illness during this stage may also take the form of mania, where the patient hallucinates and 'whirls into the chaotic turmoil of her frenzy'.

Two themes in particular that accompanied the so-called scientific medical model strongly suggest that in matters related to reproduction medical opinion only confirmed in scientific jargon the mythological constructs that persisted before. The first theme, occasionally expressed by the medical profession but more typically by women themselves, was the notion that pregnancy in particular was a period of 'possession'. This theme has been explored in both contemporary sociological and anthropological research. Lewis examines the social and political factors that have influenced the interpretation of certain forms of behaviour as characterizing spirit possession.[7] Graham[8] has adopted Lewis's perspective to see just how useful his theory is in evaluating current perceptions of, and attitudes toward, pregnancy. Informed by an interactionist perspective, she seeks to explore the various ways in which the pregnant woman is constructed by the media and, in turn, how the media reproduce and reinforce a given image women have of themselves. Pregnancy is defined by the media as a time of both physical and emotional danger to the mother, and the very language and rhetoric of pregnancy and motherhood provide yet another example of the way this episode is constructed. Graham observed that the definitions of pregnancy provided by the mothers themselves were symptomatic of the occupational, intellectual and sexual restrictions placed on women. She adopts Lewis's eight characteristics of spirit possession in a non-Western society, and points out the similarities between the characteristics of the social construction of spirit possession and the social construction of pregnancy. First, in both spirit possession and in pregnancy, the individual's body is invaded by an alien. Second, the presence of this alien provides the justification of the individual's behaviour. Third, the presence of the alien exempts the individual from any responsibility for word, thought or deed. Fourth, society manages possession by domesticity, in other words by confinement. Fifth, the cure requires the intervention of the specialist. Sixth, it can be discerned as a means of coping with stress. Seventh, it is a means of gaining a particular kind of status, and, lastly, it provides a means of manipulating superiors.

This somewhat strange analogy between spirit-possession and pregnancy is evident in a nascent and implicit form in discussions of other phenomena peculiar to or predominant among women, particularly in those conditions which can be attributed to gynaecological disorders — as for example in such biological processes as menstruation and menopause and in such mental conditions as hysteria and depression. [p. 292]

The purpose of introducing Graham's work at this juncture is to provide an understanding of nineteenth-century attitudes to pregnancy. Certainly, practitioners regarded pregnancy as an invasion. Mercier, in particular, used rhetoric that could just as readily be applied to a case of spirit possession. Maudsley draws particular attention to 'the strange longings, the capriciousness, and the morbid fears of the pregnant woman' (1870, p. 91).

The climacteric

Ehrenreich, in a contemporary analysis of the nineteenth-century view, writes that the menopause 'was the final, incurable ill, the "death of the woman in the woman"' (1974, p. 21).[9] Clouston (1906) argued that many women at the climacteric take into their minds the idea that they have neglected some duty with regard to a dead child. The medical profession shared the view that it was quite possible that women might experience hallucinations and delusions relating to sexual experience, love affairs and rape. The idea of spirit possession is also provided — Mercier likens the climacteric to the devil, which '. . . did not go quietly, but cried, and rent him sore . . .' (1890, p. 242).

Much of the evidence presented here has been derived wholly from nineteenth-century accounts. This consideration of the construction of the reproductive cycle provides only one side of the medical discursive practice of misunderstanding. Before we actually embark on an investigation of the relationship between the medico-gynaecological model and the way it informed the law and perceptions of criminality and victimology, another side of this discourse — as it defines female sexuality — must first be disclosed.

THE GYNAECOLOGICAL BASIS OF SEXUALITY

The clinical discourse of the nineteenth century generated a new set of diseases that had hitherto been defined in moral terms. Many forms of behaviour and activity were prohibited, since it was believed that they precipitated illness, just as they were a manifestation of illness. The result of this medicalization of all forms of human activity was to create a definition of normality and also of abnormality supported by medical and clinical categories. Sexual activity was ripped out of its moral enclave, and regulated not only according to accepted standards of morality, but in accordance with the medical discourse on health and disease. The disease model succeeded in intervening at every possible level of sexual behaviour. In this scenario the sexual activities of women were the most rigorously supervised.

Any possible deviation from the appropriate social or sexual role — such as smoking, laughing loudly, talking excitedly, sexual relations outside marriage, or sexual relations within marriage for pleasure rather than procreation — was frequently considered the result of a disorder of gynaecological origin. American medical practitioners also agreed that disorders of the uterine organs and appendages contributed to mental illness, lunacy and instability, which became manifest in inappropriate behaviour and various acts of sexual impropriety. Hence, Skene maintained: 'insanity is often caused by diseases of the procreative organs . . . insane women should be placed in charge of a specialist for diseases of women'.[10] Similarly, Hall's treatment of insane women arose from this particular conception of causality.[11] In 1898, he examined 78 women in an asylum for the insane with a view to establishing the gynaecological basis of their instability. He operated on 33, and found five instances of perineal laceration, six of cervical laceration, seven of retroversion with adhesions, three of simple retroversion, one of clitorid adhesion, ten of salpingitic and ovarian adhesions, eight of cystic ovaries, one of parovarian cyst, four of varicocele of broad ligament plexus and one of uterine fungoids. Hall concluded that local pelvic irritation (masturbation) may produce abnormal cerebral activity giving rise to abnormal menstruation, and that there exists some correlation between pelvic diseases and mental aberration. He was quite clearly of the view that insanity was merely a manifestation of the diseases of the procreative organs. Maudsley had also maintained that the 'irritation of ovaries or uterus' was sometimes a direct cause of nymphomania (1870, p. 82). While in 1902 Baker discovered that female criminal lunatics had a history of uterine disease and disorders of menstruation.[12]

From 1850 onwards four specific formulations of the relationship between sexuality, gynaecology and insanity were being proposed by various practitioners. First, it was maintained that the very act of sexual connection had a debilitating effect on the female gynaecological organs. Tilt asserted that sexual connection had a 'downright poisonous influence on the generative organs of some women' (1862, p. 234). More specifically he claimed that sub-acute ovaritis 'is more especially the sequel of the culpable exercise of intercourse, as seen in women in every respect unfortunate' (p. 307) and that 'Marriage may give an additional impulse to the morbidly disposed ovaries'. These views were reiterated by Dr Thomas, who contended that 'the act of sexual intercourse . . . becomes an absolute and positive source of disease'.[13] This particular theory exercised considerable control over women and sexual activity.

Second, dissension amongst gynaecologists produced the diametrically opposed view that sexual abstinence in women was harmful for mental health and the proper functioning of the gynaecological organs. Tilt maintained that the privation of sexual stimulus was a predisposing factor of sub-acute ovaritis (1862, p. 309). It was also considered to result in sexual excitement of a physical nature, which had an influence on stimulating the organs of ovulation. This view was developed and elaborated by various practitioners. Consider the views of MacNaughton Jones, who argued that to restrain a married woman from intercourse has the effect of producing erotic tendencies and the whims and fancies of hysterical encounters (1884, p. 127). Marriage 'mattered' for this school of thought and was frequently advocated as a cure for various sexual and gynaecological ailments. Tait reported a particular case study where the woman in question had been suffering with 'menstrual epilepsy'. At first the perineum had been leeched; a galvanic pessary was then introduced into the uterus and aloes and iron were administered. Finally, the physician advised the patient to 'get married' since her social condition would effect a permanent cure.[14] Such advice was by no means uncommon.

The greatest consensus of medical opinion concerned the relationship of sexual excess to gynaecological disorders, and in turn of sexual excess to insanity and aberrant behaviour, but even here a chicken—egg type disagreement arose. Tilt, for instance, suggested that sexual excess was the effect of a disorder of the genital organs (1862, p. 358). In providing evidence for his theory he cited the case of a 16-year-old girl who was known to cohabit with twelve to fourteen persons a day. Upon examination it was found that the fallopian tubes were united to her ovaries. Hewitt was more specific in proposing that sexual excess was the cause of chronic conjestion of the uterus and other secondary disorders (1872, pp. 14, 568). During both intercourse and ovulation there is an 'erection' of the uterus. In addition he maintained that the unnatural excitement of the generative organs also leads to 'uterine mischief'. Furthermore, sexual excesses occasioned pain in the ovarian region and the unnatural exercise of the generative organs was said to produce ovarian volliculitus and peritonitis. Some time later, Allbutt similarly proposed that sexual impropriety led to stupor and hypochondriasis (1899, p. 51).

The greatest preoccupation of the gynaecologist was the control of female sexual behaviour. This was achieved by creating a number of clinical categories defining the fallen, unchaste and precipitating woman. Nymphomania was the main clinical classification for the unchaste woman. The term itself, from all accounts, seems to derive from Acton's famous treatise *The Functions and Disorders of the Reproductive Organs* (1857). Very broadly speaking, nymphomania described a condition of sexual depravity and wantoness in women that amounted to unchaste behaviour and self-abuse. During the first half of the nineteenth century nymphomania was primarily associated with moral insanity. Acton wrote: 'I admit, of course, the existence of sexual excitement terminating even in nymphomania, a form of insanity which those accustomed to visit lunatic asylums must be fully conversant with' (quoted in Marcus, 1971, p. 31). Acton went further and sub-divided the category of nymphomania into three types according to the particular manifestation of sexual excess. He observed andromania, clitoromania and hypatomania. After the middle of the nineteenth century, as in most other forms of mental illness, an attempt was made to identify a pathological base, but there was a wide difference of opinion as to causality. Maudsley, for instance, identified the cause of nymphomania as an 'irritation of the uterine appendages' (1870, p. 82). Throughout the nineteenth century the relationship of masturbation to nymphomania is made particularly clear. Maudsley maintained that three-fifths of his patients were incarcarated because of self-abuse. This was especially thought to be the case amongst working-class women.

On the other hand, sexual excess or self-abuse was regarded as the effect of specific gynaecological or neurological disorders. Dr Magnan's paper, read before the Academy of Medicine in 1855, distinguished four bases within the cerebro-spinal system that predispose sexual excesses or perversion. In 1886, Routh adopted this basic categorization in order to analyse female sexuality. Within this categorization, onanism is the result of an organic disorder located in the fourth lumbar vertebrae, whilst orgasm and sexual excitement are located in the posterior cerebro-spinal area. Perverted sexuality is located in the anterior cerebro-spinal area, whilst erotomania is related to anterior cerebro or psychical causes. For instance, in the event of masturbation, the irritation of the pudenda excites an active reflex upon the genito-spinal tract. The relationship of sexual behaviour to neurological conditions was also considered by Tait. The continual practice of onanism was said to lead to a hypertrophy of the clitoris and enlargement of the nymphae and ultimately insanity. It was therefore widely believed that such tumours were particularly common among fallen and unchaste women and prostitutes.[15]

The gynaecological construction of female sexuality, its causes and its effects was class bound. Working-class women were typically thought to be of ill fame. It was believed that there was a far greater likelihood that such women were morally insane and nympho-maniacs. They were considered totally responsible for their own depravity, and it was more likely that gynaecological disorder would be seen as the result of sexual excess or self-abuse. By contrast, the behaviour of a middle-class nymphomaniac or unchaste woman — an infrequent occurrence — was considered symptomatic of an organic malfunction. Routh argued that the prostitute may be suffering from a disease of the posterior cerebro-spinal area, which strongly suggests that the causes of prostitution were negotiable irrespective of social class. However, the considered cause of sexually and socially inappropriate behaviour and the social class of the patient were factors that exercised a considerable influence on the particular methods of treatment considered most efficacious and appropriate.

TREATMENT OF GYNAECOLOGICAL, SOCIO-SEXUAL
AND MENTAL DISORDERS

The methods of treatment for nervous complaints and gynaecological disorders and for sexual and social deviancy were punitive,
varying from pouring cold water over the head, face and neck to
exercising pressure on the ovarian region. The so-called hysteric
had a special cure in store — physicians advocated that 'the face
and neck may be smartly slapped with a wet towel' (Ormerod, 1899,
p. 125). If such methods as these failed to effect a cure, then the
application of leeches to the perineum was considered a means of
curing nervous disorders. The infamous leech was used frequently
and widely until the end of the nineteenth century.

Exactly how many women were actually at the receiving end of
this kind of 'treatment' is uncertain, but if physicians regarded
expressive behaviour or individuality in women as a manifestation
of an illness then the numbers must have been considerable.
Consider, for instance, Savage's description of women suffering
from 'simple hysterical mania': 'They rapidly become less and less
conventional. Thus a lady will smoke, talk slang, or be extravagant
in dress; and will declare her intention of doing as she likes. At this
stage love affairs, and the like complications are common' (in
Allbutt, 1899, p. 355). As for the women incarcerated in lunatic
asylums, they provided guinea pigs for asylum attendants and
physicians who wanted to try out various 'cures' on them. The
principal objective was the control of the hysteric or neurasthenic
who was misunderstood and consequently mistreated. From the
application of leeches to the use of the nerve extract prepared from
the brain of a rabbit for the condition of hysteria or neurasthenia
(*British Medical Journal,* 1893, p. 1321), women were the victims of
therapeutic ignorance.

Gynaecological, socio-sexual and mental disorders were
frequently treated with electricity. Wright, remarking on this
frequently used method, commented in 1889 that like many other
forms of treatment it was 'only on trial'.[16] The galvanometer and the
local application of electrodes were nevertheless often used in
cases of disordered menstruation and in rather more serious
complaints of uterine displacement and ovarian tumours. The
principal technique involved the introduction of a platinum
electrode into the uterus. The side-effects of electrical treatment

varied from nausea and severe headaches to death in certain cases from shock. These so-called side-effects were ironically treated with the further administration of harmful and dubious drugs. If these more violent forms of cure had no effect then a much more subtle kind of treatment was administered. The Weir—Mitchell method involved a combination of rest for long periods and electrical treatment together with an emphasis on eating, if not over-eating, and local massage. In fact this method constituted a form of brainwashing whereby the patient would be persuaded to conform and to accept the appropriate role of motherhood, domesticity and passivity and subservience to men.

Local massage was instituted as a scientific cure for a variety of disorders, and was inevitably open to wide abuse. The anonymous writer of *My Secret Life* knew of doctors who exploited their power to observe the female person (in Harrison, 1967, p. 254). Newman commented on the tendency of young doctors to interfere with female patients (1889, p. 279). The emphasis on having faith in the physician was all part of the tyranny. For in fact it was reported by some that the local treatment experienced by many women was roughly equivalent to rape. Elizabeth Blackwell criticized the method of local massage as it encouraged abuse and 'seldom allowed a lady to retain her valued person' (quoted in Wood, 1974, p. 41). A letter to the *British Medical Journal* in 1866 on the subject of uterine and vaginal massage pointed to the abuses of this method and stated that many physicians insisted on 'digital exploration'. In defending themselves against such accusations, doctors maintained that women themselves were 'reduced by the constant use of the speculum to the mental and moral condition of prostitutes' (Carter, 1853, pp. 66-7).

The extent of the control over women patients by male physicians is revealed in the types of drug given in cases of mental and sexual aberration. For instance, cases of hysteria and especially onanism and nymphomania were treated by administering particularly large doses of the soporific drug potassium bromide in order to depress the nervous system and ultimately control the patient. It was generally agreed that bromide of potassium was most suitable for cases of nymphomania,[17] and for the 'irritable, excitable condition so common in women with uterine irregularities'.[18]

That is not to argue that there was general consensus of medical opinion as to the most suitable method of therapy in such cases.

Indeed, contradictions revealed themselves at each and every level of gynaecological treatment. In certain cases rest cures were advocated, whilst other physicians preferred exercise cures. For instance, the profession was deeply divided over the therapeutic value of the bicycle. Some physicians advocated the use of the bicycle in facilitating a cure in cases of hysterical and sexual aberration.[19] On the other hand, Theresa Bannan remarked on the poisonous influence of bicycling for the female sex: 'one danger is the saddle, which is physically and morally injurious to women — Moreover, the impingement and vibration of the saddle can and do act as a sexual excitant' (*Medical Record,* 1895). In this respect there was also deep concern over the use of the treadle sewing machine as this was considered to have morally harmful effects of a similar nature (Ellis, 1933, p. 104).

The most barbarous and appalling 'treatment and cure' for sexual excess, irregular sexual practices and occasionally epilepsy and hysteria, was the surgical excision of the clitoris (clitoridectomy). Contrary to popular belief, this ancient and primitive custom is not just a 'survival' from the past that persists in peasant and pastoral societies; it was advanced as a cure for a wide variety of female disorders in nineteenth-century gynaecological practice. Evidence shows that this operation was performed in both hospitals and asylums. Some female patients asked for surgical intervention for fear of going mad if they persisted with their onanistic habit. The operation was also performed experimentally on pauper women.

The actual extent of this practice was somewhat concealed, partly because of Victorian prudery. It was considered far too indelicate to discuss the female genitalia, and especially the clitoris, or to profess to any knowledge of the subject. For instance, in 1867 Sir Samuel Baker provided the *Lancet* with an account of clitoridectomy practised on Nubian women. Like so many other articles written at this time on sexual matters, it was published in Latin in order to make such matters inaccessible to the unspecialized reader who might casually peruse the journal.

At the same time, clitoridectomy was practised by many eminent members of the British Medical Association. Baker Brown pioneered this disreputable operation in the name of treatment. He claimed that the removal of the clitoris provided the most effective and guaranteed cure for 'peripheral pudic irritation' (masturbation), which precipitated amongst other things hysteria, spinal irritation, epileptic and cateleptic fits and mania. He was so utterly and resolutely convinced of the efficacy of this operation that in certain cases he removed the clitoris without first seeking the permission of the father or husband, much less the consent of the patient herself. It was with regard to this question of medical ethics and consent, not to the operation itself, that Baker Brown faced a series of charges before the Obstetrical Society in 1866-67, which resulted in his removal from the society in 1867. Dr West, in criticizing the unethicality of Baker Brown's method, said '. . . without saying one word to the lady or her husband, or hinting in any way what he was about to do, cut off her clitoris' (*The Lancet,* 6 April 1867, p. 427). In his reply and defence, Baker Brown denied performing clitoridectomy without the cognizance of the patient. He said that the patient had confessed she was in the habit of rubbing the clitoris and the labia.

Although Baker Brown was removed from the medical register this did not mean that clitoridectomy did not continue to be practised. Dr West, who had objected to Baker Brown's unethical and unprofessional approach, himself advocated clitoridectomy, and applied caustics locally in order to cure hysterical fits. In 1872, Professor Hewitt advocated the removal of the clitoris in cases of epilepsy (Vol. 2, p. 653) and, almost twenty years after the Baker Brown controversy, Dr Routh presented a paper to the British Gynaecological Society's Annual Meeting (1886, p. 509) where he reasserted the view that clitoridectomy represented the most effective cure for masturbation and nymphomania. During the course of his address he stressed that it was the duty of every physician to do the very best for the patient, despite the growing prejudice against this practice. He claimed to have performed the excision on three occasions. Mr Heydon condoned its efficacy, claiming that the operation provided an effective cure for epileptic fits and also in cases of hysterical mania. Dr Smith, for instance, performed this particular act of barbarism in cases of sexual excitement. In Britain, as in many other Western countries, the clitoris was considered to be at the very heart of female sexual aberration and disorder. In the 1860s, Baker Brown had considered that the excitement of the clitoris might lead to death in certain cases. Routh had similar reservations regarding the clitoris, which undoubtedly affected his perception of symptoms, diagnosis and treatment (1886, p. 497). In one particular case, where a patient had died, Routh stated that she had feared that she might die of the passions that devoured her. Webster maintained that the practice of masturbation might result in a nervous breakdown, besides hypertrophy of the clitoris for which a complete cure was only deemed possible through the removal of the affected parts.[20] Dr Murray, in effecting a cure, had scraped the clitoris away with a platinum loop heated with electricity, which he seemed to think was a most effective cure.[21] In 1900, and even later, the operation continued to be used. At this time, it was much more likely that the female pauper or asylum patient was at the mercy of such kinds of experimentation. The attitude toward asylum and pauper patients, and by definition the sexuality of working-class women, is reflected in the remarks of Dr Campbell Clark, who at the British Medical Association Conference in Glasgow proposed that masturbation and sexual excitement were aberrations confined solely to female pauper patients.

In both America and Germany, the medical profession shared very similar views regarding the danger of the clitoris and the advantages of its removal. In America, Dr Walker regarded the clitoris as the predisposing causal factor in instances of neurosis, chorea, and epilepsy in children, and removed the clitoris in such cases.[22] Dr Morris proposed another method of mutilating women. He maintained that the irritation of the clitoris (masturbation) led to sexual perversions of all kinds. He also claimed that as the clitoris degenerates, then sexual desire lessens. His theory embraced sexual racism in a unique way. The glans clitoris in white women was small, whilst in negroes it was large. He therefore advocated the separation of the prepuce from the glans clitoridis, which resulted in controlling the desire to masturbate and curing nymphomania. He remarked: 'The clitoris is a little electric button which pressed by adhesions rings up the whole nervous system'.[23]

The practice of clitoridectomy was yet another expression of the effort to control female sexual behaviour and to enforce, if necessary by surgical means, conformity to an appropriate pattern of femininity. It has continued until fairly recently (see Ehrenreich and English, 1979, p. 111). Furthermore, it reflects the extent of the misunderstanding of female sexuality within the gynaecological discourse.

However, the actual removal of the clitoris was in most cases suggested as a last resort in the attempt to control and cure sexual

aberrations in women. Not all physicians agreed that clitoridectomy would provide the ultimate cure in cases of onanism and
nymphomania. Forbes Winslow, for instance, maintained that in
advocating the excision of the clitoris as a cure Baker Brown 'begins
his treatment of these cases at the wrong end' (*British Medical
Journal,* 22 December 1866, p. 706). Allbutt remarked that the
female patient was frequently 'entangled in the net of the
gynaecologist' (quoted in MacNaughton Jones, 1893, p. 282).

The actual source of sexual excitement was not considered by all
physicians to be attributable to the clitoris. One school of thought
considered it more appropriate to consider the uterus and the
ovaries in this context. It was not uncommon for women whose
sexual behaviour was inappropriate to have their ovaries removed
by a physician in an attempt to provide a cure. Spratling had remarked
that 'nothing short of ovariotomy will be found to deserve the term
palliative' (*Medical Record,* 1895, p. 442). Elizabeth Blackwell
referred to this surgical interference as the 'castration of women'.

The particular fate of one young female patient in the 1880s
deserves special consideration. Dr Stewart recorded that he had
succeeded in 'obtaining a complete confessional from the woman'
concerning her onanistic habit. (The confession of sexual practices
to a gynaecologist was considered the first step in the direction of
effecting a cure.) This resulted in the perpetration of a variety of
cruel punitive forms of treatment or prevention that eventually
resulted in her total desexualization. The first method was
administered by her mother who regularly whipped her daughter's
hands. The second strategy in Stewart's arsenal was the oral
administration of bromides and chloral. The third line of attack was
the local application of carbolic acid and hydrochlorate of cocaine.
This was administered to little avail. In consequence, a pad stuck
full of sharp steel pins was placed over the vulva. Massage and
electrical treatment followed. Finally, the physician declared that
he had no alternative but to remove her ovaries.[24] The loss of her
womanhood was considered infinitely less fateful than the evil and
debasing habit of onanism.

THE GYNAECOLOGICAL DISCOURSE IN
LEGAL PRACTICE

The gynaecological discourse elaborated in the preceding pages has focused primarily on the nature and construction of female sexuality and reproduction. The narrative does not abruptly end in 1900; the beliefs regarding the relationship of gynaecology and the reproductive cycle to female behaviour have persisted, albeit in a somewhat less apparent form until the present. The primary reason for concentrating on this historical period is to reveal how such beliefs originated within a scientific frame.

It is now time to study the way legal practice has been informed by such gynaecological constructions and thereby reproduced them. Consider for instance the role attributed to the reproductive cycle in crime commission. Ellis remarked: 'It is a matter of some importance that in the exact investigation of any fact in a woman's life or organism, we ought to know its exact position in the woman's cyclic life' (1894, p. 256). This view was widely shared by members of the medical profession. It is not surprising, therefore, that in attempting to provide explanations for the female offender a gynaecological basis was posited as the predisposing cause. Nor is it inconsistent with this view that victims of sexual assault were frequently perceived as bringing false charges in consequence of some gynaecological aberration. Such opinions were not only to influence the law, but in general affected perceptions of women's fitness for public life. Women were consistently presented as unstable, irresponsible and hysterical. Whilst it was quite easy to see women as mentally unstable, since this was no more than an exaggeration of her 'normal and pathological' condition, it was virtually impossible to see women as criminals. Women who broke the law were typically described as unstable.

The taxonomies and categories available for the classification of the female offender reflect this conflation. Women were incarcerated either in lunatic asylums or in prisons where they were classified as lunatics (aberrant behaviour), criminal lunatics (rule-breaking behaviour) or as criminals (rule-breaking behaviour, no mental or gynaecological disorder present). Most women were defined as criminal lunatics as evidenced in the various statistics provided by the Commissioners in Lunacy.[25] Gynaecological disorders and the various stages of the reproductive cycle were all predisposing causes advanced by the medical profession as contributory influences in various forms of aberrant behaviour.

The gynaecological discourse influenced the formation of statute and the resolutions of select committees, as well as the criminal justice process. I have already discussed the influence of the image of female passivity. The belief in the instability of women was also extremely influential, especially regarding reform measures pressing for female enfranchisement. For instance, the Qualification of Women Bill of 1907 was opposed by Earl Halsbury and Lord James of Hereford because '. . . her mental constitution is supposed to be so ill balanced that it is practically certain that she will devote her days and nights to breaking up political meetings and assaulting the police'.[26] Remarking on the nature of women, Earl Halsbury said:

> I think they are too hysterical, they are too much disposed to be guided by feeling and not by cold reason, and they are very much disposed to refuse any kind of compromise. I do not think that women are safeguards in government; they are very unsafe guides when they argue from sentiment and not from reason.[27]

The message here is blatant: any behaviour that departed from the female role and sexual expectation was interpreted as a manifestation of mental or reproductive instability.

GYNAECOLOGY AND THE FEMALE OFFENDER

As a general rule, the very idea that a woman could or would commit a criminal act was fundamentally unthinkable — with the possible exception of paupers and prostitutes. Criminal activity was typically defined as predominantly male, and more often than not consistent with the behaviour of lower-class males. The concept of female criminality was as incompatible with the idealized bourgeois conception of female behaviour as the concept of mental illness was with the idealized conception of masculinity. The judicial statistics for this period reveal that the crimes committed by women fell into the following categories: prostitution (soliciting), procuring young children, concealment of birth, child stealing and shoplifting. It appeared that the female offender committed crimes that were regarded as an extension of her normal appropriate activity. When women were apprehended and charged with crimes of homicide, theft, assault or arson, their behaviour has been interpreted, more often than not, not as the manifestation of a criminal mind or a criminal type but as the end product of an unbalanced mentality. Indeed, since the mid-nineteenth century, the medical and legal professions have shared the view that such behaviour is more than likely related to the reproductive cycle or to gynaecological disorders.

Whether indeed episodes such as menstruation, lactation or mental sexual delusion really influence the commission of crime is not what concerns us. What is of very real importance is the extent to which such beliefs have been influential in facilitating and providing certain motivatory and mitigatory accounts to 'significant others' in the explanation of female crime.

The various nineteenth-century studies of the female offender point decidedly to the reproductive cycle as the predisposing element in criminal activity. Lombroso's classic study, *La Donna Delinquenti (The Female Offender,* 1895), concluded that the criminal offences of the hysteric revolve around the sexual function. He maintained that female crime was closely correlated with the reproductive phase, producing statistical evidence in support of his theory. Out of 80 women arrested for opposing the police or for assault, 71 were at the menstrual. Ellis corroborated these views: 'Whenever a woman commits a deed of criminal violence it is extremely probable that she is at her monthly period . . .' (1894, p. 254). Ellis maintained that a relationship between an act of violence and the monthly cycle 'should be ascertained as a matter of routine'. The belief in the existence of a correlation between menstruation and crime commission was widely supported throughout the nineteenth century, and it can be observed that menstruation has been regarded as a significant contributory factor in the offence of shoplifting by women.

Evidence suggests that in cases involving middle-class defendants it was not untypical to offer a plea of insanity. Fee maintains that an elegant lady caught stealing would be more likely to be defended on a plea of insanity than a dock worker (1978, p. 633). She quotes John Bucknill who in 1858 argued that kleptomania was urged as a defence for ladies of respectable connection. Marc alleged that kleptomania was a criminal disorder manifest in women labouring under disordered menstruation or in those far advanced in pregnancy. Tait maintained that 'special dangers' await women at this time (1889, p. 151). One of the dangers was explicated by Dr Macnaughton Jones in a seminal address to the Annual Meeting of the British Medical Association in 1900. He urged strongly that an aberration of the sexual function, menstrual disorders and physiological changes could lead to crime and erratic moral acts and should be taken into consideration in determining the responsibility of a woman who is charged with a criminal act. The view that menstruation was a predisposing factor in crime and mental conditions and also suicide was well supported by Drs Shaw and Westcott who discovered that out of 700 suicides, 200 killed themselves at the change of life and most of the others were menstruating at the time.[28]

The repercussions of such opinions resounded throughout the legal field. In trials for theft, homicide and arson, the evidence of menstruation in the life of the defendant was in certain instances introduced during the nineteenth century. In the criminal trial of *R v Brixey* (1845), a maidservant was charged with the murder of an infant in her care. She was acquitted on the ground of insanity, probably arising from obstructed menstruation (Taylor, 1865, pp. 1109-10). Disordered menstruation was also introduced as a defence strategy in *R v Shepherd* in 1845.[29] A woman charged with theft was found not guilty on the ground of insanity (kleptomania) since it was decided that she had stolen certain goods whilst suffering from amenorrhoea (Taylor, 1865, p. 1125).

This belief that menstruation and its various disorders were related to insanity and to crime was well documented throughout the twentieth century (see, for example, Ross, 1909). However, by 1927 there was growing disagreement about the influence of menstruation. Fairfield argued that menstruation had only a trivial effect on body chemistry, and rejected the thesis that physiological crises had an influence on crime.[30] Nevertheless, the view persisted. McIlroy contributed to this mythology when she maintained that dysmenorrhoea was prevalent amongst typists.[31] Vigorous dancing was prescribed to effect a return to a normal state of health. Writing in the 1960s, Dalton found that 491 women in Holloway prison had committed their crime during the pre-menstrual or menstrual period.[32]

Pregnancy has also been considered by the legal profession as a contributory factor in an act committed by a woman when a plea of insanity is offered. Taylor, a professor of medical jurisprudence, maintained that the changes in the uterus during pregnancy often resulted in women perpetrating crimes of great seriousness such as murder and arson without a motive (1865, p. 878).

There is overwhelming evidence that considerable numbers of women were regarded as temporarily insane after childbirth. The

Report of the Commissioners in Lunacy for 1879 revealed that out of 964 women admitted to private hospitals for the insane, in 11 women the cause of insanity was pregnancy, 60 women were considered insane as a result of parturition, and 10 women were considered temporarily insane as a result of lactation. For the same year, out of a total of 5761 women in pauper hospitals for the insane, in 68 the considered cause of insanity was pregnancy, 357 were admitted as the result of parturition and 137 as the result of lactation. Certainly, since 1850, maternal filicide has frequently been defended by relating it to post-puerperal states and to lactation.

Both case law and statute reflect the medico-legal assumptions frequently made regarding this crime and the tendency of courts to acquit the female defendant on grounds of post-natal conditions. In case law, the relation between childbirth, homicidal mania and maternal filicide is well demonstrated in the court processing of the case of *R v Ryder* (1856) where a mother killed her child by placing it in a pan of water. Judge Erle, in summing up, remarked that the insanity was temporary, due to the effect of childbirth (Taylor, 1865, p. 1122). The relation of lactation to temporary insanity was considered by Dr Ashwell as early as 1844. He claimed that undue lactation might give rise to an attack of mania under which the murder of the offspring might be perpetrated.[33] These and related assumptions have influenced the handling of such cases since *R v Lacey* (1858) (Taylor, 1865, p. 1122). It is also partially reflected in *R v Vyse* (1862) where the defendant poisoned two of her children. The defending counsel raised the defence of insanity not only on the ground that there were instances of insanity present in the defendant's family, but he also alluded to the fact that she was suffering from 'undue lactation': 'Whilst she was suckling her last child her health became very much deteriorated and he advised her to wean the child and to give up attending business for a time'.[34] In *R v Law* (1862) the defendant had killed both her husband and her child. It was decided that the jury might find her not guilty, 'having killed her husband immediately after an apparent recovery from a *disease* [the result of childbirth] which caused a great loss of blood and exhausted the vessels of the brain, and thus so weakened its power and so tended to produce insane delusions of the senses . . .' (emphasis added).[35] Chief Justice Erle stated that there is a state of disease resulting from childbirth, thus establishing an important precedent. By 1922 the Infanticide Bill had been introduced, which would reduce a murder charge to one of infanticide if it could be shown that the defendant was suffering from temporary insanity associated with the recent birth of the child.

Of course the belief that the reproductive cycle or else gynaecological disorders have an influence in the commission of crime has been muted in the twentieth century. For the most part it is an idea that has been subject to heavy criticism. However, what certainly requires some consideration is the way in which male and female offenders are processed differentially with regard to the Infanticide Act today. The Butler Committee Report (1974-75) stated that the medical principles of the report may no longer be relevant, since puerperal psychoses are now regarded as no different from others.

GYNAECOLOGY AND THE FEMALE VICTIM

The socio-legal construction of the sexual assault victim was aided by the belief in 'hysterization of women's bodies' and gynaecological definitions of sexuality. The sexual assault complainant, whether a working-class woman or middle-class lady, was considered to be making a false accusation of a sexual nature, either out of spite, malice or revenge, or else out of shame and an effort to conceal an act of unchastity. Allegations of a sexual kind were also frequently considered to arise from hallucinations, fantasy or delusions. It is this latter category that is of special concern, and I shall consider the way in which this particular belief became decisive in the organization of the text when a woman brought a sexual assault charge.

The interesting thing here is that the false accusation hypothesis had no class boundaries. As a general rule women of working-class origin were regarded as bringing sexual charges out of malice, spite or monetary motives, whilst middle- and upper-class ladies were thought to be subject to sexual fantasy and delusion. The only real difference lay in the responsibility attributed to these two classes of women. There was a tendency to treat the working-class sexual complainant in a punitive way since it was thought her allegation was made with the precise objective of seeing a man's ruination. The middle-class complainant, by contrast, was not regarded as responsible for her actions, for she was thought to be 'sick' and therefore her allegation had no guilty intent.

The view that women of the upper and middle classes especially suffered from hysteria that often led to sexual aberrations found considerable support in the nineteenth century. Dr Mercier discovered that the virgin and the gentlewoman were particularly prone to hysterical fits and that such hysteria was especially common amongst those who led idle lives (1890, p. 228). Mercier quotes Mercatius: 'Seldom, should you see a hired servant, a poor handmaid, though ancient, that is kept hard to her work, and bodily labour, a coarse country wench, troubled in this kind; but noble virgins, nice gentlewomen, such as are solitary and idle . . .'. This view of the idle rich was also expressed by Aveling who asserted that 'those who sit the greater part of their lives', and 'those who adopt the dorsal reclining position during the greater part of the day' were particularly prone to leucorrhoea and problems of the vulva.[36] By contrast, working-class women were not traditionally considered to be subject to hysteria. If they suffered from hysterical symptoms then the cause was related to sexual excess, vice and depravity.

The hysterical condition was at first considered more specific to women than to men. It was manifest through fits of temper, fainting, tears, sexual delusions and hallucinations. In some accounts hysteria was described as a temporary moment of possession. Hysteria served to epitomize the 'cult of female invalidism', and the various forms of fits were considered to have causes both in pathology and in certain specific external factors. However, despite the obvious ambiguity over the precise aetiological origin of the disease, it continued as a general rule to be defined in organic terms as caused by some malfunction of the reproductive organs or the irritation of the ovaries or uterus. The medical profession continued to insist that hysteria was a female ill even into the twentieth century. In 1906 Savage wrote: 'The hysterical border is chiefly inhabited by women'.

A variety of conditions was thought to accompany hysteria, especially sexual fantasies and delusions and hallucinations. Practitioners exaggerated the sexual component of women's hysteria and defined women's experiences of sexual intimidation, assault and rape, seduction and incest, as arising not from real events but either from imagined sexual longings or else from sexual excess.

> . . . thus, among younger women we occasionally meet with those who imagine that they have been injuriously affected by some man; and

such will write compromising letters, or make accusations against
gentlemen, demanding satisfaction, or that their characters shall be
cleared before the public. [Savage, 1884, p. 258]

In providing an instance of such sexual fantasies, he said that one
patient had told him that one man had caused her to feel all sorts of
sexual urges and she was convinced that by some means or other he
was going to have his way with her. Savage also observed that
delusional insanity of this nature was common amongst widows,
and referred to the particular delusions experienced by women at
the climacteric. Such women apparently complain of persons taking
sexual liberties with them and the hideous sexual tortures to which
they are subjected. Allegations of sexual assault were thus able to
be marginalized. This essentially gynaecological view provided
both the law and also the police with a powerful rationale for
treating genuine cases of sexual assault by fathers, employers and
medical practitioners as further instances of fantasy.

Sexual hallucinations were considered to be a common
occurrence in the hysterical woman. Dr Norman observed that
certain hallucinations were often associated with sexual delusions
of hearing and of smell, which particularly affected women during
the climacteric. More important in influencing attitudes to sexual
assault victims, he maintained that hallucinations of the general
sense were most common, especially delusions of persecution.

> On certain female sufferers from delusions of persecution all kinds of
> sexual outrages are perpetrated. They complain not only of being
> violated (by men, and in some cases by beasts, as a mode of torture
> and disgrace — outrages which they say occur mostly at night, or
> when they are asleep), but also of sensations produced by occult
> means in their genitalia when they are awake, such as dilation, and so
> forth. [1899, p. 393]

Tuke, in *A Dictionary of Psychological Medicine* (1892), also stated
that widows and single women are especially prone to a disease
characterized by perversions of feeling of the senses and of a sexual
nature.

Sexual delusions and hallucinations were considered by the
medical profession to affect the unmarried especially. In 1870,
Maudsley evolved the term 'old maid's insanity': 'women who believe
themselves to be seduced by lovers or ravished by persecutors
during the night, sexual hallucinations being an ovarian or uterine
excitement might also be described as the characteristic of old

maids.' This view was supported in the writings of Clouston, Mercier and Savage, who argued that old women are especially prone to bring allegations of a sexual kind against men.

The diagnosis of sexual delusions, hallucinations, longings and trauma was not confined to chaste women. It was occasionally used to understand unchaste, sexually precipitating women, although the unchaste woman (who was invariably considered to be working class) was thought to experience sexual delusions because of moral depravity.

These views on the predilection of women to experience sexual fantasy as a result of the reproductive cycle, gynaecological disorder or sexual excess leading to insanity influenced the legal consideration of the sexual victim. Any sex charge resulted in mobilizing sex-gender medical accounts. Because a literature existed on sexual delusions of rape in women, the law was immediately influenced. The way in which the relationship of gynaecology, victimology and the law affects the criminal justice system is to be explored in greater detail later (see Chapter 4).

The principal discourse during the nineteenth and twentieth century that explained femininity, female sexuality, female deviancy and female victimology was the *scientia gynaecologia*. Although there was some disagreement regarding the direction of the causal relation of gynaecology and mental health, gynaecological disorders won the day. The differences between the sexes were rooted in the social construction of female gynaecology. This resulted in a gross misunderstanding, whereby women were seen as victims of their own gynaecology, which dictated their activities and intellect. Any display of independence or individuality in women was considered the result of a gynaecologial disorder. Being the victim of a sexual offence or being an offender were both considered the result of a gynaecological disorder. The construct of woman was saturated with a belief in gynaecological determinism from which no woman could escape. The ultimate effect of this belief was to cast incredibility on women generally. They were excluded from participation in certain areas of life and denied rights and responsibilities. As victims of sexual offences they were mistrusted and their allegations treated with suspicion. As offenders they were sick and disordered, but rarely if ever criminal.

CHAPTER 4

Masochism or Fantasy:
Psychoanalysis and Rape

Do as the lasses do — say 'no' but take it. [Scottish saying]

INTRODUCTION

The emergence of psychoanalysis at the beginning of the twentieth century marked a decisive shift within the medical model as it had defined female sexuality. The period from 1850 to 1900, in particular, was characterized by a rapidly growing gynaecologization of female sexuality and behaviour, whilst from 1900 onwards psychoanalysis redefined the structural basis of female sexual expression by relocating it in the structure of the unconscious mind. The various behavioural manifestations and expressions of the subconscious mind, were, in part, regarded as deep-seated responses to the anatomical distinction between the sexes. Female sexuality was perceived not so much as the manifestation of a given gynaecological or physiological structure, but rather as the expression of the female psyche, as constructed in response to the absence of a phallus.

Lacan (1977a) elaborates a new way in which the study of the cultural acquisition of sexuality might be approached. His decisive contribution in his re-reading of Freud is contained in his axiom that the unconscious mind is structured as a language. In proceeding from a formulation whereby language and culture precede the development and growth of each individual consciousness, the unconscious mind is construed as the effect and not the cause of language; by the same token the conscious mind is also effect. The individual subject then acquires language and the conscious mind and thereby finds a place in language or 'falls ill'. In this way, women either accept a patriarchal definition of the conscious and unconscious mind, accept male definitions of their fears and longings, or else 'fall ill'.

100

Of direct consequence for an understanding of sexuality is the particular distinction between normal and abnormal behaviour made by psychoanalysis. For instance, nineteenth-century gynae-cologists and mental health physicians recognized and identified what they considered to be manifestations of sexual fantasy and masochism in women caused by a 'sick' mind — the product of a reproductive or gynaecological disorder. The psychoanalytical discipline, by contrast, considered the elements of sexual fantasy and masochism as essential characteristic features of femininity. In this sense, psychoanalysis normalized certain manifestations that had hitherto been considered 'pathological'. Any distinction between normality and abnormality was one of degree only in this particular construction.

Two extremely significant themes have emerged from psycho-analysis that have had the profoundest and most damaging effect on the interpretation and construction of female sexuality in both legal and everyday practice. The first theme is the interpretation of the female unconscious mind as masochistic. This has given support to the belief that women often enjoy violence during coitus, and therefore might precipitate or actively encourage it. The result of this particular psychoanalytical construction is particularly disastrous for a reading of the rape situation. Victims of sexual assault are interpreted via the intervention of 'vulgar' Freudianism as desiring rape and at a subconscious level consenting to sex even when at a conscious level they may say 'no'. This interpretation especially aids the false allegation hypothesis, as gynaecological constructs had aided it before. The second theme elaborates the idea that a woman's sexual fantasies of domination, violation and rape regarding the act of coitus are related to the subconscious mind. According to Lacan, sexual fantasy originates in language, which precedes the subconscious mind. This view has serious consequences for the credibility of the testimony of a woman who alleges rape.

The specific intention of this chapter is to examine and interpret the social construction of the belief in the female unconscious desire for rape through an analysis of language and psychoanalytical symbols. This involves not merely providing for an understanding of the cultural acquisition of sexuality as proffered in Lacan's re-reading of Freud, but also emphasizing the need to analyse how various constructions of sexuality are reproduced in language. This latter problem is to be interpreted from the position of 'significant others', that is, the way judges, police, magistrates, doctors, gynaecologists and jurors perceive and construct the sexuality of women.

FEMALE SEXUALITY IN PSYCHOANALYSIS

In defining the boundaries of the construction of femininity through the concepts and rhetoric of psychoanalysis, the specific intention is to trace the basis of certain twentieth-century constructs of the sexuality of women. Psychoanalysis has located the source of sexual expression and non-sexual activity in the structure of the unconscious mind. With the growth and development of psychoanalysis and the expatiation of sexuality, sexual behaviour has now become a serious field of scientific study. The various responses of women to the lack of a penis, to the father, to intercourse, to menstruation and to childbirth have been explained within the psychoanalytical discipline. Further, psychoanalysis has also provided an explanation for the emancipated woman, the lesbian and the dominant female.

> Psychoanalysts have contributed to the view of women as weak, inferior, passive, fragile, soft, vacillating, dependent, unreliable, intuitive rather than rational, castrated and handicapped. Men have been polarised as aggressive, controlling, strong, superior, proud, independent, venturesome, competitive, hard and athletic. [Miller, 1974, p. 367]

Trimmer has asserted

> Doubtless, too, many women have sexual fantasies with regard to being raped, beaten or forcibly overtaken by a male and for some women a 'little battle' is enjoyed as part of love-play. There are also recorded cases of real physical masochism in women ... At times, the masochistic elements in some women's characters can result in a subsequent rape charge being made. [Trimmer, 1978, p. 136]

FEMALE MASOCHISM IN PSYCHOANALYSIS

Freud's theory on masochism is most clearly expressed in *New Introductory Lectures*: 'Thus masochism, as people say, is truly feminine' (1974, p. 116). In 1924, Freud identified three definite types of masochism: first, the 'erotogenic' type accompanied by a lust for pain; second, 'moral' masochism, where a norm of behaviour was implicated and where it was often accompanied by a sense of guilt; third, the 'feminine' kind, which although also present in some men was a characteristic of female behaviour. On the subject of female masochism he had this to say:

> In both cases — for the real situations are in fact only a kind of make-believe performance of the phantasies — the manifest content is of being *pinioned, bound, beaten painfully, whipped,* in some way mishandled, forced to obey unconditionally, *defiled, degraded.* . . . in them the subject is placed in a situation *characteristic of womanhood,* i.e. they mean that he is being castrated, is playing the passive part in coitus, or is giving birth.[1] [Emphasis added]

Masochism is then, as Freud asserts, primarily feminine, although he explains that certain features are present in both sexes: 'In men . . . their phantasies either terminate in an onanistic act or else themselves constitute the sexual gratification'.[2] In *New Introductory Lectures* he maintains there is a significant and real distinction in the role of the sexes — the male being sexually active and the female, by contrast, passive (1974, p. 115). In one solitary act of tokenism, for there is no other similar remark throughout his work, he suggests that social conventions actually force women into passive situations, and it is the repression of aggressiveness that favours the development of masochistic impulses.

The theory of female masochism expressed in Freud is decisive for the way the victim of a sexual assault is interpreted. Whilst Freud maintained that 'feminine' masochism might be found in both men and women, other psychoanalysts have instead confined it exclusively to an appreciation of female sexuality.

Deutsch, in *The Psychology of Women* (1944), was much more specific in her analysis of rape. Deutsch maintains that the sexual act was originally an act of violence and that women secretly desire to be raped and violated. She asserts that women need to gratify masochism, and one way of achieving this is to protest violently. She insists that masochistic tendencies in women are the psychic consequences of the more fundamental anatomical sex differences. Indeed, she affirms that to be feminine is to be masochistic — a position confirmed by her clinical observations, she asserts. Deutsch develops her initial conviction in so far as she maintains that 'masochism is the most elementary power in a woman's life'. It is at this point in her analysis that the construct of masochism moves from being a characteristic of both sexes to becoming inherently and specifically feminine. She explains that women have a natural predilection for masochism because it decreases guilt and provides them with the opportunity of enjoying sexual intercourse.

Horney's theory on masochism (1967), in contrast with that presented by Deutsch, represents an important shift in aetiology. In both 'The Flight from Womanhood' and 'The Problem of Feminine Masochism' (first published in 1924 and 1935 respectively) she considers the very essential variable of social conditioning from a psychoanalytical position. In summarizing the dominant views of psychoanalysis relating to female sexuality, Horney had three things to say. First, she maintained that psychoanalysis presents the view that in intercourse women secretly desire rape and violence on the physical level and humiliation and derision on the mental level. Second, psychoanalysis presents the view that the physical experience of childbirth provides a woman with an unconscious masochistic satisfaction. Third, the psychoanalytical discourse maintains that when men indulge in masochistic fantasies their only desire is to play the female role.

Horney's main criticism of psychoanalysis was that it marginalizes the role of social and cultural conditioning. She attempts a synthesis of the biology of anatomical differences between the sexes and the sociological implications of these differences, which she confidently maintains can lead to a more complete statement of female sexuality. Consider, for example, the interpretation she gives to the suffering of a primitive tribe. Rather than representing masochism of the type described, it represents an effort to ward off danger. She maintains that it is a fairly obvious conclusion that these ideologies function to reconcile women to their subordinate role by presenting subordination as a static unalterable fact of nature. Horney demands the recognition of both social and cultural factors together with psychoanalysis in the interpretation of masochistic predilections in women. She insists that within psychoanalysis the psychic consequences arising as a response to anatomical differences are greatly over-emphasized.

Following in the tradition of Horney's work, Thompson attempts to emphasize the socio-cultural factors involved. In a paper entitled 'Some Effects of the Derogatory Attitude Toward Female Sexuality' (1950), she explains that this view is the result of cultural attitudes that impress upon women that their needs are not as insistent as men's so that the female permits herself to be used when she is not sexually interested or at most mildly aroused (in Miller, 1974, p. 61).

SEXUAL FANTASY IN PSYCHOANALYSIS

The second, similarly damaging, theme is that women experience sexual fantasies and delusions in connection with coitus and especially with respect to the rape situation. Freud asserted, in this context, that the very act of repressing an idea transforms it into psychical excitement and bodily symptoms. Freud maintains that hysterical and neurotic women manifest symptoms of sexual delusions and fantasy, which are often the result of jealous and imagined events. For instance, he says that the fantasy of seduction is an attempt to subvert the memory of sexual activity (masturbation). Many patients reported that they had been seduced by their fathers, but he interpreted these accounts as falsehoods that acted as a symbolic representation of a girl's fantasy of being raped by the father: 'I was driven to recognize in the end that these reports were untrue and so came to understand that hysterical symptoms are derived from phantasies and not from real occurrences'.[3]

Neo-Freudians have presented the sexual fantasy in the most damaging way possible for a construction of women. In her study *The Psychology of Women* (1944) Deutsch maintains that the fantasy life of girls in puberty reveals an essentially masochistic content: 'Girlish fantasies relating to rape often remain unconscious but evince their content in dreams, sometimes in symptoms, and often accompany masturbating actions' (1944, p. 255). She continues in her attempt to present the rape and sexual assault situation as a centrifugal point in the fantasy world of women:

> In dreams the rape is symbolic: the terrifying male persecutor with knife in hand, the burglar who breaks in at the window, the thief who steals a particularly valuable object, are the most typical and frequently recurring figures in the dreams of young girls. [1944, p. 255]

Deutsch also defines a series of conscious masochistic rape fantasies. These, however, are of the erotic kind since they are closely connected with masturbation. Accordingly, these conscious fantasies are less genital in character than the symbolic dreams. In addition, they involve blows and humiliations, and in rare cases the genitals themselves are the primary target of violence. Deutsch's views provide support to the false accusation hypothesis in the event of a charge of rape or of a related offence. She says 'that rape fantasies are variants of the seduction fantasies so familiar to us in the lying accounts of hysterical women patients' (1944, p. 256). She maintains that her own clinical experience of accounts of rape alleged by white women against negroes '(who are often subjected to terrible penalties as a result of these accusations) has convinced me that many fantastic stories are produced by the masochistic yearnings of these women' (p. 256). It is at this juncture that she departs from the Freudian account since she maintains that such fantasies are based upon real seductions.

Puberty and the onset of menstruation is a common stage during which such fantasies occur. Deutsch maintains that puberty is characterized by 'Ardent wishes to be desired, strong aspirations to exclusive egoistic possession, a normally completely passive attitude with regard to the first attack, and a desire to be raped that asserts itself in dreams and fears' (1944, p. 117). Deutsch similarly provides the foundation for the view that women also desire 'instrumental rape', since she writes that a frequent female fantasy is where 'The female figure ties the girl, gags her, and prepares red-hot objects; these are applied by the men to the girl's genitals' (Deutsch, 1944, p. 257). These various beliefs about the nature of female masochism and the female rape fantasy have persisted in diverse kinds of literature up until the present. In his study of the human female, Kinsey found that 6 per cent of women dream of rape and that 2 per cent of rape dreams involve sexual orgasm (Kinsey *et al.*, 1953, pp. 213-14).

The themes of masochism and fantasy within the psycho-analytical enterprise are the most central to understanding the construction of female sexuality. Yet in the context of rape or sexual assault they are the most damaging. Deutsch's particular brand of psychoanalysis has had perhaps the greatest impact in constructing in 'scientific' terms this particular image of the sexuality of women. Indeed, much of what she has had to say has been erroneously attributed to the psychoanalytical tradition in general, or else to Freud in particular.

FEMALE SEXUALITY DEFINED IN
PATRIARCHAL LANGUAGE

Some of the problems of interpretation that arise when cases of sexual assault are being 'made sense of' are the result of a basic conflation of those situations involving normal coitus and those situations where coitus is part of a wider framework of domination and violence, which leads to the normalization of rape. Trimmer has talked of paraphilia (parallels to love) and rape, thus evoking the idea of 'normal rape' (1978, p. 129).

Blom-Cooper has emphasized the many difficulties that arise as a result of this conflation: 'The problem with sex offences is that they are now being judged against a background of emotion and moralising never encountered in other cases and this emotional upheaval can only cloud the issues being judged.'[4]

The female role in coitus and the fantasies and predilections for masochism said to be experienced by women have been prescribed by men and defined in patriarchal language. To elaborate Lacan's thesis, it is a particular form of language and culture that precedes the individual. A patriarchal language imposes itself on the individual, who acquires a conscious and subconscious sexual identity and at the same time a language by which others are perceived. It is men and not women who have defined the myths regarding the female desire to be seduced, violated or dominated. And it is men who have evolved the belief that when women say 'no' they mean 'yes'. In rape, the result of all this is the attribution of blame and 'contributory fault' to the victim, and the attribution of excuses and alibis to the offender to protect male interests. The point of focus is a concern with understanding the various reasons a victim may have for reporting a rape. The motivation of the offender is not introduced in court. Male sadism, dominance and aggression are not invoked in an attempt to make sense of his behaviour, in the way that masochism and fantasy are introduced to make sense of hers. The only references are those made by the prosecuting counsel who, as he is not at liberty to cast any imputations against the character of the defendant, has this stock phrase at hand — 'He was determined to have his way'.

The 'drive reduction' or 'instinct' model provides a psycho-analytical elaboration that makes male behaviour intelligible. It constructs male behaviour as the outcome of innate impulses that are beyond immediate control. Storr emphasizes the active and passive distinction of male and female sexuality when he explains that male sexuality contains an important element of aggression because of the 'primitive necessity of pursuit and penetration, whilst the female recognises this and submits'. He maintains that the fantasies of men are invariably sadistic, and erotic literature exists where women are 'bound, restrained, rendered helpless or beaten'.[5] How very conveniently male erotic literature depicting male fantasies about women that degrade the female sex and embody the male sexual 'will to power' personified in rape is totally forgotten. It would be interesting in the rape trial to know about *his* sexual fantasies and flights. As one woman pointed out: 'It would be relevant for instance to know whether or not *he* usually took "no" for an answer'.[6]

Why is it that the myths of masculinity are minimalized in the rape situation? Throughout the ages men can be characterized by their desire sexually to dominate and to violate, to treat women as sexual objects of barter or to possess them. Yet the treatment and perception of sexual offenders reflect the tendency to exonerate the rapist whilst punishing the victim. In 1975 the Butler Committee proposed that the sexual offender receive medical treatment: 'sexual offenders were often good citizens in all but this one respect'.[7] Such medicalization and depoliticization of a crime that is more likely to be the result of unequal power relations than of hormonal imbalance are also evident in the psychoanalytical literature. The notion is obscured that men deliberately and forcibly have intercourse with women, often in callous ways as a means of demonstrating power and dominance or of getting 'value' for the cost of a meal and drinks.

FEMALE SEXUALITY IN LEGAL AND EVERYDAY PRACTICE

The two themes of masochism and fantasy as components of the rape situation are issues that have been challenged by various feminist writers. The Schwendingers (1974) provided one of the first critiques that set out to reject the popular fallacies about victims of rape. Violence and force in cases of rape are highly problematic areas for discussion, very largely because even the role of violence in 'normal' consenting sexual relations has been normalized, so that when a rape actually occurs it is frequently defined away. Corroboration warnings to the jury display the partisanship of the judiciary and often reflect the psychoanalytical assumptions of femininity. In cases where there is corroborative evidence, such as scratch marks, bruises and cuts, an alternative explanation is frequently provided that seeks to evoke the belief in the masochism of women in the minds of the jurors. The dissemination and assimilation of psychoanalytical discourse is evident in various rape trials where violence in rape has been normalized and construed by the defence as violence in sex.

Since the decision in *R v Camplin* (1845) and the statutory provision in the Criminal Law Amendment Act of 1885, the definition of rape incorporated the possibility of rape 'without her consent'. However judges have not always in practice adhered to that provision, and it is significant that jurors have not convicted in rape trials where the amount of violence is minimal (Kalven and Zeisel, 1966, p. 252).

FEMALE MASOCHISM IN LEGAL PRACTICE

The belief in female masochism has resulted in the generation and proliferation of a dialogue that incorporates some old and some new ideas. From folklore and ancient custom to modern medicine and science all these ideas have together created a Pandora's box of mischief and trouble defining female sexuality. There are two specific beliefs that have been inherited from folklore and custom. The first is expressed in Ovid: 'and when I beg you to say "yes", say "no".'[8] Within the psychoanalytical model it is given a new interpretation. The second, essentially an extension of the first, is that since women secretly desire to be violently ravished, any cry of resistance, any observation of struggle, is really indicative of a subconscious consent. These two variations on a theme of masochism in sexual relations are used not only in the interpretation of coitus, but also in the interpretation of an allegation of rape or of a related offence.

These particular interpretations find their way into every conceivable level of the criminal justice system. They are apparent in the parliamentary debating process, in case law, in judicial procedure and in judicial utterances. Consider, for instance, the second reading of The Attempted Rape Bill, 1948. The Bill was introduced by Mr Younger, the Under Secretary of State, whose primary object was to raise the custodial sentence for attempted rape from two to seven years. Mr Paget, in his opposition to the Bill, reiterated an old adage: 'Many girls say "No", but there are quite a lot of those girls who would be profoundly disappointed if they were taken at their word.'[9]

Several recent classic rape trials, which have for certain reasons become *causes célèbres*, illustrate the operationalization of this belief within the trial itself. In the notorious case of *Morgan* (1975), three men were charged with rape on a friend's wife. Morgan, the complainant's husband, was indicted on a charge of aiding and abetting the rape, since the judge's statement in *Clarence* (1888) — '... for she has no right or power to refuse her consent'[10] — made it legally impossible for a man to rape his wife. In their defence the three accused claimed that the complainant had consented (or so they believed) to all that had transpired, and had even offered to masturbate them. The defendants maintained that they believed her cries and struggles were a manifestation of her attempt to stimulate her own sexual excitement. Mrs Morgan's story was somewhat different, however. She alleged that she was forcibly dragged out of her bedroom whilst each one raped her in turn. The three defendants were found guilty of rape and Mr Morgan was found guilty of acting as an accessory.

The defending counsel for the accused appealed against conviction on the ground that the men honestly believed that Mrs Morgan was consenting. He claimed that they believed her resistance was 'no more than play acting'.[11] The appeal was dismissed. The case of *Morgan* was finally heard in the House of Lords, where it was held that 'If an accused in fact believed that the woman had consented, whether or not that belief was based on reasonable grounds, he could not be found guilty of rape'. The issue of 'reasonable belief' in a woman's consent had been raised a century earlier by Justice Denman, who, in referring to a particular rape case in which a woman had not resisted intercourse because she thought the man her husband, said: 'There may be cases where a woman does not consent in fact, but in which her conduct is such that the man reasonably believes she does.'[12]

But the entire *Morgan* case, whilst correctly attempting to bring the mental element in rape in line with other criminal offences, also involved the question of masochism in female sexuality. In a most savage cross-examination at the time of the first hearing, in which it was implied that the complainant was a masochist, the QC for the defence suggested that Mrs Morgan really did enjoy it all and asked how a man is to know whether her struggles mean 'stop it' or 'come on'. The classic statement was provided by Lord Hailsham who in the course of the deliberations of the Law Lords remarked: 'If he believes the woman is consenting to rough treatment because she likes it, it would not be rape . . . what a woman wants and what she consents to may be two different things' (*The Times* 30 January 1975, 5a). In fairness to Lord Hailsham he has asserted that this remark was ripped out of context. Sir Harold Cassell has also been credited with making similar derogatory remarks. He is reputed to have said: 'If a woman resists then a man may think she is in fact consenting and is giving him the additional thrill of a struggle' (*Private Eye*, 21 February 1975).

In *R v Cogan and Leak* (1975), Leak procured Cogan to have intercourse with his wife with the primary aim of humiliating and punishing her. Leak was indicted on a charge of aiding and abetting the crime, whilst Cogan was indicted on a charge of rape. Cogan was sentenced to two years imprisonment, whilst the husband was sentenced to seven years imprisonment for aiding and abetting, five years for attempted buggery and three years for assault. Cogan appealed on the grounds that he believed at the time that the victim was consenting. Leak also appealed on the ground that his conviction could not stand if the principal offender were acquitted. In addition, he maintained that the judge gave insufficient consideration to the fact that he had not been convicted of a sexual offence. *Morgan* was referred to in the appeal. However, Lawton, LJ said 'The fact that Cogan was innocent of rape because he believed that she was consenting does not affect the position that she was raped'. Cogan's appeal was allowed but Leak's was dismissed.

In response to this controversy, The Sexual Offences Bill 1975 was introduced by Mr Ashley. The discussion surrounding the Bill in Parliament provoked similar constructs of masochism and sexuality from Mr Lee who, in his patriarchal wisdom, asserted: 'This is, above all, an intimate field of emotional human relationships where rationality is not always to be expected of human beings. I use the phrase "She did not say 'Yes', she did not say 'No' ", and that represents a hazardous situation.'[13]

The tendency for this particular construct to inform the courts, magistrates and jurors has been considered by various writers. Lakes-Wood provides an account of a case where the complainant was beaten, raped and sodomized by two men who held her at gunpoint. The violence that characterized the attack did not deter the defending counsel from trying to cast a slur on the character of the complainant. He told the court that she was divorced, that her children were in a foster home, and that she had previously had several affairs with other men. Lakes-Wood intimates that women realise that in order to secure a conviction they must be 'bruised, bloody and damned near dead'.[14] This view receives wide support in the writings of medical jurisprudence. Professor Glaister, writing in 1902, strongly advised the victim to resist to the last, giving up only when overcome by 'unconsciousness, complete exhaustion, brute force, or fear of death' (1945, p. 377).

The significance that jurors attach to the degree of violence present in such cases is important in influencing the decisions of jurors and also the conviction rate. This aspect is considered rather more fully in a detailed study conducted by Kalven and Zeisel (1966). The authors found that in the event of a 'simple rape' (a term used where little or no violence is present) there was as much as 60 per cent jury disagreement. They observed that the jury considers the conduct of the victim in 'judging the guilt of the defendant' since past moral character is often considered to have a bearing on the contributory fault of the victim. For instance, where a woman got into a car and drinking was involved, the jury acquitted. In a savage case of rape where the jaw of the complainant had been fractured in two places, the presence of a prior relationship resulted in an acquittal. Where the victim was brutally beaten, the jury acquitted because she was a prostitute (pp. 242-57). The findings of a British study conducted by Soothill, Gibbens and Jack tend to confirm this conclusion. They found that in cases of rape with a low degree of violence, acquittals were the highest (1976, p. 69).

The belief that when women say 'no' they mean 'yes' does of course have some grounding in reality. No doubt many Victorian women said 'no' to any sexual advances but nevertheless desired sexual contact. Their verbal responses were presumably fashioned on the then considered relationship between virginity and goodness, but this does not appertain today. As for the belief that women are masochistic and enjoy an additional 'thrill of struggle' (Morgan, for instance, was alleged to have told the defendants that his wife 'was a bit kinky'), this is a view that has been increasingly mobilized and operationalized as the general status of women has improved.

FEMALE SEXUAL FANTASIES IN LEGAL PROCEDURE

The belief that many women experience sexual fantasies of being raped, seduced and violated has been evoked in discussions and debates relating to rape and sexual offences in Parliament, and has also considerably influenced decisions arrived at in rape trials. Consider, for example, the comments of Mr Paget in The Attempted Rape Bill, 1948: 'It is in female psychology to wish, to some extent, to be overcome by a superior male.'[15] Over twenty years later, introducing the Anonymity of Victims Bill, Mr Crowder made an emotive remark concerning female psychology, the rhetoric of which belongs more appropriately to the nineteenth century: 'We know only too well that Hell hath no fury like a woman scorned, and that there are women who, out of spite and venom, will quite unjustly and wrongfully accuse persons of having raped them.'[16]

In the case of *R v Buttolph* (1974) Buttolph, a village policeman, was charged with the rape of a professional dancer. The defending counsel spent a considerable length of time putting questions to the complainant that related to her sexual desires and her subconscious longings, reflecting the assimilation of psychoanalytical theory in the courtroom procedure. The overwhelming emphasis the defence placed on female fantasy, masochism, lying and vanity was certainly, by all accounts, unwarranted and, as far as rape cases go, the savage cross-examination was unprecedented. At every available opportunity defence counsel made full use of the fantasy notion — as he told the court: 'Women, like men, have fantasies in sexual matters.' He went on to construct a picture of the complainant as a masochistic, fantasizing female who was the kind to bring false allegations against men: 'Please don't start with the idea that women do not make up stories like this; they do . . . Her claim that she was raped at gunpoint by a masked man could be what she would have liked to have happened.' And just in case any member of the jury might still have missed his point, he said: '. . . a subconscious desire for rape cannot be ruled out . . .' This onslaught against the complainant was accompanied by a tongue-in-cheek criticism of her profession: 'There is no one better at putting on a show than someone who has spent most of her life on the stage' (*The Times,* 14 June 1974; *Daily Mail,* 15 June 1974). Consider also the attempt to discredit the complainant by recourse to the now obsolete notion that women feel ashamed after intercourse: 'I am not saying that she is a promiscuous whore . . . I am suggesting that on this occasion she fell to a temptation that presented itself and was bitterly ashamed later.' In his summing up, Judge Melford Stevenson warned the jury: 'A complaint by a woman may be a deliberate lie — sometimes vanity.' He continued by advising the jury not to wander into the jungle of amateur psychiatry, as if they were not already deep in the thicket. Buttolph was found guilty and received a seven-year prison sentence.

What is important about *Morgan, Cogan and Leak* and *Buttolph* is that in each case, whilst past sexual experience did not constitute the basis of cross-examination, imputations were made involving psychoanalytical constructions of female sexuality. Masochism and fantasy intervened in the cross-examination to discredit the complainant. Despite the fact that in all these cases the victims experienced violent and terrifying ordeals, it was imputed in defence that either she was that 'type of woman', or she was 'kinky', or else the defendants had been led to think this was so, or, as in *Buttolph,* rape was the private fantasy of the complainant.

Although I have referred to only a handful of cases, the point is made I think that certain features of the psychoanalytical discourse defining the nature of female sexuality have informed legal and everyday consciousness. By explaining human behaviour in terms of the unconscious mind, psychoanalysis provides an account of the mechanisms of passivity, masochism and fantasy that ensure the subordination of women. In this context it provides a precise way of structuring the text when a complaint of a sexual nature is alleged, such that the belief in the false accusation hypothesis is mobilized and reproduced.

PART III

The Routine Management of Discretion

CHAPTER 5

The Routine Management of a Rape Allegation

Something that the police ought to do something about.
[Leslie Wilkins]

INTRODUCTION

Since the early nineteenth century increasing importance has been placed on the collection of official statistics as a research tool in estimating the incidence of rape. The pursuit of the 'real' rate has been accompanied by a refinement of the methods and techniques of data collection, with the result that the apparent rise or fall in sexual assault has been interpreted as an index of a 'real' increase or decrease in its commission. This positivist method of interpretation has contributed to a series of erroneous assumptions regarding the incidence of rape and has driven the real issues involved in its social construction deep into a cul-de-sac of obscurantism. The most critical and decisive component in the process of social construction is the role played by the complainant herself in the production and formulation of the official rate. This has not been studied, either because it has been considered of little importance or else because it has gone unnoticed.

The official rate discloses absolutely nothing whatever regarding the practical workings of the police, of probation officers, of judges or of jurors. Criminal statistics provide no information about the use of discretion in the several decisions involved in taking up a charge or in the police decision to caution or to prosecute, or, at the other end of the criminal justice system, about the decisions involved in the process of plea bargaining and sentencing. Yet these 'dark areas' are the very concerns that require investigation, for it is these decisions that influence the way in which official statistics are constructed and the way the complainant of a sexual assault is managed — such that '*rates of deviant behaviour* are produced by *the actions taken by persons in the social system* which define, classify and record certain behaviours as deviant' (Kitsuse and Cicourel, 1963, p. 135).

The question that is considerably overdue in this arena of sex crimes is dual pronged. The first element considers to what extent the actual operations of the administrative legal system have created and sustained a 'systematic distortion' of the official statistics relating to rape (see Biderman and Reiss in Box, 1971). The second element considers the role of the complainant in the actual mobilization of the criminal justice process. These two questions are interrelated, but the specific nature of the second element is the main focus of this chapter. The starting point of analysis is an attempt to ascertain to what extent the routine activities of those agencies involved in the criminal justice process are informed by theories of the complainant, and by background assumptions of sexuality and femininity. Whilst it is certainly true, and has been suggested elsewhere, that certain complainants are more likely than others to report the offence to the police and to prefer charges, and are more likely to be thought legitimate by the police, the complainant of rape and related offences presents a unique case because a medico-legal discourse has evolved over time to define such a complainant and to prescribe the way she is most suitably dealt with.

It is curious that those writers whose chief concern has been to provide a critique of official statistics should treat as non-problematic the very decisive role of the complainant in the production of criminal statistics. This anomaly is doubly strange in the case of the crime of rape, since there has been an unnecessary and often unwarranted focus on the complainant. The content and preoccupations of the medico-legal discourse alone provide sufficient evidence to suggest that the concern since 1800 with the complainant and her motives for bringing such a charge has verged on the obsessive. And yet, whilst this dialogue between medical and legal men persisted as to the state of mind and the psychological predilection of the complainant, there have been no attempts to explain the origin and reproduction of such impressions.

From this viewpoint, two features are of particular significance. On the one hand it seemed important to consider the background assumptions 'significant others' came to share regarding the nature and typicality of a sexual assault complainant. On the other, it was also important to consider those particular assumptions that the victim of a sexual assault can assimilate about herself as a 'sexual assault complainant' and in turn uses to define her own behaviour. In fact, in the case of rape and related offences, it is the complainant and not the offender who is placed right in the centre of the drama. The action taken by members in the criminal justice process in instituting criminal proceedings depends very largely on *her* police statement, *her* testimony and *her* answers provided in cross-examination, together with a whole spectrum of cues *she* gives at each and every successive stage of the legal process.

Official records may also be shaped and influenced by particular theories and typifications that assist policemen in their routine activities of recognizing and detecting the criminal, and recognizing the 'true' complainant. In an effort to make sense of the world and to assess 'what *really* happened', the police — as do other 'significant others' — rely on a series of typifications about the nature of crime and of criminals. Cicourel maintains that the police develop certain theories about certain individuals and groups, about morality and immorality, good and bad people, good men and good women and about institutions, practices and also typifications of community settings; such theories or conceptions are employed in routine ways: 'Thus the officer's preconstituted typifications and stock of knowledge at hand lead him to prejudge much of what he encounters ... particular ecological settings, populated by persons with "known" styles of dress and physical appearance, provide the officer with quick inferences about "what is going on" ' (1968, p. 67). The police settle the world by a set of assumptions that, erroneous or not, result in them developing 'a lay sociology of crime and enforcement which will direct them' (Rock, 1973, p. 176).

In the same way that the police have a shorthand, or series of signs and symbols that they look for in order to make sense of crime and criminal offenders, they also share certain common assumptions about the 'typical' rape complainant. For instance, Skolnick's work on 'symbolic assailants' is of particular significance in understanding the typical perception of the rape complainant, since the police and 'significant others' have come to regard certain gestures, language, signs and attire as indicative of consent (Rock, 1973, p. 177). Piliavin and Werthman have discovered in their study of gang delinquency that the police develop 'indicators of suspicion by a method of pragmatic induction' (Rock, 1973, p. 177). In the same way, certain 'indicators of suspicion' are developed of sexual assault complainants. In certain instances the police may actually be instrumental in neutralizing the criminality of the offender because certain cues the complainant may give may lead to the complainant being regarded with suspicion and her legitimacy being called into question. Since it is the police who bring the prosecution, the rape may, or may not, be officially recorded — depending on an innumerable series of factors and of circumstances of negotiatory stages. What follows is a scenario of the assumptions that have influenced the various negotiatory stages of the criminal justice system and their outcomes.

THE COMPLAINANT IN MEDICO-LEGAL DISCOURSE

Theories about the rape complainant are derived from medical and psychoanalytical discourses of knowledge that since 1800 have been assimilated into statutory law, legal procedure and pre-trial processing, and have had an enormous influence on the way a rape allegation is routinely managed. Whilst the various institutional agencies and individual agents within the criminal justice system have absorbed medical and psychoanalytical considerations from medical and psychoanalytical literature, it is from within the discourse of medical jurisprudence itself in particular that police, police surgeons, counsel, judges and 'significant others' are most likely to derive and assimilate ideas on the nature of femininity and female sexuality in the context of formulating impressions of rape allegations and of the predilections of sexual assault complainants.

Symbolically, medical jurisprudence forms a bridge between law and medical and psychological theory, whereby medical concepts are incorporated and also reproduced in the everyday practices of the criminal justice system. Whilst the field of forensic science has developed along scientific lines, perceptions of the rape situation, and especially of the complainant, are by contrast imbued with mythological constructs of female sexuality derived from fundamental misconceptions. Within medical jurisprudence, the construction of the crime of rape and the perception of the rape complainant echo the assumptions of femininity found within the paradigms of medicine, gynaecology and psychoanalysis. For instance, a view constantly reiterated is that rape is an impossibility and that rape allegations are more typically made by hysterical and lying females. Although these two assumptions have persisted throughout time, various twists, turns and moments of disagreement can be detected within the medico-legal field. For this reason, it seems apt to discuss the development of this discourse in roughly four historical phases, since at some moments certain assumptions dominated and others were totally denounced, and certain beliefs have persisted up until the present.

IGNORANCE AND THE PERPETUATION OF CERTAIN IDEAS, 1800–1850

The origin of the science of medical jurisprudence as it relates to rape and related offences — crimes known in the nineteenth century as seduction, attempted ravishment and indecent or outrageous assault — can be traced to the early nineteenth century. It is perhaps significant that the first professor of forensic medicine was appointed in 1807. The most prominent pioneers were Drs Farr (1815), Male (1816), Paris and Fonblanque (1823), Smith (1824), Beck (1825) and Traill (1840). The extent to which the views expressed by these eminent men affected and significantly informed the routine management of a rape allegation is a matter for speculation, since at this time few criminal trials for rape were recorded and the police force was only just being formed. (For instance, the police surgeon, who was later to perform a crucial role in the management of a rape allegation, was not even created until the Metropolitan Police Act of 1829. Even then, the police surgeon was not a typical feature of police investigations of rape until the twentieth century.) Nevertheless, the views propounded by the early jurisprudents were undoubtedly assimilated by some police officers, magistrates and judges.

Three key assumptions relating to the rape allegation dominated medical jurisprudence at this time: first, that it was impossible to commit rape on a grown woman; second, that the virginity and chastity of the complainant were an index of the credibility of her allegation; and third, the highly controversial opinion that in cases where a rape victim conceived following the offence, this could be taken as evidence of her consent.

The impossibility of rape

The belief in the impossibility of rape figures prominently throughout medical jurisprudence and may well have influenced police decisions against prosecution and also jurors' decisions in favour of acquittals. However, since a conviction for rape resulted variously in the death penalty or life imprisonment, police were certainly very reluctant to prosecute, and jurors were reluctant to convict, unless there was evidence of extraordinary circumstances, as in instances of extreme violence and brutality or as in the rape of a respectable lady by a ruffianly villain of the lower orders. Farr, in *The Elements of Medical Jurisprudence* (or 'a succinct and compendious description of such tokens in the human body as are required to determine the judgement of a Coroner and Courts of law in cases of Divorce, Rape and Murder, etc.'), emphatically maintained that rape was not possible 'unless some very extraordinary circumstances occur' (1815, p. 44). The 'extraordinary circumstances' consisted of evidence of profound physical violence and mutilation of a specific kind on the body of the hapless victim. Even so, signs of violence were regarded only as necessary, but by no means sufficient evidence of corroboration and therefore did not automatically secure a conviction. Although it was not explicitly stated, it seemed most likely that signs of violence to the female genitals were regarded as of greater import and corroborative significance than evidence of violence to other parts of the female body. Consider, for instance, the assertion made by Belloc: 'Where a rape has been committed not only will the *parts* of the woman have suffered violence, but there should be marks of bruises on different parts of her body, in consequence of her struggles and endeavours to preserve her chastity' (quoted in Farr, 1815, p. 45; emphasis added. See also Traill, 1840, p. 66). This conviction was to persist in the minds of many, not only throughout the nineteenth century but even up to the present day.

Virginity and chastity — rape or consent?

The belief that the past sexual character of the complainant determines both her credibility and the likelihood of consent, reflects the rules of procedure introduced in *R v Hodgson* (1811-12) and followed in *R v Clarke* (1817). Farr, Paris, Fonblanque, Smith, Beck and Traill all consistently announced that 'female harlots', or unchaste women, frequently made false charges of rape. And so, jurisprudents were already advocating the differential treatment of rape or related offences alleged by chaste and unchaste girls. Undoubtedly this differential treatment influenced the construction and the collation of official records on rape. The wide discrepancies between the law in theory and the law in practice are expressed in the various legal claims frequently made concerning the law's pledge to ensure that prostitutes were also protected. I have already raised this question with reference to case law. However the opinions of various writers in medical jurisprudence deserve special and separate consideration here. Smith, in a chapter headed 'Stuprum (Violation of the Female)' asserted: 'The crime is not only equally atrocious, whether committed on the person of a virgin or of a married woman, but also if the subject be of ill fame — *even a common prostitute . . .*' (1824, p. 394; emphasis added). Despite the various utterances about the non-partisanship of law in theory, medical jurisprudents recognized and conceded the practical impossibility of bringing a prosecution, let alone securing a conviction, where the moral character of the complainant was in question. Hence, case law categorically stated that the strongest possible corroboration is required if the complainant is unchaste or a 'strumpet'. Even the chaste woman had very often to be severely beaten in order to prove her resistance.

'The responsive womb' — conception and consent

A particularly provocative idea influencing the management of the rape complainant is the belief that conception is only possible when sexual intercourse is accompanied by desire. This theory is propounded in several works of medical jurisprudence, which reveals just how readily the medical opinion of gynaecologists on aspects of fertility and infertility in women influenced legal precepts and beliefs. Farr remarked: 'It may be necessary to enquire how far lust was excited, or if she experienced any enjoyment. For without the enjoyment of pleasure in the venereal act no conception can probably take place' (1815, p. 46). Paris and Fonblanque similarly argued that if pregnancy followed a rape then the complainant had most probably consented to all that had taken place. The consequences of this particular belief were catastrophic for the victim of rape. In certain cases where victims conceived after a forcible rape then the charge would be dropped.

There was considerable disagreement even in the early nineteenth century regarding this belief, however, and some jurisprudents dismissed such views as misleading and erroneous. In 1803, East wrote 'It was formerly supposed that if a woman conceived it was no rape, because that showed her consent; but it is now admitted on all hands that such an opinion has no sort of foundation either in reason or law' (1972, p. 445). Male maintained that the conception of the complainant in no way excused the ravisher. Smith also asserted that it had been 'erroneously imagined that forcible copulation was never followed by pregnancy' (1824, p. 415).

The controversy persisted throughout the nineteenth century. Consider, for instance, the views expressed by Gardner, who maintained that women who were raped rarely conceive: 'To this impassionless performance of the act from personal repulsion to the male, is ascribed the fact that women raped, and virgins forcibly deflowered, are rarely impregnated . . .' (1856, p. 48). Taylor pointed out that pregnancy following rape had actually been put forward by defending counsels in recent rape trials with a view to discrediting the evidence of a woman. He said that if this view was believed by jurors it would lead to great injustice (1865, p. 1010). The work of Duncan and Edis continued to promote the view that women who displayed a positive aversion to the sexual act still became pregnant.[1]

By the turn of the century it was conceded that the nineteenth-century belief in the relation between impregnation and consent was erroneous, and it was no longer used as a defence tactic. By the 1930s the tide clearly seemed to have turned and pregnancy following a rape was accepted as grounds for abortion. In the case of *R v Bourne* (1938) Mr Bourne, an obstetrician and surgeon of some considerable excellence, was charged with the criminal offence of procuring the miscarriage of a girl of 15. The girl in question was the victim of a rape and Bourne had considered that the health of the mother was seriously at risk since the very thought that she had conceived following this dreadful event was particularly distressing and obnoxious to her. Bourne was acquitted, so establishing a precedent in such cases. But the differential construction and management of 'good' or 'bad' victims persisted with impunity. Consider, for instance, remarks made in defence of Bourne's actions. Defending counsel said that the girl would be marked by nine months of labour, unless she is a girl of very exceptional character such as a feeble-minded girl, or one belonging to the prostitute class or a Dolores 'marked cross from the womb and perverse', clearly suggesting that whilst a good girl would be marked a bad girl would not.[2]

By 1960 the tide had begun to change yet again. Advances made in the field of coital physiology, demonstrated first in the work of Masters and Johnson, introduced new evidence pointing to a positive correlation between consent and conception, thereby reiterating in physiological terms certain nineteenth-century suspicions. In a series of laboratory studies they showed the various changes in myometrial irritability and contractility of the uterus during coitus, which they discovered had a special sucking effect that facilitated conception (Masters and Johnson, 1966, p. 122). In 1978, Dr Fox published the results of aspects of his work that demonstrated a positive correlation between female orgasm and conception. He monitored changes in intra-uterine pressure during female orgasm, and suggests that it is possible that some form of suction facilitates the passage of sperm into the uterus.[3]

MEDICAL JURISPRUDENCE GATHERING MOMENTUM, 1850–1900

During the second half of the nineteenth century there was growing concern about the importance of corroborative evidence in allegations of rape. It was considered insufficient evidence in itself if bruising was found; but evidence of violence to the genito-vaginal area was considered corroborative, which seemed to reassert earlier views. At the same time, belief re-emerged in the false allegation hypothesis, which cast doubt on the credibility of the complainant. The earlier notion that implied that false accusations were made by unchaste 'female harlots' was now accompanied by the view that such actions might also be made by all kinds of women — hysterical virgins, or particularly wilful or spiteful women, or women with blackmail in mind.

It is certain that by this time the ideas of medical jurisprudents began to have a far greater influence on the workings and negotiations of the criminal justice system. It is worth pointing out that the first police surgeon was appointed in 1830 and by 1850 each force had a divisional surgeon. However, the medical investigation of a rape complaint and thereby the rape complainant was still rudimentary and inadequate.

False allegations — 'rape in a railway carriage'

From the mid-nineteenth century the belief in the false allegation hypothesis gathered increasing momentum, supported in all disciplines of medicine, psychology, law and medical jurisprudence. Taylor, a professor of medical jurisprudence, reproduced the belief that rape could not be committed on a woman of good health except in 'instances of stupeficiation'. This followed the ruling established by the presiding judge in *Camplin* (1845). The belief in the impossibility of rape received further confirmation by the eminent gynaecologist and police surgeon Dr Tait: 'I am perfectly satisfied that no man can effect a felonious purpose on a woman in possession of her senses without her consent' (1889, p. 56). This belief was held by numerous gynaecologists. Taylor also asserted that the false accusation was made both from wilful and from hysterical motives (1865, p. 989). Marks of violence considered to be in the wrong places on the victim were regarded as an indication of the falsity of an allegation. Thus it was the task of a victim to ensure the rapist used violence against her, but in the right places, lest she be considered to be inventing the circumstances of the offence. This meant that rape prosecutions were increasingly difficult to effect. The allegation of a prostitute in particular continued to be treated with great suspicion, and more usually with disinterest.

A number of factors were quite clearly responsible for the emergence of a 'moral panic' regarding false allegations. The media, especially, were culpable. In the same way that Cohen singles out the media for delineating boundaries and exacerbating suspicions and fears about mods and rockers,[4] the late nineteenth-century 'gutter' press helped to create and maintain a belief in the lying, imagining, hysterical and malicious rape complainant. Certain newspapers began to report with greater frequency and brashness incidents of rape and cases of committal proceedings and trial details. The style of reporting ranged from the less dramatic and more factual reporting encountered in *The Times* to the salacious sensationalization of horrible and gross detail. In particular, the press created a new type of complainant — the railway compartment complainant.

It is certainly very possible that the design of railway compartments in the nineteenth century was such that men were provided with an opportunity to molest and harass with impunity. However, the press, the courts, the police and the magistrates did not see it that way at all. Instead, the complainant was considered to be probably bringing a false charge. From 1870 to 1900 a rapid succession of sex offence charges were alleged against those whom the legal process preferred to define as poor unsuspecting innocent gentlemen.

The medico-legal profession was readily inclined to believe that any allegation of rape made by a woman was pure fantasy. Pearsall seems to treat this as non-problematic and acquiesces with the dominant and powerful mood of the late nineteenth century: 'many neurotic women imagined that they had been interfered with in the unlightened sojourn of the tunnels' (1969, p. 396). The press played the main part in accelerating the sense of panic. Headlines typically read 'Rape in a Railway Carriage', 'Another Rape in a Railway Carriage', 'The Alleged Assault in a Railway Carriage', and so on. There were a few rather more sympathetic men who were prepared to accept that this 'moral panic' of false accusation was perhaps wrong and that men were actually taking certain liberties with women. In 1892, the matter was discussed in the House of Commons. One solution to the 'attempted outrages' on women was provided by Mr Spencer who suggested separate compartments for men and women.[5]

This 'moral panic' reflected a particular view of femininity that was eagerly exploited by various powerful interest groups who sought to protect their indiscretions with domestic servants, patients, clients and others in similarly powerless positions by attributing the blame to the lying, malicious or deluded complainant. It was generally considered that virgins and whores alike, for a variety of motives, made false accusations against employers, masters, doctors and police surgeons. In *The Transactions of the Medical Defence Union* (1885-6) it was reported that a medical member had been charged with indecent assault 'under the most unjust circumstances'.[6] This particular case was made public before a bench of magistrates and by the media. The message was clear and loud—medical men must be protected. In the *Annual Report of the*

Medical Defence Union for 1888, the president reported that he had been applied to in numerous cases concerning charges of improper conduct towards patients. The Medical Defence Union considered that in four cases the charges were unjustly made without the slightest evidence, in one case the patient was suffering from delusion and in other cases charges had been brought for the purposes of extorting money.[7] In the case of a woman patient who complained about injuries sustained as a result of an examination, the Medical Defence Union said that there were no grounds for such a charge, claiming that she was hysterical.[8]

Routh's address to The British Gynaecological Society in 1886 reveals the extent of such views among gynaecologists. The medical attendant was considered to be in a most vulnerable position and was frequently said to be most unjustly accused of sexual assault. Routh strengthened his case by suggesting that the complainant was frequently the victim of sexual delusions. Women, he said, were the 'most decided liars in creation' and it was the duty of men to protect themselves from such women. In giving advice to medical jurists and police surgeons, he recommended a full examination of the complainant of sexual assault, 'physically, historically and locally', since it was the duty of the physician to determine which cases arose as a result of the 'perverted sex instinct'.

The 'moral panic' concerning the rape allegation was no doubt instrumental in the creation of the police surgeon, who by the 1890s was a routine element in the investigation of a rape charge. Tait was appointed as police surgeon to the Birmingham City Police in the early 1890s. In a particularly vitriolic article that appeared in *The Provincial Medical Journal* of 1894 Tait summarized some of the observations arising out of his gynaecological work and having a direct bearing on matters of jurisprudence. He explained that with 'the extension of railway travelling and the introduction of anaesthetics and new hypnotics, the ease with which an errant maid, when discovered, sheltered herself by making a charge of crime against her lover was then apparently made so much easier' (1894, p. 226). He also described complainants as 'vile conspirators and blackmailers'. Tait's influence was profound — out of nearly 100 reported cases of rape/assault, he advised prosecution in only 6. He explained that in most cases the charges were based on malevolent motives. Tait was critical, too, of the provision in the Criminal Law Amendment Act, 1885, that raised the age of consent from 14 to 16. He considered that it would result in a far greater number of women bringing charges of rape against men and would increase the possibility of blackmail. The protection of young girls from the advances of elderly men did not seem to concern him unduly.

In this respect, the so-called 'male protectors' — the judges, the police and the medical profession — instead of protecting women, made it even more difficult for them to bring charges against powerful men. It was especially significant and perhaps ironical that these very same men suggested that there was no need whatever for women to protect themselves. Yet the experience of case law shows the reverse to be true. Doctors, choirmasters, clergymen and dentists had all taken advantage of their prestigious and powerful positions. Gynaecological therapeutics, in particular, revealed the extent of this malpractice since the vaginal and uterine massage that was recognized as a form of treatment was no doubt in certain instances administered by gynaecologists for their own vicarious sexual excitement.

Signs of rape — forensic matters

The growth and development of forensic science techniques at the end of the nineteenth century tended also to have some bearing on the way in which the rape allegation was perceived, handled and socially constructed. The signs of rape and the presence or absence of virginity, or the recent loss of virginity, were certain technical matters considered of great importance when sexual assault was alleged. The presence of the hymen was considered an indisputable proof of virginity; by the same token the absence of the hymen was regarded as evidence of loss of virginity. However, MacNaughton Jones, in a paper published in *The Provincial Medical Journal*, maintained that the intact hymen was not indisputable proof of chastity or virginity and therefore did not automatically prove conclusively that a false allegation was being made (1894, p. 193).

EVERY WHICH WAY AND LOSE — 1900–1950

The medical jurisprudence of the early twentieth century as it relates to sexual assaults treated the rape allegation with even greater suspicion than ever before. Either way, every which way and lose was the experience of the unchaste woman and also of the respectable virgin. Sudnow's formulation of the normalization of certain criminal activities provides a method for examining the tendency of official agencies to 'normalize' certain rape allegations. The emphasis at this time focused essentially on the issues of the signs of rape and false accusations; it is clear that there was an increasing readiness to accept the possibility of the false accusation, and that an increase of violence was required to secure a conviction.

Signs of rape — forensic questions

In 1902 Glaister emphasized the necessity for physical signs of violence to be visible on the body of the victim if the complainant's account was to have any credibility. In the absence of these 'signs of rape', 'at first a healthy scepticism as to the truth of her statements' should be displayed (Glaister, 1945). Despite the provisions laid down in the Criminal Law Amendment Act, 1885, in practice it seemed an impossible task to convince a jury of the commission of the crime in the absence of violence. The signs of virginity are enumerated in Glaister as the presence of an intact hymen, the normal condition of the fourchette and posterior commisure, a narrow vagina and an underdeveloped condition of the nipples. However, there is evidence to show that this is not a definitive statement since in some cases a hymen is absent and hypertrophy of the labia and clitoris is often present. McCann, in a paper on gynaecological questions of medico-legal importance, asserted that the presence of the unruptured hymen does not prove virginity absolutely, despite the position adopted by the court that it was evidence of *virgo intacta* (1926-7, p. 34). Throughout the traditional writings on jurisprudence, there is an implicit tendency to differentiate between good girls and bad girls. The work of Glaister is no exception here. He asserted that a virgin could not be raped during sleep, although a woman of sexual experience could very well be (1945, p. 399).

False allegations and fantasies

From the beginning of the twentieth century, the belief that any woman — chaste or unchaste — might bring a false allegation was nurtured to the full. Poore believed that it was quite common for women to make accusations of a sexual kind against their dentists and medical practitioners. His treatise on medical jurisprudence is of special significance here, since he introduced a new presentation of the rape victim in his work: 'rape must often be regarded as one form of insanity' (1901, p. 321). Glaister held similar views on the subject in that he considered that medical men and dentists were liable to false charges being made against them. He further maintained that women frequently simulated a rape by inserting an object into their vagina and bruising themselves. Glaister's son, in his text on *Legal Medicine* of 1925, developed several of his father's ideas:

> It must be remembered that every alleged case of rape is not necessarily one. There are many adult females of loose morals who, although consenting parties to sexual connection at the time, later become conscience-stricken, and to alter the complexion of their act after it has been committed, lay a charge of rape against the partner of their illicit intercourse.[9]

Arnold, writing in 1906, similarly suggested that women bring false allegations of rape. However his emphasis was slightly different in that he considered the false accusation to arise from the state of mind of the complainant at the time and after the event: she 'sometimes really does believe subsequently that she did not consent to sexual intercourse at the time.'[10]

All writers on medical jurisprudence concluded for one reason or another that an allegation of rape was to be treated with great caution. Possibly the most damaging interpretations of women are to be found in the writings of Gross and Wigmore, who are still quoted by eminent judges and professors of law and medical jurisprudence.

In 1911, Professor Gross, police magistrate and professor of criminal law, published *Criminal Psychology for the judiciary and legal practitioners*. In this work he maintained that women are hysterics and liars, and warned the judiciary to be wary of the lack of female credibility. Like medical practitioners and gynaecologists of the 1890s, he pointed out that the menstrual condition in women gave rise to unjust complaints regarding seduction and rape. He wrote 'Every one of us is sufficiently familiar with such accusations, every one of us knows how frequently we can not sufficiently marvel how such and such an otherwise quiet, honest, and peaceful girl could perform things so incomprehensible' (1911, p. 313). He continued by directing the lawyer to consider the 'erotic propensity' in women, 'for many a sexual crime may be more properly judged if it is known how far the woman encouraged the man, and in similar cases the knowledge might help us to presume what attitude the feminine witnesses might take towards the matter'. Gross then generated a taxonomy of female types according to their tendency to bring false charges. His classification includes old maids and hysterical, pregnant and single women (p. 319), a theory very much reminiscent of the views of nineteenth-century medical practitioners such as Maudsley, Mercier and Tait. Gross also had something to say with regard to the conflict between conscious and subconscious desires: 'Even her simplest affirmation or denial is not honest. Her "no" is not definite; e.g. her "no" to a man's demands' (p. 342).

Gross's *Criminal Psychology* was received with great enthusiasm by British medical and legal experts and practitioners. *The Spectator* took a more reserved and bigoted view, in one breath declaring the work of foreign criminologists as 'mildly ridiculous' and, in another, congratulating Gross for attempting a 'truly heroic task'.

Possibly the most significant single influence on medical jurisprudence in this country is Wigmore's treatise on evidence, which Radzinowicz has claimed is the greatest treatise on criminal law ever produced (1961, p. 115). Wigmore was acclaimed as one of the greatest judges ever. His work was to influence the development of British jurisprudence and law up to the present. It was especially informed by medical beliefs relating to the rape complainant. Consider the following passage:

> There is, however, at least one situation in which chastity may have a direct connection with veracity, viz. *when a woman or a young girl testifies* as complainant against a man charged with a sexual crime, — *rape, rape under age, seduction, assault.* Modern psychiatrists have amply studied the behaviour of errant young girls and women coming before the courts in all sorts of cases. Their psychic complexes are multifarious, distilled partly by inherent defects, partly by diseased derangements or abnormal instincts, partly by bad social environment, partly by temporary physiological or emotional conditions. One form taken by these complexes is that of contrary false charges of sexual offences by men. The unchaste (let us call it) mentality finds incidental but direct expression in the narration of imaginary sex — incidents of which the narrator is the heroine or the victim. [1940, pp. 459-460]

MEDICAL JURISPRUDENCE, 1950–1976

From 1950 the principal concern of the police, courts and judiciary was the false accusation. Even this recently, false accusations were still thought to be made out of spite, malice and revenge by unchaste women, virgins and young girls. The views of Gross and Wigmore have been reiterated by legal practitioners, eminent judges and professors of both law and medicine. The various writings of Williams, Napley, Hughes and Heydon, together with those of police surgeons and doctors, go towards the reproduction of mythologies of the complainant in several significant ways.

Professor Williams's belief in the probability of charges of rape and sexual offences being largely false is evident in his writings on corroboration. In 1955, he first justified the necessity for such cases to be corroborated. In a revised edition he elaborated on this: 'There is a sound reason for this, because these cases are particularly subject to the danger of deliberately false charges, resulting from sexual neurosis, phantasy, jealousy, spite or simply a girl's refusal to admit that she consented to an act of which she is now ashamed' (1963, p. 159). In examining the possibility of false accusations, Williams cited the deliberations of Wigmore on the 'unchaste mentality' and asserted that the evidence of a complainant is open to doubt since it may 'be warped by psychological processes' (1962, p. 663). Indeed, Williams independently refers to the mental complexes in women that may influence the making of a complaint. He contends that the danger of false evidence is present in all cases where a prosecutrix may be actuated by sexual motives. Hughes (1962) further elaborated and articulated the false accusation hypothesis, relying heavily on psychological and psychoanalytical theories on the nature of female sexuality.

During the 1960s such ideological beliefs continued to inform the law and were reiterated in legal and medical journals. Camps, the eminent forensic pathologist, in his article in *The Practitioner* (1962), disclosed just how much importance is placed on the opinion of the surgeon. In providing an illustrative case he says that many allegations of rape are in fact untrue. He reiterated the well-worn adage that rape is impossible: 'In fact, if it were not for the fact that rape can take place from fear, the problem might be fairly easy to solve, for a fully conscious woman of normal physique should not be able to have her legs separated by one man against her will'

(1962, p. 34). Dame Josephine Barnes in 1967 continued to reproduce the ideology of the precipitating and fantasizing complainant. In justifying the need for corroboration in a rape charge, she explained that the story of rape is frequently fabricated. She also pointed to the need to ask questions about prior sexual relations.[11]

The mythologies about the characteristics of the rape victim continued to be promulgated in the seventies. Adding significantly to the reproduction of the false allegation hypothesis, Forbes wrote,

> Rape under anaesthesia given for dental or minor surgical operations is sometimes alleged. No medical or dental practitioner should be unaware of the very serious risk he runs by giving a general anaesthetic to a female in the absence of an impartial witness. Some women experience erotic dreams during anaesthesia and may genuinely believe they have been sexually assaulted though this is quite without foundation. [1972, p. 289]

Bernard Knight, barrister at law, similarly wrote:

> There is a particular risk in medicine and dentistry of unfounded allegations of indecent assault, either through malice or through confusion following anaesthetics for dental or minor operations. The allegations of a woman when recovering from the effects of gas and oxygen or intravenous barbiturates are not always malicious, the effects of the narcosis sometimes leaving the genuine belief in a woman's mind that she suffered sexual interference . . . Though the majority of allegations of sexual interference are unfounded, especially when young teenage girls are concerned, . . . It must again be emphasised that the majority of allegations are false usually because consent was given at the time, and later regretted. [1972, pp. 167-72]

Gee illustrates the extent and pervasiveness of mythology on rape when he records how the late Grace 'recommended that the victim be seated on the least comfortable chair; if she does not fidget, the genuineness of her complaint is suspect' (Polson and Gee, 1973, p. 500). Miers (1974) takes up the issue of victim precipitation and examines the extent to which it is related to a psychological disposition of victim proneness. The notion of the lying, hysterical, fantasizing female, of the wicked and malicious woman, or of the precipitating woman persists even in contemporary consciousness:

> Remember that the young girl with heavy make-up, false eye lashes, plunging neckline and grossly short mini-skirt seen at the time of the medical examination may be vastly different from the well-scrubbed,

pony-tailed schoolgirl in gym tunic who subsequently gives evidence at a criminal trial. [Paul, 1975, p. 156]

The idea that complainants are suffering from sexual fantasies is still present in the medico-legal accounts: 'The victim's account of events surrounding the material time should be consistent, as some women allege rape after consenting to sexual intercourse and subsequently change their minds. Some emotionally unstable women enjoy rape fantasies and may allege rape when no offence has taken place' (Power, 1976, p. 120). In 1974, Napley, an eminent solicitor later to become the president of the Law Society, reiterated the views of Wigmore, Gross and Williams on the tendency of women to bring false charges of rape. Napley maintained that false allegations were brought by women who had realized that they had 'gone too far'. His main support for the false accusation hypothesis is that 'sexual matters are known to create, particularly in women, a high degree of fantasy' (1974, p. 1226). In reference to Wigmore, Heydon maintains that false accusations proceed from all kinds of psychological neuroses and delusions (1975, pp. 80-4).

Attitudes to the rape complainant have not really changed that much since 1800. In various ways the preoccupations of medical jurisprudents of the early nineteenth century continue to plague the theorists of today. In fact the issues of false accusation, female masochism and female sexual fantasy have become so readily assimilated into legal practice that they often go unnoticed. Yet the medico-legal discourse has had profound consequences for the day-to-day routine management of the rape complainant ever since the early nineteenth century.

ASPECTS OF THE ROUTINE MANAGEMENT OF COMPLAINTS

The decision to report a rape or related offence is influenced by a variety of contingencies that follow the commission of the crime — the response of the woman concerned to the rape, her expectations of the criminal justice system and certain interesting class differences. The factors involved in whether she reports an offence or not, and whether she withdraws the charge, are all 'dark areas' that have gone unexplored within the criminal justice system. It is well known that victims of rape and sexual assault are deterred from reporting the offence to the police because they share the background assumptions of the police and other officials and are aware of the inquisition and further humiliation they will be exposed to.

THE WORKING-CLASS COMPLAINANT IN THE NINETEENTH CENTURY

The decision to report

Working-class women were deterred from reporting a sexual assault primarily from economic motives. The grinding poverty in which they lived meant that holding on to their means of livelihood was of paramount importance, and their jobs would certainly be denied them if they were absent from the workplace for any reason. Indeed, in many households, wives and daughters were the main, and often the only, breadwinners. So important and vital was that source of income, pittance that it was, that the Factory Commissioners' Report of 1844 described vividly how many women returned to work 'their breasts dripping with milk'. Leach reports having seen women in the last period of pregnancy fined 6d for sitting down to rest (Engels, 1974, pp. 172 and 208). Was it likely under such circumstances as these that victims of sexual assault would risk instant dismissal, which would surely follow if they failed to arrive at the appropriate time at the workplace? The pressures of work, the long hours and sheer physical drudgery militated against a substantial section of working-class women from making a complaint.

Working-class women were further deterred because of the attitude of the police toward them. Rather than protecting working-class women, the police actively controlled their behaviour. The rape of a working-class woman was of little consequence and was often perceived as a 'just desert' for such low women. The legislation reflected this attitude. The Vagrancy Acts of 1824 and 1844 and The Town Police Clauses Act, 1847, demonstrate just how mythical and how fallacious the notion of 'male protectiveness' was, especially where working-class women were concerned. As I have shown earlier, these statutes provided the police and magistrates with the power to charge any woman with 'acting suspiciously'. The arm of the law fell particularly heavily on the working women of the factories and mills who were returning home late at night or in the early hours of the morning and were liable to be arrested for 'sus'. Working-class women were very well aware that if they made a complaint of a sexual kind to the police, the final outcome might well be that they would be charged for loitering or acting suspiciously, rather than a charge being brought against their attacker for sexual assault.

The contagious diseases legislation of 1864 and 1866 provided perhaps the most powerful deterrent against reporting a sexual crime, since it gave the police the power to demand that any woman should undergo a medical examination with the precise intention of establishing the presence of venereal disease. These compulsory examinations fell particularly heavily on working-class women and also upon women engaged in 'inappropriate' occupations or who contravened social norms. Butler gives an account of a professional singer who was forcibly examined under the provisions of these Acts and was perpetually harassed by the police.[12] Her only misdemeanour was that she had dared to choose a profession considered incompatible with the female role and disreputable, especially for a woman. A working-class woman who brought a charge of a sexual nature knew only too well that she was inviting perhaps yet another assault, or at least harassment and intimidation. The routine medical examination required of victims of rape also provided the police doctor with the excuse to examine a woman for venereal disease under the Contagious Diseases Act. Indeed, many women who were examined according to the provisions of this Act described their experience as a form of 'instrumental rape' (Walkowitz, 1977, p. 72).[13] Evidence submitted to the Royal Commission on the Contagious Diseases Acts referred to certain cases where chaste women had been interfered with by the police.[14] It is more than likely that the experience of a medical examination for the victim of a sexual assault was but a repetition of the rape she had sometime earlier experienced. In a reading of the Criminal Law Amendment Bill (1884), the Earl of Milltown remarked that it placed injudicious powers in the hands of the police, some of whom were black sheep.[15] The examination was a degrading and humiliating experience, carried out in inadequate clinical conditions, with poor lighting and by inexperienced doctors.

Working-class women were also deterred from reporting instances of sexual assault because the very men who had perpetrated these dastardly acts were more often than not their employers or their relatives. This rendered women powerless in every way since their reputation and livelihood depended upon their often unwilling yet passive and discrete submission. It would require tremendous courage and tenacity for an employee to make an accusation of this kind against her employer since it would inevitably result in instant dismissal; she would be denied any references for further employment and, in some cases, the workhouse might even be the ultimate end of her attempt to defend her right to say 'no'. In this respect, factory and mill girls, seamstresses and domestic servants, were particularly at risk. Thomas Fellows' evidence in The Chadwick Papers (1838-40) described how girls were invariably seduced by their masters and turned out into the streets.[16] On 11 January 1868, the *Illustrated Police News* carried a story of a mill manager who, it was alleged, had committed an outrage on a 12-year-old girl. The report stated that the manager had taken the girl into his office where he committed the offence, threatening to take her life. Such instances were everyday events.

It was not until 1884 that any real attempt was made to protect women and young girls in particular from rape and seduction by masters and employers. In the debate on the Criminal Law Amendment Bill, the Bishop of Lichfield said that no offence was more frequent.[17] Yet, when finally the Bill became law the clause that was intended to protect young women was considerably diluted in its effect: section 7 announced that a guardian or master was to be charged with only misdemeanour or assault, and further that 'it shall be a defence to any charge under this section to show that such a girl had been unchaste previously to the time of the offence charge'.

Anyway, it was widely believed that allegations by working-class women were falsely made. They were often considered to bring such charges to extort money from men. Indeed, it was believed that such women made big business out of blackmailing men. This view was expressed in an earlier parliamentary discussion of the Criminal Law Amendment Bill in 1883, when Lord Brabourne said that it was a very common thing to have false charges of such a nature brought. He remembered a woman jumping out of a train at Canterbury and making a charge of sexual assault. He maintained that it was later proved that this particular woman 'regularly practised the system of making these false charges in order to extort money'.[18]

Women also tended not to report instances of sexual assault because of their own self-definition of the situation. Perhaps in the nineteenth-century moral climate it was preferable to be raped than murdered or exploited by procuresses. In an environment where violence seemed to be very much the order of the day and violence against women in marriage was given statutory assent, perhaps a rape here or there was not so terrible. One must assess this possibility in the context of the legal and social status of women at that time. Judge Jefferson in the eighteenth century declared that a husband could beat his wife with whips and sticks, but he could not hit her with a cudgel or knock her down with an iron bar.

Thus rape amongst the working classes was very rarely reported, unless the assault involved grave brutality or was perpetrated upon a child. Rape was often obscured if the victim was found dead or else dying from the injuries sustained since it was recorded as murder. In such cases it was left to the coroner and inquiring officers to pronounce a verdict. The coroner's role from 1860 onwards was hegemonic in the detection of crime since the actual factors occasioning death were determined by the coroner, and the decision to hold an inquest was at the fancy and whim of the particular coroner concerned. Consider the case of William Rose. He was convicted of murdering his wife who had initially been pronounced dead from natural causes. The coroner Mr Todd, in calling an inquest, said 'I had no suspicion, nor had, I believe, any one else; but upon a *post-mortem* examination, the death was found to be occasioned by a pointed stick being thrust up the vagina in three different directions; and thereupon the husband was convicted and executed'.[19] We are left to speculate whether this was an attempt to procure an abortion or the perverted behaviour of a sexual psychopath. Atkinson discloses the way coroner's definitions are influenced by background assumptions — many cases of rape might be obscured if strangulation marks alone were present.[20] Consider, in this context, Wilson's interesting and macabre theory about Jack the Ripper. Documentary evidence available states that at none of the coroners' inquests on the dead victims was there any mention of sexual assault. Wilson points out that three of his victims had teeth missing, and suggests that one possible interpretation is that an act of fellatio took place, although it was not known whether doctors who performed the post mortems looked for any signs of seminal fluid in the throats of the victims (Kelly and Wilson, 1973, p. 9; see also Katz and Mazur, 1979, p. 164).

The decision to prosecute

For those women whose accounts were accepted, the magistrates hearing and the trial procedure was set in motion. But few cases ever resulted in a conviction. Defending counsels and judges frequently alluded to the possibility of the allegation being falsely made. This account was readily operationalized in most cases in an attempt to discredit the witness, especially where there was little corroborative evidence or where the defendant was of a higher social standing than the complainant. Indeed the readiness of the courts to invoke the false accusation hypothesis in order to secure acquittals was not uncommon. Consider the following reports of rape cases and the way they were disposed of.

In 1867, a domestic servant alleged that she had been indecently assaulted on a train by her employer (*Illustrated Police News,* 12 January). The case was tried summarily and dismissed for lack of corroborative evidence. This did not deter Mr Hutchison, QC, the trial judge, from asserting that he believed the charge to be false. On 11 July 1868, the headlines of the *Illustrated Police News* read 'Unfounded Charge of Indecent Assault'. In this particular case the false allegation hypothesis was stressed once again. An imputation of blackmail was also made. So, although questions relating to particular events of past moral character could not be put in cross-examination, the actual imputation had the required effect.

The false accusation hypothesis was frequently introduced because powerful class interests were at stake. In *Day and Night* (7 October 1871) the headlines read 'Young Lady who Dreams of Indecent Assault'. It described the trial of a policeman who was charged with indecently assaulting a young woman. The policeman alleged that the complainant was in the street, late at night, half naked and in a drunken and disorderly disposition. The complainant explained that she was in the street at this late hour because she was intimidated by the behaviour of some of the men who lived in the same house. She believed it was their intention to beat and outrage her. In seeking the protection of a policeman she was assaulted by him. Mr Justice Flowers said in his summing up:

> I think that a woman who brings a charge of the description alleged against the police and behaves in an extraordinary manner is not in a fit state to be at large. *I must remand her for one week for enquiries to be made.* [The defendant was then removed.] And it is to be hoped that before the end of the week her father will have found a husband for her so that she will cease to dream of these perpetual assaults on her virtue. [*Day and Night* 7 October 1871; emphasis added]

No doubt this was a warning to women not to bring charges against police officers, the servants of the state. The judge's prescription of marriage was not untypical. Marriage was frequently prescribed by medical practitioners in instances of hysteria and sexual delusion. Drysdale maintained: 'The only one who can cure an hysterical young woman is a young man whom she loves . . .' (1859, p. 180). The judgment passed by Mr Justice Flowers was indeed coloured by the intervention of certain beliefs, superstitions, fears and theories regarding the nature of female sexuality. This particular case was also unusual in that a policeman, an upholder of the moral and consensual order, a man considered to be beyond reproach, stood in the dock. The complainant, by contrast, was a woman who was certainly not a virgin and was of the lower classes.

Nevertheless, in most cases of rape or indecent assault on working-class or lower middle-class women the defendant was acquitted, especially if the defendant was a gentleman. Defending counsels obviously exploited the mythologies that a woman cannot be raped, women precipitate assault, unchastity means consent, since such ideas would conform to both the judges' and jurors' perceptions of women. Whether counsel ever believed in the questions they put is largely immaterial — what the judge and jury believed is the important issue. Although, in law, past moral character was evidence of the credibility and consistency of her story, in the jurors' minds it was seen also as evidence of consent.

In such cases the corroborative evidence provided by the police surgeon or else by a doctor called in by the police to administer a routine examination has been of crucial importance in supporting the complainant's allegation. Even after the judgment in *Camplin* (1845), it was necessary to find substantive 'signs of rape' on the body of the complainant to sustain a rape charge. In a case in 1843 the defending counsel and the judge both advised the jury of the danger of convicting on uncorroborated evidence. The defending counsel intimated that, within the law, her story is given greater credibility if she tries to resist, to get away from her assailant or at least to make some kind of struggle. The presiding judge in his summing up reiterated Lord Justice Hale's famous dictum 'a rape charge is easy to be made' and clearly directed the jury to return a verdict of not guilty. The police surgeon said that he had found no marks of external bruising and that, in consequence, there was little support for her allegation (*The Times,* 21 March 1843).

The relative social class positions of defendant and complainant, their reputations, respectability and character, influenced the credibility attributed to the testimony of the complainant. The word of respectability always took precedence over the word of the disreputable or simply of a woman of lower social standing. In a case of alleged rape in 1868 the defendant was a respectable man of the middle class. (Indeed, the notion of respectability influenced the newspaper headlines: the *Illustrated Police News* carried the caption 'Serious Charge Against a Respectable Man'.) Mr Justice Flowers remanded the prisoner for 'Close enquiries into the character of the complainant', thus shifting the focus of the criminal justice system onto the complainant. He was strongly influenced by the school of medico-legal thought advocated by Taylor and later by Tait and Routh that consistently stressed that women frequently brought false charges of a sexual kind.

The working-class victim of sexual assault was afforded little if any credibility in a court of law. In nearly all cases the defendants pleaded 'not guilty'. The result of this plea exposed the complainant to questioning as to general character, but she could not be cross-examined as to particular facts. Nevertheless, defence counsels from that day to this have got part way round that obstruction by putting a question to a witness about the type of woman the complainant was, thereby suggesting that the defendant knew she was a woman of loose morals and acted towards her on the basis of this information. The number of acquittals at this time was, of course, the result of the number of 'not guilty' pleas. But an acquittal did not necessarily mean that the case could not be proved — the judge, the defence counsel and especially the media made sense of acquittals according to the false accusation hypothesis. Even in cases where the accused was found guilty, the sentences were extremely light — varying from a fine to several months imprisonment — especially in view of the fact that in the statute rape was said to be a most heinous offence.

The severity of the sentence was influenced by the social status of the complainant and of the defendant and also by the amount of violence inflicted upon the victim. The legal and economic status of a working-class woman valued her life and right to say 'no' at the price of a few days' imprisonment or a few shillings. Two conflicting interests were at stake — the complainant and the defendant. On the one hand, the judiciary had little desire or interest to protect the poor. Engels had written earlier that to the judiciary the women of the poor were not women. Besides, since the majority of working-class women were unchaste there seemed little to protect. On the other hand, many rape allegations were made by factory girls and domestic servants and in most instances the defendant's status was so superior that he was acquitted automatically. Feminists were justifiably angered by a law that permitted the perpetuation of rape, seduction, intimidation and sexual harassment of such women by men who had the power to hold their livelihood in the palms of their hands. Matilda Blake and other vehement feminists exposed the utter hypocrisy of the belief in 'male protectiveness':

> It may be argued that men who physically assault women are mostly of the lower and uneducated classes, but the inadequate prison sentences are passed by judges and magistrates who occupy a high position in society, and who profess to be chivalric gentlemen.[21]

THE MIDDLE- AND UPPER-CLASS COMPLAINANT
IN THE NINETEENTH CENTURY

The decision to report

Women of the middle and upper classes were also deterred from making complaints of a sexual nature. However, the reasons differed significantly from any that might have dissuaded women of the poorer classes from bringing such charges. In the very allegation of a sex crime charge, the complainant was publicly declaring that she was no longer a virgin. In Victorian society a woman's 'most treasured' asset functioned very much in the same way as a 'commodity', and its loss had a number of essentially economic consequences. First, it was very likely that a woman's marriage prospects would be ruined. There would certainly be no prospect of marriage to a man above or equal to her family's social status — now considerably diminished. Second, it was extremely likely that her dowry would be reduced. Interestingly, the economic factor reveals itself most clearly in the event of rape on a married woman, when the husband could bring an action for damages, as has been shown.

Middle-class women were also deterred from reporting sexual incidents because of the tremendous shame and dishonour to their families that such exposure would bring. In addition they knew that their allegations might be considered false or else the result of fantasy and wishful thinking. They also knew that their allegation of rape or indecent assault was much more likely to be treated as seduction. Finally, they were deterred because sexual assault was usually committed by family, friends or acquaintances and very rarely by strangers, since women were chaperoned or confined to the home.

The decision to prosecute

Nevertheless, many actions for indecent assault and rape were brought in the nineteenth century. Two significant class differences can be observed. In the first case the law agreed that indecent assault on a woman ranged from attempted intercourse to froterism, but for a middle-class complainant indecent assault was given a far wider interpretation to include a brush of the hand against an arm or leg. In the second case, middle-class women who had been raped by acquaintances could bring an action for seduction. This was not available to the women of the lower classes and besides was slightly more respectable for all concerned.

Indecent assault. Many charges of indecent assault were boldly made by ladies of the middle and upper classes for behaviour varying from a touch upon an ankle, a kiss, a passionate embrace or a hand on the thigh. There did not seem to be any single trend in the treatment of these minor indiscretions, although the class relation of complainant and defendant again assumed an important role. In some cases a minor indecent assault by a gentleman on a lady was treated with great seriousness. These cases became *causes célèbres* and functioned as devices to reiterate the conventional code of morality, restating and reaffirming the belief in the 'gentlemanly code of conduct'.

In the case of *R v Baker* (1875) for example, Baker — a gentleman, a public figure, a colonel and a friend of the Queen — was indicted on three counts: attempt to ravish, indecent assault and criminal assault. The evidence for the prosecution was that Baker had passionately embraced, kissed and fondled a Miss Dickenson in a railway compartment.[22] Two extremely dubious and incredible witnesses for the prosecution alleged that when the train drew to a halt they had noticed that Baker's trouser buttons were 'three parts' undone. That in sum was the case for the Crown. Miss Dickenson was not cross-examined. The case for the defence was that Baker had kissed Miss Dickenson. Baker was convicted on the second count of indecent assault, while the other two charges were dropped. Considering his offence, a small fine might have been expected. Instead, Justice Brett fined Baker £500 and sentenced him to one year in prison. This was far more severe than the sentences passed on most working-class or middle-class men who had raped and brutally assaulted working-class women. So why was Colonel Baker sentenced to a one-year term of imprisonment for a kiss?

Society's reaction was angry and hostile and far surpassed any punishment the law might have meted out. The press eagerly reported the case in detail. One paper wrote that it was an offence 'Only men of the lowest type would be deemed capable of contemplating' (Playfair, 1969, p. 58). Some felt that Justice Brett had been far too lenient with Baker, and compared Baker's sentence with a sentence Brett had passed on another case involving a similar charge. On 9 January 1876, *Reynold's Newspaper* reported a trial where a 'ruffianly looking' labourer had attempted to ravish a young 'respectable' daughter of a local farmer and landowner. Mr Justice Brett in his summing up made these remarks: 'If a respectable young lady cannot go through the fields unprotected without being made the victim of a villain, the country soon will not be fit to live in.' Brett sentenced the defendant to two years' imprisonment, which he declared he considered most lenient under the circumstances. *Reynold's News* said of Brett: '. . . no man has the keener eye to distinguish between the broad cloth and fashion than Brett. And he will assuredly meet his reward for the discrimination he displays in dealing with an uneducated lout and the friend and associate of a Prince.' The class bias in sentencing policy was most explicitly stated by Mr Justice Greenwood. In a case where the defendant was found guilty of indecent assault and fined £4, Mr Justice Greenwood explained that if the woman in question had been 'respectable' the defendant would have received a prison sentence of six months.

Breach of promise. Few middle-class women reported rape and few middle-class women were the chief prosecution witness in such cases. The conclusion that respectable ladies were not raped is erroneous — the delicacy of this class deterred such ladies from bringing charges. A number of alternative courses of action lay open to them. They could, of course, take no legal action whatsoever, or they could prosecute for less or alternative offences thereby safeguarding their social reputation, which would invariably be ruined in a rape case.

There are several indicators that the breach of promise action was used very widely, and was often alleged by women in the event of rape, especially when the assailant was a relative or an acquaintance. Breach of promise, an offence under the Matrimonial Causes Act of 1857, provided the injured party with the legal means to sue for breach of contract. In doing so, it gave women some protection against the ruination of future marriage prospects. One particularly important feature is that in most cases the woman had been seduced and the promise of marriage broken. It doesn't take much imagination to work out exactly what had transpired here.

The response of the law to such actions paralleled the response to the allegation of rape and indecent assault. It was a commonly held assumption that such actions were brought by malicious, lying and spiteful women, who sought only one goal, vengeance against the man who had broken his word. *Smith v Ferrers* (1846) was perceived as one such fabricated breach of promise action. It was brought by Mary Smith against the Rt Hon. Washington Sewalls Shirley 9th and present Earl Ferrers. Mary Smith was described as a woman of 'high character', 'respectable', 'well connected' and 'well accomplished'. The case for the plaintiff was that it was Mary Smith herself who had written certain letters to Ferrers persuading him to marry her, although she denied this. The case was finally dismissed. Whether her charge was false or not, it is certain that she had had some relationship with Ferrers and it is also very likely that a woman of her position would have expected marriage. The Attorney General, in his summary of the case, provides valuable evidence of conceptions of femininity at that time. He remarked of Mary Smith:

Having flattered herself for some time that she might warm the heart of my Lord Ferrers, *turning her daydreams into realities, inventing,* perhaps innocently and unintentionally almost at first, the notion of his having given her any proofs of his attachment, and then finding herself so far involved as to be compelled to advance in the *career of wickedness to prop up one falsehood by resorting to twenty others, and thus to weave her intricate web,* in which, but for the most unexpected and providential circumstances, my Lord Ferrers must have been entangled, and from which he would in vain have attempted to escape.[23] [Emphasis added]

One might have thought that the Attorney General was describing the everyday life of a spider. In addition, during the course of the trial certain references were made to the menstruating woman and the imbalances accompanying this reproductive phase; emphasis was also placed on the female proclivity for lying. In providing an account of the case, Harrison fully agrees with the attitude to Mary Smith held by The Attorney General: 'In 1846, both judge and jury realized that girls on the verge of womanhood often do get up to some odd behaviour' (1962, p. 24).

The nineteenth century was characterized by such breach of promise actions. A few were false, but it is very probable that many were not simple cases of broken engagements after lengthy courtships but involved instances where marriage was promised to secure a submission to intercourse. This situation was not rape, but the carefully planned intimidation involved in the seduction does not fall far short. The distinctions depend on the complainant's submission and the defendant's intent. The characteristics of each case varied only marginally: first, the parties were acquainted; second, an agreement was made; third, there was a degree of intimacy between them; finally, the man broke the agreement. In *Allison v Cairns* (1885) Helen Allison brought a breach of promise action against Cairns, who she claimed had intended to marry her and also had made all the promises necessary for the happy occasion. In cross-examination, evidence was brought forward relating to the mental condition of Helen Allison's mother, who was said to be in a lunatic asylum. Cairns said that this was his reason for not wishing to honour his agreement to marry.[24] In August 1885 a breach of promise case was brought by Miss Newton against Coupland at

Liverpool Assizes. The defendant seduced the plaintiff during courtship and when she told him she was pregnant he pretended to offer to marry her; afterwards he refused to do so.

The growing concern over breach of promise actions resulted in parliamentary intervention. In 1879, Mr Herschell was extremely keen that the breach of promise action should be dropped from the statute book, since he maintained this was only an action for wounded feelings and nothing more. In 1884 a Bill was introduced whose single clause read: 'From and after the passing of this Act no person shall be entitled to maintain an action in respect of a breach of promise to marry. Provided always that this shall not apply to any action commenced before the passing of this Act.' Sir Hugh Gifford, who opposed the Bill, declared that it would deprive women of protection. He argued that it was too common for a man to pursue a girl and having obtained all he wanted cast her off without any prospects in life.

Since breach of promise actions were also attempts by jilted women who had been seduced to make some provision for their child or else for the loss of status that would result from this loss of chastity and the effect it would have on future marriage prospects, then it was more than compensation for 'wounded feelings'. Sexual assault on middle-class women must be examined by looking beyond charges brought for rape to instances of seduction and abduction implicit in breach of promise actions.

THE TWENTIETH-CENTURY COMPLAINANT

The apparent increase in sexual assaults since 1900 is as much the result of the actual increase in the crime as of an increasing tendency to report the offence to the police, of certain changes in police procedures of investigation and of changes in attitudes of the police to the complainant that may have influenced decisions to prosecute.

Since the turn of the century women have been more ready to report that a rape has occurred. This is possibly attributable to their increasing emancipation resulting in a greater readiness to discuss sexual matters and a growing feeling that their right to say 'no' had to be protected. Women's organizations and groups over the years called for justice and protection for such women, instead of the shame and often criticism of their morals that a rape or indecent assault trial frequently invoked.

On the side of the establishment, the mandatory presence of the police surgeon in the examination of victims of sexual assault became a routine aspect of police procedure. Perhaps more than any one other agent in the criminal justice system, the police surgeon personified the decisive fusion of medical and legal knowledge. The police surgeons' theoretical references were the texts on medical jurisprudence that constituted a main part of their background assumptions about the female sexual complainant. Moreover, traditionally the police surgeon was male and the medical examination for many complainants was a 'double violation'. So the emergence of the police surgeon in early years did little to encourage women to report such cases.

In 1927, the Manchester Watch Committee, persuaded by a woman councillor, appointed a woman police surgeon for the investigation and examination of sexual assault complaints made by women and children. Dr Wells became the first part-time female police surgeon in England and most probably in the world. It was thought that a woman could deal with women and child victims with greater efficiency and care and create the necessary rapport. The contradiction that must inevitably have presented itself to those appointing her is obvious. On the one hand, the job of the police surgeon involved in the investigation of sexual assault would entail inquiries into details of the most indelicate, foulest and often most perverted kind — a field most inappropriate for the 'passive', innocent woman. Yet, at the same time, it was recognized that children and female victims of sexual assault would be much more likely to provide an accurate account of their ordeal to a female police surgeon.

However, this appointment in Manchester was unique and unfortunately did not represent a trend throughout all police forces in Great Britain. It appears that there was something rather peculiar to the social and economic conditions in certain areas of Manchester that forced councillors to recognize the extent of sex crimes. Dr Wells's victims came from deprived areas of the city where Engels had, almost a century earlier, discovered that sex crime and incest were commonplace. According to Wells, the social and economic conditions of the past had not undergone sufficient improvements to alter this state of affairs substantially.

The appointment of a woman police surgeon in Manchester

played a decisive role in influencing the number of sex crimes reported and the number of prosecutions and disposals. The rape victim or child victim of sexual assault was certainly more likely to report the offence to the police and undergo the police investigation that followed if a woman was present. In 1941, continuing in her efforts to make the police aware of the desperate need for women in this field, Dr Wells proposed that it should be compulsory in all cases of sexual assault for a woman doctor to be called in to conduct the examination. She recognized the double trauma for the victim: 'in cases where the examination involves looking at and feeling the "private parts", it seems wrong that women and girls should have to undergo what to them may very well appear like another assault.'[25] (It is interesting to compare her remarks with the writings of feminists in the 1970s; for instance, Julia Schwendinger (1974) also speaks of a double violation in that women can be 'twice victimized'.)

The recruitment of women police officers no doubt influenced the tendency of the complainant to report, as police women from the 1940s onwards came to play an increasing role in their routine management. But whether or not the presence of women officials in the criminal justice system has really assisted the complainant is a point of conjecture. The medico-legal discourse from which both women and men draw certain assumptions about the nature of female sexuality is a field in which women often accept and assimilate assumptions about women even more fervently and indignantly. One female police surgeon, for instance, had said to a conference of policewomen that a man seeking intercourse picks up a girl who has 'asked for it'. Another female police surgeon has talked of the 'female rape fantasy'.

So what about all those statistics and attempts to derive theories of the incidence of rape from factors within the social structure? Just how valid are they? Amir, in his study of Philadelphia court files (1971), discovered that in 86 per cent of all cases known to the police a degree of violence or force was used. Two possible interpretations follow from this observation: either violence is perceived as a feature integral to most rapes and by extension rape is a crime of violence; or else violent rapes are more likely to be reported to the police. The former interpretation is most typical, and yet to attempt to derive any theory of rapists and social conditions seems a rather misleading exercise. For instance, Gilley (1974) explains that only 1 rape in 10 is reported; 56 per cent of reports of rape in America lead to arrest and 36 per cent of prosecutions lead to conviction. So only 0.9 per cent of actual rapes result in a conviction.

Violence appears as a typical component because women recognize that unless marks, cuts and bruises — 'signs of rape' — are present then as far as the police and others are concerned 'there is no case to answer'. For the most part statistics have been treated as non-problematic; very little attention has been paid to the way in which the routine management of the complainant may influence their compilation.

The process that begins with the commission of a crime and ends with an individual law-breaker being sentenced or acquitted is negotiable and is at each successive stage informed by ideas and assumptions, discourses and theories external to the legal process itself. Previous work in this area of the negotiation of crime has been confined to a consideration of male offenders, but it is certain that in rape cases the complainant plays the most decisive role. The medico-legal discourse (which over the years has promulgated a series of notions on femininity and female sexuality that have prescribed and reproduced a monolithic view of female complainants as precipitating and not passive) has played a significant part in informing decisions made by policemen, magistrates and the judiciary in their daily routine activities and has influenced the way they handle complaints and dispose of them. Such beliefs have also informed jurors' decisions to acquit.

The handling of complaints is a task in which the police learn by certain 'rule of thumb' methods to sort out the legitimate complaint from the false allegation. However, this discretion also becomes institutionalized and routinized. Certain ideas about the complainant have become so much a part of the criminal justice system that when rape is alleged an image of the complainant rather than the offender is immediately evoked — she is a liar, unchaste and invariably hysterical, a woman or young girl who 'asked for it' anyway and is sufficiently malicious to bring a false charge against an innocent man.

CHAPTER 6

The Death of a Precedent —
Not of an Ideology

Now, here, *you see, it takes all the running* you *can do to keep in the same place. If you want to get somewhere else, you must run at least twice as fast as that!* [The Red Queen, *Alice Through the Looking Glass*]

INTRODUCTION

This excursion into the complex and contradictory arena of the 'objective' reality of female sexuality in the law has attempted to expose the discrepancies between statutory law and the legal process through an examination of the way conflicting models of female sexuality have influenced these two facets of law. In so doing, it has been amply demonstrated how a given set of ideas of sex-gender relations has been assimilated in statutory law and reproduced in legal practices during the trial procedure. This in turn has had certain consequences for the perception of female sexuality and female identity.

The preoccupation of this final chapter is in no way an exception to the general endeavour, since it seeks to reveal the discrepancies between a particular statute and its implementation. More specifically, I intend to disclose the continued reproduction of the various assumptions of female sexual precipitation both in the scenario of parliamentary law-making and in the conduct of a rape trial in contemporary as opposed to historical practice.

In several decisive ways the royal assent of the Sexual Offences (Amendment) Act, 1976, announced the death blow to certain cross-examination strategies whose history spanned some 150 years and that, in effect, had latently controlled female sexual expression through the public exposure of socially and sexually inappropriate behaviour. This practice was first authoritatively implemented in *R v Clarke* (1817), where moral character was introduced in evidence. So, until 1976, the sexual assault complainant in a defended trial for rape or related offence had to varying degrees encountered a tortuous barrage of questions put in cross-examination that set out to protect the defendant and almost inevitably assassinated the character of the prosecutrix. This inquisition disclosed some of the most intimate details of the complainant's sexual, social and medical experiences for the scrutiny, judgement, moral indignation and often derision of the court.

The 1976 Act proposed to restrict the scope of defence counsels' freedom to investigate any detail as to character that might work to the discredit of the principal prosecution witness. In addition, the definition of 'rape' was significantly restated as 'sexual intercourse without her consent'. Furthermore, there were certain provisions relating to publicity of such criminal trials especially with a view to protecting the anonymity of the complainant.

However, certain of the prominent reform measures proposed by the Advisory Group on the Law Relating to Rape (the Heilbron Committee) and later presented in the Sexual Offences (Amendment) Bill were met not with resounding enthusiasm but with fierce opposition, especially the proposals relating to the moral character of the complainant. The Committee suggested that past sexual history should no longer be required by the medical examiner in the course of his examination of a complainant of a sexual assault. Although a change in the existing state of the law was generally desired, it was also evident that belief in the possibility of false accusations persisted most fervently in certain quarters.

Since the passing of this legislative measure, various criticisms have been made of its uneven implementation because of individual proclivities of judges and because of the absence of specific guidelines for interpreting the Act. Like many other statutes before, several sections of the 1976 Act are wide open to a variety of interpretations. This can be explained, first, by the general way in which the judge has absolute discretion to allow or disallow the cross-examination of the witness as to details of past moral character and, second, by the numerous assumptions about sexuality and coitus that inform discretionary judgements. The law cannot enforce allegiance to certain ideological constructions or particular interpretations. It cannot prevent, or avert the perpetuation of, sexist ideology, even though it may indirectly restrict certain procedures that would otherwise be more likely to exacerbate the reproduction of sexism.

Since 1976, judges have differently interpreted sections of the Act relating to the admissibility of evidence as to character, the lifting of the ban on anonymity and the general conduct of the trial process. Although specific guidelines were suggested at the Bill stage, they were amended as the Act reflects.[1] The judge can give leave for the submission of evidence 'if and only if' he is satisfied that to exclude such evidence might be prejudicial to the defendant. The decision of a judge to lift the ban on anonymity in cases where the defendant is acquitted might be construed as a judge's belief that the complainant has lied or else made a false allegation.[2] The Act is also deficient in that it does not place any limit on counsel in their tendency to 'get round' the restriction placed upon questions 'as to sexual experience of a complainant with a person other than the defendant'. Besides, this clause does not seem to be so qualitatively different from the previous restriction on the admissibility of evidence as to specific facts of any sexual experience with particular men other than the defendant.[3]

Counsel thus still has considerable scope to make inferences regarding the complainant's demeanour and character. An excellent instance of the dexterity of counsel in word manipulation and suggestion and the effect of perspicacious judicial intervention is provided in the cross-examination of Marie Stopes by Sergeant Sullivan in a criminal libel case brought against Sutherland in the 1920s. Sutherland had written that the method of contraception advocated by Dr Stopes was 'monstrous' and published the remarks of Professor McIlroy who at the Proceedings of the Medico-Legal Society of 1921 had said that the method of contraception was 'the most harmful . . . of which I have had experience'. Marie Stopes was not allowed to escape the imputation of encouraging sex outside marriage, either by counsel or by the presiding judge, Lord Hewitt.

SERJEANT SULLIVAN . . . Have you, in the course of your investigations considered whether the apprehension of the responsibility of parenthood might be a deterrent to acts of impropriety?

A. I consider that insulting to womanhood.

Q. I do not know that you understand the question I put to you?

A. Perfectly.

Q. I want to know have you considered that among young people, apprehension of the possibility of parenthood has acted as a restraining influence in favour of propriety?

A. I consider that an insult to womanhood; we are not moral because we are afraid, we are moral because it is right and intrinsic in our nature to be moral.

A. Are you able to answer the questions?

A. You ask me: I have considered that question. I have considered it, and I consider it an insult to womanhood.

A. Will you answer the question?

A. I understand the question to be: Have I considered that possibility and I say, Yes, I have considered it.

Q. In your opinion?

A. Might I have the question explained. I do not understand.

Q. Perhaps you do not, and your answer suggested to me that you did not understand it, though I thought it was clear. Have you ever considered that the apprehension of resulting parenthood may be a restraining influence on the conduct of young people towards one another?

A. My answer is I have considered that, and I consider it an insult to womanhood.

Q. Very well, that is formal and I pass from it.

Lord Chief Justice: Do you mean unmarried people?

Serjeant Sullivan: Yes, unmarried people.

Dr Stopes: He means, does he not, that women are moral because they are afraid, and I say no.

Lord Chief Justice: I do not think he means that.

Dr Stopes: Would you explain to me what he means.

Lord Chief Justice: *I should put it the other way round.* Do you suggest there are not some cases, perhaps many cases, in which persons refrain from fornication because they do not want to produce illegitimate children?[4] [Emphasis added]

In the case of a rape trial no complainant would be as tenacious as Dr Stopes, but counsels have made similar imputations and judges have intervened at opportune moments, thus making known their preferences at the trial stage.

The Sexual Offences (Amendment) Act, 1976, makes no

provisions for restricting such interventions by judges, nor does it stop judges from expressing personal impressions on the nature of female sexuality when warning the jurors of the danger of convicting on uncorroborated evidence. Nokes writes: 'it is the practice to require corroboration of the evidence of the prosecutrix, as on charges of rape and connected offences' (1962, p. 504). In most texts on evidence, various reasons are posited for the need for such a warning — Hale talks of 'malicious and false witnesses' (1971, I, pp. 635-6). However, although the corroboration warning also applies to sexual offences against boys and men, the same sexual rhetoric, ideology and myth are not implied. Heydon sets out the case for and against corroboration in sexual assaults on women:

> ... women may bring a false charge for a variety of special motives. A woman may wish to repudiate an act of which she is ashamed or which she fears will result in pregnancy with consequent criticism from her family and circle. A woman jilted by a man may revenge herself by falsely alleging rape. A false sex offence may be alleged as part of a blackmail scheme, particularly against persons who have much to lose by the revelation of sexual improprieties and ample opportunity for them, e.g. doctors and dentists. A spitefully motivated woman may allege a sex crime as the best way of destroying a man, particularly since sometimes unproved allegations are as damaging as proved ones. . . . Then false accusations may proceed from all kinds of psychological neuroses and delusions. A woman who is frustrated and unconsciously desires sexual experience, or who is afraid of men may allege that sexual incidents happened to her. She may desire notoriety on the basis that it is better to be raped than ignored. . . . The danger here is that it is very difficult to detect when some bizarre motive of this kind is operating, and the supposed victim may have so high a social standing or so innocent-seeming an exterior as to disarm suspicion and attract sympathy (see Williams, 1963, pp. 173-8). *The current improvement in the status of women is said to lessen the chance of such fantasy, but this is doubtful.* [1975, p. 81; emphasis added]

Whilst the legislation may in some ways improve the conduct of a rape trial, the real test of its effectiveness is its practical application in a court of law. Certain more obvious difficulties have already been indicated. In addition, its effectiveness depends on the various discourses, apparently external to the legal process, that have some considerable bearing on legal practice itself. Despite the restrictions relating to the admissibility of evidence, women, even now, are presented as liars, hysterics and sexual fantasists — as a perusal of the medico-legal literature in the post-1976 period will inevitably disclose (see, for example, Burges, Knight and Trimmer). Such ideas also characterized some elements of opposition to certain clauses at the Bill stage and therefore were influential in the law-making process. Even with the advent of this statute, the very same constructions of female sexuality that dominated medical, legal, police and popular literature prior to 1976 continue to be reproduced and reiterated. Whilst it is true that the various cases that follow are highly selective, the object is to reveal the persistence and perpetuation of sexist ideologies in the courts.

THE SETTING UP OF AN ADVISORY COMMITTEE

From the early 1970s a growing awareness of the apparent increase in the incidence of sexual assault on women made rape a cause for concern. This concern was exacerbated by certain elements of the media contributing to the 'moral panic' created by, in particular, the notorious Cambridge rape case and later the case of the Yorkshire Ripper. At the other end of the spectrum, in cases arousing far less concern, public figures and eminent judges were remarking 'what's an occasional rape here or there', 'it was a pretty anaemic rape as far as rapes go'. In the majority of cases, an image of 'normal' rape was created. Public reaction blamed the victim, and emotions were only high when the rape had been perpetrated on a child (Gagnon, 1965-6; see also *R v O'Dwyer*[5]) or when rape on a woman was particularly violent (Amir, 1971). Samuels considers an 'ordinary' rape to be devoid of any 'mitigating or aggravating features' (1978, p. 677), while grave cases are those involving violence. Where sentences of 8—15 years have been passed, the circumstances have involved rape, buggery and attempting to choke[6] or the use of a knife as a threat.[7]

Since the 1970s, many women's organizations have adopted the anti-rape campaign as a rallying issue. Indeed, rape as an issue has had a bandwaggon effect, in that many women with a variety of personal and political grievances have regarded it as a central feature of female oppression. It has also become a point of unification for feminists world-wide, although in some countries, where the oppression of women is extreme and virginity prized beyond all else, victims of rape are forcibly married to their rapists and thereby silenced for ever (Saadawi, 1980, p. 20). Much of the anger, hostility and criticism has been directed to the actual processing and management of the victim, which reflects other social and political processes.

There has been a rapidly expanding literature on the subject from a feminist perspective.[8] These readings have either maintained that the act of rape itself is a quest for power through dominance and has nothing at all to do with sexual gratification, or else have concentrated on exposing the unnecessary probing of the moral character of complainants.

During the early 1970s certain trials became *causes célèbres* in the growing campaign to bring about a change in aspects of legal practice. If one particular trial could be isolated for its contribution in accelerating legal change then Morgan and his co-defendants have a case to answer (see Chapter 4). And although the point of law raised in *Morgan* resulted in only part of the change in rape legislation, the furore following the decision in *Morgan* regarding reasonable belief in a woman's consent had a wider precipitating influence.

Following the cases of *Morgan* (1975), *Cogan and Leak* (1975) and Patrick Moving (a self-confessed rapist, given a suspended sentence), Mr Ashley asked the Secretary of State to consider revising the law on rape. On 18 June 1975, Roy Jenkins, the Home Secretary, set up the Advisory Group on the Law Relating to Rape with a view to assessing those areas in most need of reform. The committee comprised Professor Gibbens, Dr Pringle, Professor Simpson and Mrs Wright, with Mrs Justice Heilbron as the chairwoman. The composition was perhaps unusual — psychiatrists, children's officers and lawyers — and was much opposed by Mr Rees-Davis who considered the group insufficiently experienced to carry out its task.[9]

The committee took less than six months to publish their recommendations, which reflected the urgency with which they viewed their task. They sought opinions and advice from numerous agencies, groups and individuals who had, during the years, expressed concern over the existing state of the law. These organizations submitted written evidence or oral statements for consideration by the committee. Their comments fell broadly into two camps. On the one hand, certain groups reflected the view that women should be protected from unwelcome advances by men and also that the current legal and medical interrogation was unnecessary. However, a substantial number of organizations gave further impetus to the false allegation hypothesis, in that they maintained either that the law was perfectly adequate as it existed or else that further measures should be taken to protect men from false charges against them. It was, in part, the opinions expressed by the first group that contributed to the formulation of the committee's recommendations. On the whole they pressed for changes securing the anonymity of victims, for restrictions on cross-examination and for more sympathetic management of victims in the pre-trial and post-trial stages. Katz and Mazur (1979) have pointed out that it is precisely these pre-trial and post-trial stages that have been ignored.

The Medical Women's Federation, Women in the Media and Justices Clerks' Society were some of the organizations welcoming a change in the law in the direction of limiting the distress incurred by a victim of sexual assault. Groups were divided over the question relating to anonymity, and whilst some groups agreed with the general rule, they could not agree that a complainant's name should never be published. Some groups felt that any attack on the character of the complainant should remove the shield of protection from the accused.[10] A substantial element in the evidence submitted dealt with the decision in *Morgan* to acquit on the grounds that the defendant had honestly believed that the complainant consented, however unreasonable that belief may have been. This decision was widely supported, although the fears it gave rise to (some called it a 'rapists' Charter') were also acknowledged and conceded.[11] Certain organizations also advocated a more sympathetic consideration of the complainant in the pre-trial police investigation. Some emphasis was placed on the necessity for a woman police officer to be present and for a woman practitioner to conduct the examination.[12]

The Association of Police Surgeons of Great Britain stressed the need for the improvement of the techniques and skill of the examiner in such examinations. They considered it relevant that the police surgeon should be at liberty to ask specific questions relating to gynaecological and sexual history, including evidence of miscarriage and menstrual disorders and the use of internal tampons. Questions should also be asked about medical history (including psychiatric history). At this point they disclosed the persistence of their belief in the false accusation hypothesis, pointing out that it is common knowledge among police surgeons that a large number of cases of alleged rape examined 'are in fact not rape at all'. Trimmer made similar assertions when remarking on the beliefs and ideologies of police surgeons.

> There is no doubt that sexual fantasies with a strong rape component play a part in the sex life of some women. Many police surgeons claim that the majority of allegations of rape are ill-founded although this is hotly denied by 'action groups' on rape the world over. [1978, p. 153]

The false accusation hypothesis was expressed by a considerable number of organizations. The opinions of Justice (the British section of the International Commission of Jurists) are especially interesting. They explained that the false allegation arose from a variety of reasons: the need to explain away adultery or seduction to a husband, parents or boyfriend; the need to exculpate a pregnancy; quarrels over failure of the man to 'pay up' after sex; malice, especially against a discarding lover; and the possibility of sexual fantasy experienced by some women. The possibility of false accusation was similarly upheld by the Royal College of Obstetricians and Gynaecologists, who maintained that the victim should remain anonymous unless the defendant was found 'not guilty'; then the identity should be revealed in order to prevent 'frivolous cases being brought'. The Royal College of Psychiatrists conceded that false allegations were made but that these were mainly made by children. When such false allegations were made by women, they were either made by 'frustrated housewives and women who have been rejected' or were motivated by blackmail.[13]

THE REPORT OF THE ADVISORY GROUP

In December 1975, the advisory group's report was published. The committee announced five main recommendations.

(1) They advised that any evidence relating to past sexual history of the complainant should no longer be admissible, on the basis that such procedures result in unnecessary suffering, humiliation and distress for the victim and are irrelevant (paras 86, 89, 91, 92, 128, 131, 133). The committee further stressed that a certain line of questioning 'in effect puts the woman on trial' and may give a totally

wrong impression of the complainant to the jurors. They pointed out that many discrepancies in practice occurred because of the reluctance of the court to interfere with the conduct of the defence.

(2) The committee proposed that questions relating to moral character ought not to be admissible unless an application is made by the defence counsel to the judge, in the absence of the jury. The judge then decides whether moral character is, or is not, relevant. The committee envisaged that evidence might be admissible in cases involving prostitutes, because such evidence may be relevant to the issue in hand. They also were of the opinion that other examples might occur, although such cases were probably exceptional (para. 135). Furthermore, if the prosecution counsel, in his opening speech, remarks that the complainant is a happily married woman or a virgin and such evidence is challenged, the judge should have the discretion to allow cross-examination and submission of evidence in rebuttal. Therefore the history of the complainant with other men is admissible only where it is directly relevant to issues before the court (para. 141).

(3) The committee considered that the character of the accused might be relevant and this should be a matter for the judge to decide. This proposal followed the Criminal Law Revision Committee's 11th Report which cited the *Straffen* case, where the defendant had strangled a girl and had admitted to two similar offences.

(4) They recommended that the publication of the complainant's name be restricted from the moment the allegation is made to the police (paras 166-9) in both rape and related offences. The reasons for this are that publicity may be distressing and harmful (paras 152 and 153), although the committee had also received a number of representations from certain organizations to the effect that there should be no anonymity, on the basis that women in rape cases are 'not always innocent' and are possibly responsible for perjury and blackmail, which puts the defendant at a disadvantage. Similar objections to publicity were made almost a century earlier in 1883 in a parliamentary debate on the Criminal Law Amendment Bill,[14] although the anonymity proposed here was to prevent the publication of impure or immoral details.

(5) The report also recommended that it was crucial that both sexes be equally represented on juries (para. 180). The evidence submitted by Women in the Media had gone even further. They

asserted that in cases where particular women were objected to, then they should be replaced by women in order to maintain the correct balance of sexes. In the nineteenth century Newman had stated in a similar manner, 'In every case of alleged seduction, it appears to me obvious that half the jury ought to be *women*' (1889, p. 270).

The Report of the Advisory Group on the Law Relating to Rape appeared in the form of the Sexual Offences (Amendment) Bill 1975, which incorporated only some of the key recommendations of the group. For instance, evidence was admissible 'for the purpose of showing that the complainant behaved on a specific occasion in accordance with her disposition in sexual matters'. However, it laid down explicit provisions for restricted matters concerning the 'sexual experiences at any time of the complainant with a person other than the defendant', 'a complainant's disposition in sexual matters' and 'a complainant's reputation in sexual matters'.

The parliamentary debates on the Bill reflected much dissension. Clauses 2 and 4, which specified under what precise conditions judges might allow the admissibility of cross-examination as to character, provoked the most heated controversy. Opposition to these clauses was so strong that at one stage it was thought that a death blow might be dealt to the Bill by a filibuster. Mr Lee, in putting forward an amendment to leave out clause 2, did not agree with limiting the scope of cross-examination. He explained that 'we are dealing with situations in which there is a high degree of emotion—situations made for the neurotic, the unbalanced and, indeed, the exhibitionist kind of person'. He continued that the argument for making rape an exception was because of 'the neurotic obsession with sexual matters which somehow affects some non-members...'[15] The clause relating to the anonymity of complainants also created considerable dissension.

1976 AND ALL THAT!

The Sexual Offences (Amendment) Act received royal assent in November 1976. Many of the crucial recommendations and provisions made by the Heilbron Committee and introduced in the Bill were not given statutory credence. For instance, the Heilbron Committee had argued that judicial discretion should be guided by certain principles laid down in legislation, but the principles proposed in the Bill were subsequently rejected. Section 2 of the Act states:

> then, except with leave of the judge, no evidence and no question in cross-examination shall be adduced or asked at the trial, by or on behalf of any defendant at the trial, about any sexual experience of a complainant with a person other than the defendant.

The main objection was to the power of the judge provided by this section. The anonymity of the complainant was also provided for in this statute, but again the trial judge was given the power to authorize the publishing of names if he/she saw fit.

THE USE AND ABUSE OF JUDICIAL DISCRETION

The 1976 Act provided the trial judge with absolute discretion as to the admissibility of evidence, the lifting of the ban on anonymity of complainant and defendant and the corroboration warning in particular.

The advisory committee had considered the extent to which the complainant's previous sexual history ought to be revealed in rape trials. It was suggested that evidence should be admitted where the association of the complainant with the accused is relevant 'subject always to the power of the judge to control questioning' or where an issue arising in the trial 'relates to a previous incident (or incidents) which is or are strikingly similar . . .' (paras 134 and 136). The committee also stated that the trial judge should have the discretion of evidence in rebuttal.

In those matters where the trial judge has absolute power in the exercise of discretion, wide differences can be observed in judicial practice. Some judges do not intervene with the conduct of the trial. But in one case the presiding judge persistently interrupted, whilst in another the judge conducted the defence and prosecution cases. In the course of the trial and in the exercise of discretion, it is very often clear to the court that the judge is by no means an impartial observer. In one case the judge's belief in the defendant's guilt was clear throughout the trial. Since there are no guidelines provided for the interpretation of the statute, it appears that guidelines are being evolved by the judges themselves. It is this aspect, more than any other, that has become a cause for grave concern. In the case of

R v Lawrence and Another (1977) the defending counsel applied to the judge to admit past moral character. The judge ruled that such matters should not be admitted since it would lead to a situation whereby it could be said 'Well, there you are, members of the jury, that is the sort of girl she is'.[16] He emphasized that a distinction existed between cross-examination designed to 'blacken her sexual character' and cross-examination 'as to the trustworthiness of her evidence'. In the case of *R v Leroy Mills* (1979) the circumstances in which previous sexual history may be admitted were raised, and in the appeal it was decided that cross-examination as to moral character was properly disallowed.[17]

Following these guidelines, in a recent case tried at Manchester Crown Court, the defending counsel made an application to the trial judge according to section 2 of the 1976 Act to render admissible the past moral character of the complainant. The female defending counsel considered that the complainant's sexual past was relevant to the defendant's state of mind, since he had been told that she was easy. The judge disallowed the application, deciding that if cross-examination of the complainant on such matters were allowed then the jury might get a totally wrong impression. Despite the persistence of the defending counsel, the judge remained undeterred.

The judge also has the power to lift the ban on anonymity. In one case in February 1978, where a man was charged with raping and beating a woman, it was agreed that the name and address of the complainant should be published to aid the defendant in his efforts to prove that the complainant 'is not only a prostitute, but one who holds out a special kind of rather attractive sideshow for clients who preferred it'.[18]

The corroboration warning to the jury continues to provide defending counsel and judges with the opportunity of indirectly discrediting the complainant. There are wide variations in the way the warning is given — from impartiality to an expression of the judge's own personal predilections. Consider the corroboration warning given by Judge Sutcliffe in 1976: 'It is known that women in particular and small boys, are liable to be untruthful and to invent stories.'[19] Defending counsels in their warning to the jury have made some equally astounding remarks. In a trial heard in Birmingham in 1980, the defending counsel said: 'Over the years experience has proved that allegations of a sexual nature are made for motives often not revealed and cast doubt on the veracity of the complainant.'[20]

Prior to the 1976 Act, defending counsels raked up every and any aspect of the moral and sexual history of the complainant that might work to her discredit. For instance, in *R v Lang,* the defending counsel made much out of the complainant's drinking habits in an effort to cast doubt on her allegation of rape (*The Times,* 17 October 1975). In November 1975, in a trial for a lesser crime of attempted rape, the complainant was asked if it was not true that she had been convicted for prostitution in 1960. This historical 'skeleton in the cupboard' did much more than to cast an aspersion on her character.[21]

Since 1976 the Act announced the restriction of cross-examination of the complainant as to sexual experience with men other than the defendant, it was assumed that past moral character would no longer be admitted and the complainant no longer discredited. This was not entirely to be the case, since the Act made no provisions for restricting the way the defence is conducted. As a result, defending counsels are still relatively free to make suggestions, imputations and innuendos, as long as they are made indirectly. Such inferences, although they cannot be pursued in cross-examination, nevertheless blemish the character of the witness in court. Consider, for instance, one post-1976 case where the complainant was asked whether she had had thrush.[22] (The 'thrush myth' is that only bad girls get it.) It was not explained to the jury that it is a complaint associated with taking an antibiotic or a contraceptive pill, and that most women at some time in their lives are bothered by it (Trimmer, 1978, p. 36).

The Scylla and Charybdis of masochism and fantasy has been given some attention in rather more recent cases of sexual assault. In a case in February 1980 where twin brothers were charged, one with rape, the other with assault and theft, the notion of female masochism was given vent. The police surgeon in giving evidence explained that he had found the complainant in great distress, and blood smears were found on her mouth and face. A 1cm long incision, 4mm deep, was found on the left side of her mouth, together with several other abrasions on her body. The defending counsel said that although she was hit, she had asked to be, saying 'Hit me, hit me, I'm kinky'. What the jury were to make of it is unclear. However the prosecuting counsel said that it is difficult to believe that a girl will ask to have her face hit.[23] Undoubtedly the suggestion was meant to evoke the model of female masochism. If adhered to, that model would explain the defendant's story, especially when the defendant's counsel put it to the complainant 'When you were having sexual intercourse you were really quite excited'!

The interference of defending counsels in the interpretation of facts is left entirely to their discretion, and often, if a suggestion fits preconceived notions of sexuality or rape complainants, then it sticks. In one recent case the medical witness explained to the court that he had found suction marks on the thighs of the complainant. The defence counsel saw the opportunity to use this for the advantage of his client. He suggested to the doctor that there were similarities between love bites and suction marks. Having successfully compared the two, he was able, some time later, to say to the court 'You can't have a love bite and be raped'. The words of the medical witness had been manoeuvred and ripped out of context. Perhaps such judgements are motivated by a belief that 'The pleasure—pain syndrome is so characteristic of ordinary love-making that the boundary across which such activity becomes a perversion is not easy to draw' (Hughes, 1962, p. 684).

In a rape case in 1980 where the complainant had sustained bruises to the upper limbs whilst being forcibly held, the defendant was nevertheless acquitted. His explanation for the bruises illustrates a most interesting theory. Apparently, after intercourse the defendant had explained to the complainant that he was unable to see her the following evening. She became hysterical and the defendant held her because she was moving her arms about. The defendant acceded that she screamed, but claimed they were screams of self-pity since, according to the defendant, she had said 'You just used me, you will tell the boys at work'. The defendant's account and interpretation of what happened is certainly convincing, especially in the light of psychoanalytical theory. Freud wrote about 'women who after the first act of intercourse — and, indeed, after every renewed act — openly express their enmity against the man by reviling him, threatening to strike him or even actually striking him'.[24]

The rape fantasy and the instability of the female sex were ploys exploited by a defending counsel that 'paid off'. In October 1978, a general practitioner was accused of indecently assaulting four of his female patients. The defending counsel asked the jury to consider whether it was a coincidence that three of the women had been receiving treatment for illness involving depression or mental problems. This account undoubtedly fitted in well with the construction that a correlation exists between mental instability and sexual fantasy. Indeed, part of the medical examination of the victim of rape and sexual assault involves questions relating to psychiatric history. In this context, it is worth noting that a particularly horrific case of rape and murder was doubted at first because the girl was known to have previously had psychiatric treatment (*Daily Mail,* 23 July 1973).

Counsel not only resort to various well-accepted myths about the victim of rape in order to imply consent; at the same time they make use of various well-defined strategic efforts to excuse the defendant.

There is a wealth of literature examining the various excuses provided by defendants in the reconstruction of their actions. Blum and McHugh have proposed that 'motive' is a public method deciding the sociological existence of action.[25] The degree to which the various 'vocabularies of motive' provided by the defendant and by his counsel are acceptable depends on the assimilation by 'significant others' of 'sexual scripts' (Gagnon and Simon, 1973). In the rape situation the defendant is provided with the resource of 'blaming the victim' or evoking a series of 'techniques of neutralization' (Sykes and Matza, 1957). For example, Taylor, in examining the responses and explanations provided by convicted sexual offenders, describes the typology of justificatory accounts available (1972, pp. 29-30). Offenders claimed that something had come over them (breakdown in mental functioning); others evoked the idea of an inner impulse, describing a desire which prompted them to act against their will; whilst some explained their behaviour as the result of defective social skills, in that they said they didn't mean to commit the offences — it was a mistake.

Most studies of this kind have tended to concentrate on the motivatory accounts provided by the offenders themselves, but the motivatory accounts provided in mitigation by counsel is an area worthy of exploration. Counsel tend to resort to several clearly identifiable models of male sexual proclivity in order to neutralize and thereby excuse a defendant's predilections. The 'uncontrollable impulse', or the 'seething volcano of sex'[26] notion of masculinity, has typically been evoked. In the case of a rape on a wife, defending counsel resorted to this strategy with a view to gaining the sympathy of the court for his client. The wife had obtained an injunction and the husband had persistently harassed and intimidated her. The defending counsel explained that the husband loved his wife, and he made repeated analogies to a 'hot water tap', which was supposedly a reference to the husband's sexual passion when aroused. The counsel explained to the jury that there was a difficulty in turning off such a tap — the inference being the difficulty in abating a man's sexual passions.[27]

With the restatement in the Sexual Offences (Amendment) Act of 1976 of *mens rea*, the prosecution must prove guilty intent in order to secure a conviction. Thus in a defence of consent or 'no guilty intent', it is left for a jury to decide whether the defendant 'honestly' believed that the complainant had consented. Cases have shown that it is not enough merely to allege that the defendant thought she was consenting or that he had 'no guilty intent'. In one particular case the defendant revealed his conception of rape when he said he had not raped her since he didn't attack or injure her, although he said he knew she wasn't willing. Poor benighted fool perhaps, but not so much the fool as a later part of his statement suggests: 'after getting her drinks all night I thought I was on.'[28] Parker encountered a similar excuse. One rapist had said 'I had intercourse with her but I didn't hurt her at all. I didn't knock her about or anything like that' (1970, pp. 193-4).

There are other techniques of neutralization. In a case reported in the *Daily Mail* (24 July 1976) the defendant was constructed as lonely and sexually frustrated, a man who 'had been unable to form a friendship with a girl and began reading pornography'. In a similar case, defending counsel said of the defendant '. . . part of his trouble lies in his feeling of inferiority and the need for reassurance' (*Daily Mail,* 10 May 1979). In the same year it was reported that the defending counsel said of the accused 'he is a man of no previous experience who found himself overwhelmed by the proximity of the female' (*Daily Mail,* 1 July 1979). The loss of self-control model is often proposed in mitigation. In one particular case where the complainant was raped and beaten with a clawhammer, the defending counsel said the accused had lost control after fourteen pints of beer.

WILD ACCUSATIONS — MEDICO-LEGAL DISCOURSE

Despite the recommendations of the advisory group on rape, the 'routine management' of the victim of a sexual assault has undergone little change. The various forensic techniques and technical aspects of examination have greatly improved, but social attitudes toward the complainant seem to have undergone little change.

As regards the possibility of false accusation, Knight (1976) claims that the presence of the chaperone was for the protection of the examiner, and says that examiners should adopt rule-of-thumb methods for distinguishing the spurious from the legitimate accusation. This is a view widely shared by police surgeons. The female Medical Officer for the Greater Manchester Police reiterates an old adage:

> I am sure that everyone agrees that men and youths must be protected from wild accusations which can be made very easily by a woman seeking to get herself out of trouble with her husband, boyfriend or parents, out of spite or, simply, fantasy. [Blair, 1977, p. 16]

Blair contends that from her wide experience in psycho-sexual clinics women use the term 'rape' very loosely; often the so-called rapes are where 'a man or youth has at some time tried to take her knickers down: all the rest of her story is pure fantasy or wish fulfilment'.

Dr Burges expresses profound disagreement with the view expressed by the Heilbron Committee, maintaining that marital status, pregnancies and previous experience of conception are all important matters.

> Many allegations of sexual assault are based upon the perjured evidence of an amoral accuser for such oft quoted reasons as the establishment of an alibi to appease her parents, husband or lover, fear of pregnancy, fear of venereal disease, revenge or blackmail. [1978a, p. 227]

Burges points out the discrepancies that have arisen in theory and practice and that have plagued legal practitioners for years. He acknowledges that the investigation of the rape complainant may be an 'inquisitional ordeal' and that a prostitute also deserves the courtesy and understanding of the examining doctor, but at the same time the 'virtuous-looking maiden may later be proved a liar and a cheat' (1978b, p. 737). Clarke (1978) also advises police surgeons to be wary of complainants of sexual offences, although he does not discriminate between men or women.

I do not wish to present all medico-legal literature in the past four years as being always prejudicial to the sexual assault complainant; I merely wish to make the point that the continued perpetuation of the false accusation hypothesis is a myth that medico-legal advisers should make every effort to remove, and texts and articles seem a very good place to start. There is some positive literature, which avoids the question altogether by concentrating on improving facilities for the medical examination or else openly criticizing the perpetuation of sexual ideologies. But such literature is scarce.[29] It is certainly worth drawing attention to Puxon's very fine and erudite paper presented to the Medico-Legal Society in 1979. I wish that there were more with her views.

The Heilbron Committee optimistically anticipated that with the introduction of the 1976 Act there would be a significant rise in offences known to the police and in convictions: 'We think that this improvement in the victim's lot is justifiable, both on humanitarian grounds and on the ground that it will encourage victims to come forward and give evidence which leads to the conviction of the guilty.' However, statistics do not reflect any real increase in rape complaints since 1976 (see table).

On the face of it, the Sexual Offences (Amendment) Act appeared as an innovatory watershed that promised to prohibit any harassment of the complainant in future court hearings. The immediate practical effect would be a greater tendency for women to report rape and to continue with prosecution proceedings in defended trials. It has been widely regarded and acclaimed as a progressive step towards the gradual erosion of certain prejudicial and erroneous ideological constructions of female sexual expression. The dreamchild of various womens organization's has functioned as a palliative, but the questions still remain as to how effective the

Rape and related crimes known to the police

Year	Rape	Indecent assault on a female
1970	884	12,609
1971	784	12,400
1972	893	11,977
1973	998	13,294
1974	1052	12,417
1975	1040	11,809
1976	1094	10,901
1977	1015	11,048
1978	1243	11,814
1979	1170	11,834

Source: Home Office *Criminal Statistics England and Wales*
Cmnd. 8098, London, HMSO, 1979.

Act is and how it can ever eradict sexist ideology. The conduct of the rape trial continues to perpetuate beliefs about 'good' and 'bad' girls. Even though the 1976 Act redefines rape as 'sexual intercourse without consent', it remains an allegation that evokes ancient mythologies and stereotypes that have little foundation in reality.

Conclusion

The Queen shouted 'No, no! Sentence first — verdict afterwards!' An ironic comment on the workings of the criminal justice system. Certainly such a pronouncement sums up the nature of the double bind that entraps women, reflecting the way *a priori* judgements are pronounced on women in their everyday lives. Understandings of women in our culture have proceeded from conceptions of their sexuality. These so-called analyses have provided nothing more than a series of misunderstandings couched in authoritative rhetoric, which has given some element of respectability and soundness to what are essentially fallacies.

Within this book of interdisciplinary endeavour, I have directed the attention of the reader to the key discourses that have individually and collectively provided a contradictory and paradoxical vision of female sexuality. These ideologies, whether of medicology or more specifically gynaecology, have principally turned out to be cul-de-sacs of mythology.

The history of misunderstanding about the nature of female sexuality has its origin in antiquity. I have intercepted this seamless web of mystery at a particular historical moment because the changes occurring at that time pointed at least superficially to enlightened thinking on female nature. The beginning of the nineteenth century signalled the development of the medicology of human behaviour and especially of human sexuality. More specifically, it announced the development of gynaecology as a science, and hence it was supposed that all knowledge must of necessity be enlightened. In this context, it marked the growth and emergence of a powerful group of professionals in the field of medicine who developed patriarchalism *par excellence*. From this point onwards, and even before, men had access to female patients and thereby power over women, having denied and disinherited female midwives from areas they had controlled, although not altogether wisely, for centuries. Man, the gentleman, the protector, now became the God of the female sexual organs. Male physicians possessed the mechanisms of control over female sexuality. As scientists, they claimed to offer truth; but they masqueraded with the head of truth and the body of a lie. With the name of science, an image was advanced of women as lying, hysterical fantasists, who were nymphomaniacs and made false accusations against men with greater panache and new credibility.

The medical profession were not alone in their beliefs about womankind. The law, in particular, from the nineteenth century onwards reflected the conflicting imagery of women, which became enshrined in legislation and legal practice up until the present. During the nineteenth century, even where statutes avowed that better opportunities and prospects for women lay ahead, the practical application and implementation of law militated against anything other than the most marginal improvement in their status.

The beliefs about female sexuality that arose in this particular climate were readily assimilated into the law. This assimilation and reproduction of such ideas is essentially a dialectical process, in that the law acts as the agent of both production and reproduction. This two-way process is particularly heinous since law is in itself a symbol of justice and truth. Law is also perhaps the greatest symbol and practical enactment of power and it is within this system that women were to experience profound injustice.

Historical analysis of ideas and legal practices sheds considerable light on contemporary legal practice. Although the position of women has improved considerably, certain laws and legal practices have been founded on the very discourses that have been discussed here. Since the nineteenth century the law has not merely assimilated these various ideas and constructs of the nature of female sexuality; it has supported the discriminatory ideologies in its very institutional practices. But it is not merely the reproduction of ideologies *per se* that has been the chief concern here. The control of female sexuality in its multifarious guises has much deeper implications.

The oppression of women arises fundamentally from the control over female sexual expression and the patrolling of the boundaries of thought on the nature of the sexuality of women. This control is achieved through a variety of means, one of which is the criminal justice system. It is worth giving some consideration to the statement by Garfinkle, Lefcourt and Schulder:

In essence, the laws are a formal codification of attitudes toward women that permeate our culture. They are used as a means of coercion to obtain conformity with norms and mores. The law is not then an instrument for altering the unequal male—female relationship; rather, it is an institutional barrier to change. [1971, p. 120]

This statement is a guide to only half the solution. Certain laws have announced substantial changes in the position of women. However, the actual interpretation of law depends on a variety of discourses essentially external to the law, but that have come to have a significant bearing upon it. Garfinkle *et al.* add: 'The change must come, therefore, from outside the law' (p. 120). Ideologies of female sexuality commonplace in the nineteenth century are still, despite significant improvements in the status of women, being reproduced today in language and in discourse. The Red Queen was right!

Notes and References

Introduction: The Social Control of Female Sexuality

1. M. Glucksmann 'The structuralism of Levi-Strauss and Althusser' in J. Rex (ed.) *Approaches to Sociology* London, Routledge &|Kegan Paul, 1974, p. 232.
2. I. Terrades 'Organizacion Economica Y Proteccion De La Virginidad' *Ethnica, Revista De Antropologia* no. 3, 1972, pp. 183-97. See also: Abou Zeid (1965).
3. Cited in K. Sacks 'Engels revisited: women, the organization of production, and private property' in R. Reiter (ed.) *Toward an Anthropology of Women* New York/London, Monthly Review Press, 1975, p. 215.
4. P. Dews 'The *nouvelle* philosophie and Foucault' *Economy and Society,* 8, no. 2, 1979.
5. R. Barthes *Elements of Semiology* London, Cape, 1967, pp. 35-42.
6. For instance, Amir (1971) found that 27% of his victims had been subjected to other sexual acts. Katz and Mazur (1979, p. 164) observed a similar pattern. Certain individual cases are worthy of consideration: see *R v Holdsworth* (*Daily Mail*, 23 June 1977). See also a more recent case at Warwick Crown Court processed as grievous bodily harm (*Birmingham Post and Mail,* 26 February 1980). Other countries are more progressive: California in 1979 introduced a 'rape by instrumentality law' whereby such offences are punishable with up to five years (*Daily Express,* 10 October 1979).
7. *R v Coney* [1882] 8 QBD 534 at 537.
8. *R v Donovan* [1934] 25 Crim App Rep 1.

1 *Female Sexual Passivity in Sexual Offences Statutes*

1. W. R. Greg 'Prostitution' *The Westminster Review* no. 53, 1850, p. 457.
2. J. Ruskin *Sesame and Lilies* London, George Allen, 1894, p. 107.
3. J. Ruskin *Ruskin Tracts* 'Letter to Young Girls' London, George Allen, Kent, 1976, p. 2.
4. *Parliamentary Debates* vol. 211, 3rd Series, 1872, c. 59-60.
5. J. S. Mill 'The ladies petition' *The Westminster Review,* 31, 1867.
6. *Parliamentary Debates* vol. 281, 3rd Series (Lords) 1883, c. 402-3.
7. *The Lancet* Letters to the Editor, 1860, pp. 609 and 643.
8. E. J. Tilt 'On the diagnosis of subacute ovaritis' *Obstetrical Transactions (London),* 15, 1874, p. 214.

9. W. L. Reid 'The clinical teaching of midwifery and the diseases of women' *Obstetrical Transactions (Edinburgh),* 12, 1866-67, p. 60.
10. P. Chambers *A Doctor Alone* (a biography of Elizabeth Blackwell) London, Bodley Head, 1956, p. 39.
11. *Parliamentary Debates* vol. 187, 3rd Series, 1867, c. 827.
12. *Parliamentary Debates* vol. 142, 3rd Series, 1856, c. 1276.
13. *Parliamentary Debates* vol. 192, 3rd Series, 1868, c. 1357-60.
14. *Parliamentary Debates* vol. 187, 3rd Series, 1867, c. 833.
15. *Macfadzen v Olivant* [1805] East 6, p. 387.
16. *Lynch v Knight* [1861] ER11, House of Lords, 7-11 at 577. For a historical account of these and related issues see O'Donovan (1978) p. 217.
17. *Keyse v Keyse & Maxwell* [1886] XI Probate Division, pp. 100-2.
18. *Butterworth v Butterworth* (1920) 36 Law Times Rep. 265 at 266 and 271; P.D. at 126.
19. *Comyn v Comyn & Hump* (1860) 32 Law Journ. (P), p. 210.
20. *Darbishire v Darbishire* (1890) 62 Law Times Rep. p. 664.
21. *Smith v Kaye* (1904) 20 Times L.R. at 263.
22. *Ibid.* at 268.
23. *R v Clarence* [1888] 22 QBD 1889 at 23; 16 Cox C.C. at 511.
24. *R v Jackson* [1891] I QBD at 671.
25. *R v Clarke* [1949] 2 All E.R. at 448; 33 Crim. App. Rep. at 216.
26. *R v Miller* [1954] 2 All E.R. at 529.
27. *R v O'Brien* [1974] 3 All E.R. at 663-4.
28. *R v Steele* (1977) Crim. Law Rev. at 291; 65 Crim. App. Rep. at 22. See also the suggestion of the Criminal Law Revision Committee that marital rape should be a criminal offence (*Working Paper on Sexual Offences,* October 1980). P. Matthews, 'Marital rape' *Family Law*, 10, no. 7, 1980, pp. 221-4.
29. W. N. East in *Journal of Criminal Science* (ed. L. Radzinowicz and J. W. C. Turner) 1948, vol. I, p. 62.
30. *R v Camplin* [1845] I Cox C.C. at 220.
31. *R v Case* [1850] E.R. 169 at 382; 4 Cox C.C. at 220.
32. *R v Flattery* [1877] 2 QBD 410 at 411; 13 Cox C.C. 388.
33. *R v Barrow* [1868] L.R., 1 CCR at 158.
34. *R v O'Shay* [1898] 19 Cox C.C. at 76.
35. *R v Williams* [1923] I KBD 340 at 341; 17 Crim. App. Rep. 56.
36. *R v Hare* [1934] I KBD at 354; 24 Crim. App. Rep. at 108.
37. *Fairclough v Whipp* [1951] 35 Crim. App. Rep. at 138; 2 All E.R.
38. *R v Mason* [1968] 53 Crim. App. Rep. at 12.
39. *Justice of the Peace* 49, 1885, at 745.
40. M. Kettle *Salome's Last Veil* London, Granada Publishing, 1977.
41. *Parliamentary Debates* vol. 145, 5th Series, 1921, c. 1780.
42. *Ibid.,* c. 1801.
43. *Ibid.,* c. 1804.
44. *Kerr v Kennedy* [1942] I KBD at 409; I All E.R. at 412.
45. *Gardner v Gardner* [1947] I All E.R. 630.
46. *Spicer v Spicer* [1954] 3 All E.R. 208.

47. *R v Stone* [1910] 6 Crim. App. Rep.
48. *R v Dimes* [1911] 7 Crim. App. Rep. 43 at 46; 74 J.P. at 47.
49. *R v King* [1920] 15 Crim. App. Rep. 44 CCA.
50. *R v Webb* [1848] 3 Cox C.C. at 183.
51. *R v Clarence* [1888] *op. cit.*
52. *R v Wood* [1877] 14 Cox C.C. at 46.
53. *Evans v Ewels* [1972] 2 All E.R. at 22.

2 *Female Sexual Precipitation in the Legal Process*

1. Manchester Crown Court, 25-29 February 1980, Court 1.
2. *R v Barker* [1829] 5 Cox C.C. at 146; E.R. 172 at 558.
3. L. Blom-Cooper and G. Drewry *Final Appeal* London, Oxford University Press, 1972, p. 65.
4. *Report of the Royal Commission upon the Administration and Operation of the Contagious Diseases Act, 1871* c. 7448.
5. See M. Peckham 'Victorian counterculture' *Victorian Studies,* 18, no. 3, March 1975, p. 259; see also: A. S. Wohl 'Sex and the single room; incest among the Victorian working classes' in *The Victorian Family* London, Croom Helm, 1978, pp. 197, 216.
6. A. Mearns *The Bitter Cry of Outcast London,* 1883 (Leicester University Press, 1970 edition, p. 61).
7. *Report for the Select Committee on the Contagious Diseases Act 1866* 1869, Minutes of Evidence, c. 1416.
8. *Stock v Central Midwives Board* [1915] 2 KBD at 56. For further discussion of this case see *The Times,* 13 May 1915; *Nursing Notes and Midwives Chronicle,* 28, no. 330, June 1915, pp. 139-40 and 150.
9. F. Tannenbaum 'The dramatization of evil' in *Crime and the Community* Boston, Ginn and Co., 1938, pp. 19-20.
10. K. Burke *A Grammar of Motives* New York, Prentice Hall, 1945.
11. E. Goffman *Stigma* Harmondsworth, Penguin, 1970.
12. Marsh B. Ray 'The cycle of abstinence and relapse among heroin addicts' in H. S. Becker *The Other Side* New York, Free Press of Glencoe, 1964, pp. 163-77.
13. *R v Holmes & Furness* [1871] L. R. (I) CCR at 334; 12 Cox C.C. at 137.
14. *R v Hodgson* [1811-12] E.R. 168 at 765. See also: Radzinowicz (1957) p. 384.
15. *R v Barker* [1829] *op. cit.*
16. *R v Hallett* [1841] E.R. 173, at 1038.
17. *R v Tissington* [1843] I Cox C.C. at 48-9.
18. *R v Clay* [1851] 5 Cox. C.C. at 146.
19. *R v Greenberg* [1923] 17 Crim. App. Rep. at 106.
20. *R v Greatbanks* (1959) Crim. Law Rev. p. 450.
21. *R v Bashir & Manzur* [1969] 3 All E.R. at 692.
22. *R v Krausz* [1973] 57 Crim. App. Rep. at 466.
23. Manchester Crown Court, 25 November 1975, Court 1.
24. *R v Martin* [1834] E.R. 172 at 1364.
25. *R v Cockcroft* [1870] 11 Cox C.C. at 410.
26. *R v Riley* [1887] 18 QBD 481 at 485; 16 Cox C.C. at 191.

27. *R v Clarence* [1888] 22 QBD 1889 at 23.
28. *R v Bradley* [1910] 4 Crim. App. Rep. at 225; 74 J.P. at 247.
29. *R v Horn* [1912] 7 Crim. App. Rep. at 200.
30. *Daily Mail* 4 April 1973.
31. *R v Riley* [1887] *op. cit.* at 483.
32. *R v Bashir & Manzur* [1969] *op cit.*
33. *R v Barker* [1829] *op. cit.*
34. *R v Hodgson* [1811-12] *op. cit.* at p. 765.
35. *R v Clarke* [1817] E.R. 171 at p. 633.
36. *R v Holmes & Furness* [1871] *op. cit.* at p. 336. See also: *R v Riley* [1887] *op. cit.*
37. *R v Lillyman* [1896] 2 QBD 167.
38. *R v Jones* [1909] 3 Crim. App. Rep. 67 at 69. CCA.
39. *R v Cargill* [1913] 2 KBD at 271.
40. *R v Winfield* [1939] 4 All E.R. at 164.
41. *R v Parks* [1961] 3 All E.R. at 633.

3 *The Gynaecology of Offenders and Victims*

1. O. Weininger *Sex and Character* London, William Heinemann, 1906, Part II, Ch. 2.
2. C. W. Mills 'The professional ideology of social pathologists' *American Journal of Sociology,* 49, no. 2, 1943, p. 171.
3. J. Coulter *Approaches to Insanity* London, Martin Robertson, 1973.
4. J. L. H. Porteous 'A case of vicarious menstruation' *Obstetrical Transactions (Edinburgh)* 4, 1877, p. 407.
5. C. Martin 'The nerve theory of menstruation' *British Gynaecological Journal,* 9, 12 October 1893, p. 272.
6. T. S. Clouston 'The epochal insanities' in Allbutt (1899) pp. 295-303.
7. I. M. Lewis 'Spirit possession and deprivation cults' *Man,* 1, no. 3, 1966, pp. 307-30.
8. H. Graham 'The social image of pregnancy: pregnancy as spirit possession' *Sociological Review,* 24, no. 2, 1976.
9. See also: C. Smith-Rosenberg 'Sexuality, class and role in 19th century America' *American Quarterly,* 25, 1973, pp. 131-54; C. Smith-Rosenberg 'The hysterical woman: sex roles and role conflict in nineteenth century America' *Social Research,* 39, no. 4, 1972, pp. 652-78; C. Smith-Rosenberg 'The female animal' *Journal of American History,* 60, no. 2, 1973; Wood (1973-4).
10. A. J. C. Skene *Treatment of the Diseases of Women* London, H. and K. Lewis, 1892, p. 930.
11. E. Hall 'The gynaecological treatment of the insane' *British Gynaecological Journal* Part 63, 1900, pp. 242-51.
12. J. Baker 'Female criminal lunatics' *Journal of Mental Science* no. 48, 1902, pp. 13-28.
13. T. G. Thomas *Practical Treatise on the Diseases of Women* Philadelphia, Henry C. Lea, 1868, p. 56.

14. L. Tait 'Menstrual irregularities and their relation to diseases of the nervous system' *Obstetrical Journal,* 1, 1873-4, pp. 94-104.

15. This opinion was expressed by a vast number of physicians; see S. Ashwell *A Practical Treatise on the Diseases Peculiar to Women* London, S. Highley, 1844, p. 708. See also: E. J. Tilt (1862) p. 312; W. R. Rogers 'Elephantine development of the clitoris' *Obstetrical Transactions (London)* 11, 1869; G. Hewitt (1872) p. 653; G. Peckham 'Tumours of the clitoris' *American Journal of Obstetrics,* 24, 1891, p. 1153.

16. Fraser Wright 'Gynaecological cases treated by electricity in Professor Simpson's clinique' *Obstetrical Transactions (Edinburgh)* 15, 1889-90. See also: W. E. Steavenson 'Note on the use of electrolysis in gynaecological practice' *Obstetrical Transactions (London)* 30, 1888, p. 229.

17. J. M. Bruce *Materia Medica and Therapeutics: an introduction to the rational treatment of disease* London, Cassell, 1889, p. 134.

18. W. Hale-White *Materia Medica, Pharmacology and Therapeutics* London, 1889.

19. Dr Hammond 'The bicycle in the treatment of nervous diseases' *Journal of Mental Science,* 38, 1892, p. 612.

20. J. C. Webster 'The nerve-endings in the labia minora and clitoris, with special reference to the pathology of the pruritus valvae' *Obstetrical Transactions (Edinburgh)* 16, 1890-91, p. 51.

21. Milne Murray, referred to in Webster, *ibid.*

22. E. Walker 'Is evolution trying to do away with the clitoris' *American Journal of Obstetrics,* 2, 1892, p. 851.

23. R. T. Morris, quoted in Walker, *ibid.,* pp. 847-58.

24. W. S. Stewart 'A remarkable case of nymphomania and its cure' *Transactions of the American Association of Obstetricians and Gynecologists* 1899, pp. 260-1. See also: L. W. Mason 'Hypertrophy of the clitoris: report of two cases' *American Journal of Obstetrics* no. 25, 1933, pp. 144-6. He wrote that much harm had been done in the past and was still being done now with operations such as clitoridectomy as a cure for masturbation. Ehrenreich and English (1979, p. 111) write that the last record of clitoridectomy was in 1948 on a girl of five in an attempt to cure her of masturbation.

25. *34th Report of the Commissioners in Lunacy 1879* Table XXII.

26. *Parliamentary Debates* vol. 175, 4th Series, 1907, c. 1347.

27. *Parliamentary Debates* vol. 175, 4th Series, 1907, c. 1355.

28. Referred to in H. MacNaughton Jones 'The correlation between sexual functions, insanity and crime' *British Gynaecological Journal* Part 63, 1900, p. 128.

29. See *Cormacks Edin. Journal* 1845, p. 632.

30. L Fairfield 'Some psychological aspects of the physiological crisis in women' *Transactions of the Medico-legal Society,* 21, 1926-7, pp. 105-12.

31. Quoted in Fairfield, *ibid.,* p. 112.

32. K. Dalton 'Menstruation and crime' *British Medical Journal* 30 December 1962, p. 1752.
33. Ashwell, *op. cit.,* Appendix.
34. *R v Vyse* [1862] E.R. 176, pp. 111-15.
35. *R v Law* [1862] E.R. 175, pp. 1309-11.
36. J. H. Aveling 'The influence of posture on women' *Obstetrical Journal of Great Britain and Ireland* 1875-6, p. 149.

4 *Masochism or Fantasy: Psychoanalysis and Rape*

1. S. Freud 'The economic problem in masochism', 1924; in *Collected Papers* (1954) Vol. II, p. 258.
2. *Ibid.,* p. 258.
3. S. Freud 'Femininity'; in *New Introductory Lectures* (1974) p. 120.
4. L. Blom-Cooper and G. Drewry *Law and Morality* London, Duckworth, 1975. See also: Trimmer (1978) p. 129.
5. A. Storr *Human Aggression* Harmondsworth, Penguin, 1970, pp. 89 and 91.
6. *The Guardian* Letters to the Editor, 20 March 1975.
7. *The Report of the Committee on Mentally Abnormal Offenders* 1975, Cmnd. 6244, at 324.
8. Ovid, quoted in S. Griffin 'Rape: the all American crime' *Ramparts,* 10, no. 3, 1971, p. 29.
9. *Parliamentary Debates* vol. 446, 5th Series, 1948, c. 2022.
10. *R v Clarence* [1888] 22 QBD 1889 at 23.
11. *R v Morgan* [1975] 2 All E.R. p. 347; 1 All E.R. p. 8.
12. *R v Flattery* [1877] 2 QBD 410 at 414.
13. *Parliamentary Debates* vol. 892, 1975, c. 1416.
14. P. Lakes-Wood 'The victim in a forcible rape case' *The American Criminal Law Review,* 2, Pt. 2, 1973, pp. 335-54.
15. *Parliamentary Debates* vol. 492, 1948, c. 2022.
16. *Parliamentary Debates* vol. 878, 1974, c. 498.

5 *The Routine Management of a Rape Allegation*

1. J. Matthews Duncan *On Sterility in Women* London, J. & A. Churchill, 1884; A. W. Edis *Sterility in Women: including its causation and treatment* London, H. K. Lewis, 1890.
2. *R v Bourne* [1938] 3 All E.R. p. 615. See also: *The Medico-Legal and Criminological Review,* 6, 1938, pp. 381-3.
3. C. A. Fox 'Recent research in human coital physiology' Part I, *British Journal of Sexual Medicine,* 1978, p. 16. See also: J. H. Clark and M. X. Zarrow 'Influence of copulation on time of ovulation in women' *American Journal of Obstetrics and Gynecology,* 109, 1971, pp. 1083-5.
4. S. Cohen *Folk Devils and Moral Panics* London, MacGibbon and Kee, 1972, pp. 9-12.

5. *Parliamentary Debates* vol. 3, 4th Series, 1892, c. 1244-5.
6. *Transactions of the Medical Defence Union* no. 1, 1885-6, p. 18.
7. *Transactions of the Medical Defence Union* 1888, p. 3.
8. *Transactions of the Medical Defence Union* 1889, p. 12.
9. J. Glaister *Legal Medicine* for Members of the Legal Profession and Police Forces, Glasgow, 1925, p. 146.
10. G. F. Arnold *Psychology Applied to Legal Evidence* Calcutta, Thacker, Spinck and Co., 1906.
11. J. Barnes 'Rape and other sexual offences' *British Medical Journal,* 2, 1967, p. 293.
12. J. Butler *Personal Reminiscences of a Great Crusade* London, Horace, Marshall and Son, 1913, p. 112.
13. Annie Clark said of the examination 'I would rather spend fourteen years in prison than submit to it'. *Shield* 17 December 1870. See also: J. J. Garth Wilkinson *The Forcible Introspection of Women for the Army and Navy by the Oligarchy, Considered Physically* London, 1870, p. 15.
14. The Royal Commission on the Contagious Diseases Acts *Minutes of Evidence* 1871, c. 8496-19883.
15. *Parliamentary Debates* Vol. 288, 3rd Series, 1884, c. 1161.
16. The Chadwick Papers, Box 10, Thomas Fellows Evidence, 1838-40.
17. *Parliamentary Debates* Vol. 288, 3rd Series, 1884, c. 407.
18. *Parliamentary Debates* Vol. 281, 3rd Series, 1883, c. 400.
19. *Report from the Select Committee on the Office of Coroner* House of Commons, 1860, 615, p. 20.
20. M. Atkinson 'Societal reactions to suicide: the role of coroners' definitions' in S. Cohen (ed.) *Images of Deviance* London, Penguin, 1973.
21. M. M. Blake 'Are women protected?' *The Westminster Review,* 137, 1892, p. 44.
22. *R v Baker* [1875] Annual Register 1875, p. 55.
23. P. Burke *Celebrated Trials Connected with the Aristocracy in the Relations of Private Life* London, William Benny & Co., 1849, p. 505.
24. *Allison v Cairns, Illustrated Police News* 8 August 1885.
25. N. Wells 'Medical women and the police force' *The Medical Press and Circular* 22 October 1941, p. 317.

6 *The Death of a Precedent — Not of an Ideology*

1. *Parliamentary Debates* vol. 911, 1976, c. 1982-99.
2. *Parliamentary Debates* vol. 919, 1976, c. 1686-78.
3. *R v Hodgson* [1811-12] E.R. 168.
4. Quoted in R. Hall *Marie Stopes, A Biography* London, Virago, 1977, pp. 222-3.
5. *R v O'Dwyer* [1975] Crim. L.R. 247.
6. *R v Jones* [1976] Crim. L.R. 203.
7. *R v Benjamin* [1976] Crim. L.R. 641.

8. Schwendinger and Schwendinger (1974). See also: E. Figes 'Rape war zone of sexual politics' *Psychology Today,* 2, no. 4, April 1976, pp. 13, 19; C. LeGrand 'Rape and rape laws' *California Law Review,* 61, no. 3, 1973, p. 919; S. Griffin 'Rape: the all American crime' *Ramparts,* 10, no. 3, 1971, pp. 26-35; J. Gillott 'Rape: the unthinkable crime that needs thinking about' *Cosmopolitan* July/August 1976, pp. 87-89; P. Lakes-Wood 'The victim in a forcible rape case' *The American Criminal Law Review,* 2, Pt. 2, 1973, pp. 335-54; Boston Women's Health Collective *Our Bodies Ourselves* 1973, p. 92; S. Weis and S. Borges 'Victimology and rape: the case of the legitimate victim' *Issues in Criminology,* 8, no. 2, 1973, p. 71.

9. *Parliamentary Debates* vol. 911, 1976, c. 1993.

10. From the written evidence submitted to the Advisory Group on the Law Relating to Rape 1975 by the Medical Women's Federation and Justices Clerks' Society.

11. From the written evidence of The Association of Police Surgeons of Great Britain.

12. From the written evidence submitted by Women in the Media.

13. Excerpts from the written evidence submitted by Justice, The Royal College of Obstetricians and Gynaecologists and The Royal College of Psychiatrists in *British Journal of Psychiatry* News and Notes, December 1975, pp. 7-8.

14. *Parliamentary Debates* vol. 281, 3rd Series, 1883, c. 403.

15. *Parliamentary Debates* vol. 911, 5th Series, 1976, c. 1982-84.

16. *R v Lawrence and Another* (1977) Crim. Law Rev. p. 493.

17. *R v Leroy Mills* [1979] 68 Crim. App. Rep. at 327.

18. Rape Counselling and Research Project *Second Annual Report* 1978, p. 11.

19. Old Bailey, 18 April 1976.

20. Victoria Law Court Birmingham, 26 February 1980.

21. Manchester Crown Court, 25-26 November 1975.

22. Old Bailey, 11 & 12 August 1977.

23. Victoria Law Court, Birmingham, 26 February 1980.

24. S. Freud 'Contributions to the psychology of love, the taboo of virginity', 1918; in *Collected Papers* (1954) p. 217.

25. A. F. Blum and P. McHugh 'The social ascription of motives' *American Sociological Review,* 36, no. 11, 1971, pp. 98-109.

26. J. Tweedie *The Guardian* 3 January 1972.

27. Manchester Crown Court, February 1980.

28. Manchester Crown Court, March 1980.

29. K. Huntington 'Forensic gynaecology' *The Practitioner,* 216, no. 1295, 1976, pp. 519-28; 'Rape and the laboratory' *British Medical Journal* 15 July 1978, p. 154. See also: D. Paul (1975).

Select Bibliography

Aaby, P. (1977) 'Engels and women' *Critique of Anthropology,* 3, nos 9 and 10, pp. 25-54.

Abou Zeid, A. (1965) 'Honour and shame among the Bedouins of Egypt' in J. G. Peristiany (ed.) *Honour and Shame. The Values of Mediterranean Society* London, Weidenfeld and Nicolson.

Acton, W. (1857) *The Functions and Disorders of the Re-productive Organs, in Youth, in Adult Age, and in Advanced Life* London.

Allbutt, T. C. (1899) *A System of Medicine* vol. VIII, London, Macmillan.

Althusser, L. (1971) 'Ideology and ideological state apparatuses' in *Lenin and Philosophy and Other Essays* London, New Left Books, pp. 123-73.

Amir, M. (1971) *Patterns in Forcible Rape* Chicago, University of Chicago Press.

Beck, T. R. (1825) *Elements of Medical Jurisprudence* London, John Anderson.

Blair, L. M. (1977) 'The problem of rape' *Police Surgeon* Spring, p. 16.

Bland, L., Harrison, R., Mort, F., Weedon, C. (1978) 'Relations of reproduction, approaches through anthropology' in *Women Take Issue: Aspects of Women's Subordination* London, Hutchinson, pp. 155-75.

Box, S. (1971) *Deviance, Reality and Society* London, Holt, Rinehart and Winston.

Brazier, R. (1975) 'Reform of sexual offences' *Criminal Law Review* pp. 421-9.

Bromley, P. M. (1976) *Family Law* London, Butterworth.

Burges, S. H. (1978a) *The New Police Surgeon* London, Hutchinson Benham.

Burges, S. H. (1978b) 'The role of the police surgeon in sexual offences' *The Practitioner,* 221, no. 1325, November, pp. 737-42.

Camps, F. E. (1962) 'The medical aspects of the investigation of sexual offences' *The Practitioner,* 189, no. 1129, pp. 31-5.

Carter, R. B. (1853) *On the Pathology and Treatment of Hysteria* London, John Churchill.

Cicourel, A. V. (1968) *The Social Organization of Juvenile Justice* New York, Wiley.

Clarke, M. D. B. (1978) 'General duties of the forensic medical practitioner' *The Practitioner,* 221, no. 1324, October, pp. 597-614.

Clouston, T. S. (1906) *The Hygiene of Mind* London, Methuen.

Cohen, S., Green, S. *et al.* (1978) *The Law and Sexuality* Manchester, Grass Roots Books.

Cominos, P. T. (1963) 'Late-Victorian sexual respectability and the social system' *International Review of Social History,* 8, nos 1 and 2, pp. 18-48, 216-50.

Coward, R. (1980) 'On the universality of the Oedipus complex: debates on sexual division in psychoanalysis and anthropology' *Critique of Anthropology,* 4, no. 15, pp. 5-28.

Coward, R., Lipshitz, S. and Cowie, E. (1976) 'Psychoanalysis and patriarchal structures' in *Papers on Patriarchy* Oxford, Women's Publishing Collective, pp. 6-21.

Cross, R. (1967) *Evidence* London, Butterworth.

Deutsch, H. (1944) *The Psychology of Women* London, Grune & Stratton.

Drysdale, G. R. (1859) *The Elements of a Social Science* (3rd edition) Published anonymously.

Durkheim, E. (1964a) *The Rules of Sociological Method* Glencoe, Free Press.

Durkheim, E. (1964b) *The Division of Labour in Society* New York, Free Press.

East, E.H. (1972) *A Treatise of The Pleas of the Crown,* vol. 1, London, Professional Books. (First published 1803.)

Edholm, F., Harris, O. and Young, K. (1977) 'Conceptualising women' *Critique of Anthropology,* 3, nos 9 and 10, pp. 101-30.

Edwards, S. S. M. (1979) 'Sex crimes in the 19th century' *New Society* 13 September.

Ehrenreich, B. and English, D. (1974) *Complaints and Disorders. The Sexual Politics of Sickness* London, Compendium.

Ehrenreich, B. and English, D. (1979) *For Her Own Good* London, Pluto Press.

Ellis, H. H. (1894) *Man and Woman* London, Walter Scott.

Ellis, H. H. (1930) *Studies in the Psychology of Sex* vols. 1-7, Philadelphia, F. A. Davis and Company.

Ellis, H. H. (1933) *The Psychology of Sex* London, Heinemann.

Engels, F. (1972) *The Origin of the Family, Private Property, and the State* New York, Pathfinder Press.

Engels, F. (1974) *The Condition of the Working Class in England* Great Britain, Panther.

English, P. (1976) 'The husband who rapes his wife' *New Law Journal,* 126, nos 5731-82, p. 1223.

Farr, S. (1815) *Elements of Medical Jurisprudence* London; translated and abridged from *Elementa Medicinae Forensis* by J. Faselius.

Fee, E. (1978) 'Psychology, sexuality, and social control in Victorian England' *Social Science Quarterly,* 58, no. 4, pp. 632-46.

Forbes, G. (1972) 'Sexual offences' *The Practitioner,* 209, no. 1251, pp. 287-93.

Foucault, M. (1972) *The Archaeology of Knowledge* London, Tavistock.

Foucault, M. (1978) *The History of Sexuality* vol. 1, An Introduction, New York, Pantheon Books.

Foucault, M. (1979) 'Truth and power' *Critique of Anthropology*, 4, nos 13 and 14, pp. 131-44.

Freud, S. (1954) *Collected Papers* vols I-V, Oxford, Hogarth Press.

Freud, S. (1974) *New Introductory Lectures* Oxford, Hogarth Press.

Gagnon, J. H. (1965-6) 'Female child victims of sex offenders' *Social Problems*, 13, nos 1-4, pp. 176-92.

Gagnon, J. H. and Simon, W. (1973) *Sexual Conduct* Chicago, Aldine.

Gardner, A. K. (1856) *The Causes and Curative Treatment of Sterility* New York.

Garfinkle, A. M., Lefcourt, C. and Schulder, D. B. (1971) 'Women's servitude under law' in R. Lefcourt (ed.) *Law Against The People* New York, Vintage, pp. 105-22.

Geddes, P. and Thomson, J. A. (1899) *The Evolution of Sex* London, Walter Scott.

Gilley, J. (1974) 'How to help the raped' *New Society*, 28, no. 612, 27 June.

Glaister, J. (1945) *Medical Jurisprudence and Toxicology* (8th edition) London, E. & S. Livingstone.

Godelier, M. (1977) *Perspectives in Marxist Anthropology* Cambridge University Press.

Goody, J. (1973) 'Bridewealth and dowry in Africa and Eurasia' in J. Goody and S. Tambiah (eds) *Bridewealth and Dowry* Cambridge University Press, pp. 1-58.

Gorham, D. (1978) 'A "maiden tribute of modern Babylon" re-examined, child prostitution and the idea of childhood in late Victorian England' *Victorian Studies*, 21, no. 3, Spring, pp. 353-79.

Gross, H. (1911) *Criminal Psychology* London, William Heinemann.

Hale, M. (1971) *The History of the Pleas of the Crown* London, Professional Books.

Harrison, B. (1967) 'Underneath the Victorians' *Victorian Studies*, 10, no. 3, pp. 239-62.

Harrison, M. (1962) *Painful Details, Twelve Victorian Scandals* London, Max Parrish.

Hewitt, G. (1872) *Diseases of Women* London, Longmans.

Heydon, J. H. (1975) *Cases and Materials on Evidence* London, Butterworth.

Honore, T. (1978) *Sex Law* London, Duckworth.

Horney, K. (1933) 'Psychogenic factors in functional female disorders' *American Journal of Obstetrics and Gynecology* no. 25, pp. 694-704.

Horney, K. (1967) *Feminine Psychology* London, W. W. Norton.

Howard, R. M. (1954) 'Rape of a wife' *Justice of the Peace*, 118, pp. 99-100.

Hughes, G. (1962) 'Consent in sexual offences' *Modern Law Review*, 25, pp. 672-86.

Kalven, H. and Zeisel, H. (1966) *The American Jury* Chicago, University of Chicago Press.

Katz, S. and Mazur, M. A. (1979) *Understanding the Rape Victim* New York and Oxford, John Wiley.

Kelly, A. and Wilson, C. (1973) *Jack the Ripper* London, Association of Assistant Librarians.

Kinsey, A. C., Pomeroy, W. B., Martin, C. E. and Gebhard, P. H. (1953) *Sexual Behaviour in the Human Female* Philadelphia and London, W. B. Saunders.

Kitsuse, J. I. and Cicourel, A. V. (1963) 'A note on the official uses of statistics' *Social Problems,* 11, no. 2, pp. 131-9.

Knight, B. (1972) *Legal Aspects of Medical Practice* London, Churchill Livingstone.

Knight, B. (1976) 'Forensic problems in practice VIII, sexual offences' *The Practitioner,* 217, no. 1298, pp. 288-90.

Kristeva, J. (1977) *About Chinese Women* London, Marion Boyars.

Lacan, J. (1977a) *Ecrits: A Selection* London, Tavistock.

Lacan, J. (1977b) *The Four Fundamental Concepts of Psycho-Analysis* London, The Hogarth Press.

Levi-Strauss, C. (1969) *The Elementary Structures of Kinship* London, Eyre and Spottiswoode.

Lewis, I. (1966) 'Spirit possession and deprivation cults' *Man* 1, no. 3, pp. 307-36.

Lombroso, C. and Ferraro, C. (1895) *The Female Offender* London, Fisher Unwin.

Mackesy, A. N. (1956) 'The criminal law and the woman seducer' *Criminal Law Review* pp. 446-56, 529-42.

Mackintosh, M. (1977) 'Reproduction and patriarchy: a critique of Claude Meillassoux "Femmes, Greniers et Capitaux" ' *Capital and Class* Pt 2, pp. 119-27.

MacNaughton Jones, H. (1884) *Diseases of Women* London, Baillière, Tindall, and Cox.

MacNaughton Jones, H. (1893) 'Uterine reflexes: distant lesions and remote symptoms due to uterine irritation' *Provincial Medical Journal,* 12, no. 138, pp. 282-5.

MacNaughton Jones, H. (1894) 'A gynaecological question of importance in forensic medicine relating to the hymen' *Provincial Medical Journal,* 13, no. 148, pp. 193-5.

MacNaughton Jones, H. (1900) 'The bearing of sexual function and disease of the sexual organs on insanity and crime' *Journal of Mental Science* no. 46, October.

Maidment, S. (1978) 'Rape between spouses? — A case for reform?' *Family Law,* 8, no. 3, pp. 87-90.

Male, G. E. (1816) *An Epitome of Judicial or Forensic Medicine; for the use of Medical Men, Coroners and Barristers* London.

Marcus, S. (1971) *The Other Victorians* Corgi Books.

Marshall, F. H. A. (1910) *The Physiology of Reproduction* London, Longmans.

Masters, W. H. and Johnson, V. E. (1966) *Human Sexual Response* London, J. & A. Churchill.

Maudsley, H. (1870) *Body and Mind* London, Macmillan.

McCann, F. (1926-7) 'Some cases of medico-legal interest in the practice of gynaecology' *Transactions of the Medico-legal Society,* 21, pp. 83-102.

McLay, D. (1975) 'Sexual assault. The role of the police surgeon' *Police Surgeon* no. 8, October.

Meillassoux, C. (1972) 'From reproduction to production. A Marxist approach to economic anthropology' *Economy and Society,* 1, no. 1, pp. 93-105.

Mercier, C. A. (1890) *Sanity and Insanity* London, Walter Scott.

Mercier, C. A. (1899) 'Vice, crime and insanity' in Allbutt (1899) pp. 248-94.

Miers, D. R. (1974) 'Victim participation in criminal behaviour' *Anglo-American Law Review,* 3, pp. 86-97.

Miller, J. Baker (1974) *Psychoanalysis and Women* London, Penguin.

Mitra, C. L. (1979) '. . . For she has no right or power to refuse her consent' *Criminal Law Review* p. 558.

Napley, D. (1974) 'The law, the press, and public opinion' *Law Society Gazette,* 712, no. 45, 4 December.

Newman, T. L. (1889) *Miscellanies. Vol. III, Essays, Tracts or Addresses, Political and Social* London, Kegan Paul, Trench.

Nokes, G. D. (1962) *An Introduction to Evidence* London, Sweet and Maxwell.

Norman, C. (1899) 'Systemised delusional insanity' in Allbutt (1899) pp. 389-99.

O'Donovan, K. (1978) 'The legal recognition of the value of housework' *Family Law,* 8, no. 1.

O'Laughlin, B. (1974) 'Why M'Bum women do not eat chicken' in Rosaldo and Lamphere (eds).

Ormerod, J. A. (1899) 'Hysteria' in Allbutt (1899) pp. 88-127.

Panken, S. (1967) 'On masochism: a re-evaluation' *Psychoanalytical Review,* 54, pp. 527-41.

Paris, J. A. and Fonblanque, J. (1823) *Medical Jurisprudence* London, W. Phillips.

Parker, T. (1970) *The Twisting Lane* Panther Modern Society.

Paul, D. M. (1975) 'The medical examination in sexual offences' *Medicine, Science and Law,* 15, no. 3, pp. 154-62.

Pearsall, R. (1969) *The Worm in the Bud* London, Penguin.

Playfair, G. (1969) *Six Studies in Hypocrisy* London, Secker and Warberg.

Playfair, W. S. (1896) 'The nervous system in relation to gynaecology' in T. C. Allbutt and W. S. Playfair (eds). *A System of Gynaecology* London.

Polson, C. J. and Gee, D. J. (1973) *The Essentials of Forensic Medicine* Oxford, Pergamon Press.

Poore, G. V. (1901) *A Treatise on Medical Jurisprudence* London, John Murray.

Power, D. J. (1976) 'Sexual deviation and crime' *Medicine, Science and Law,* 16, no. 2, pp. 111-28.

Puxon, M. (1967) *The Family and the Law* London, MacGibbon and Kee.

Puxon, M. (1979) 'Sexual violence — fact and fantasy' *Medico-Legal Journal,* 47, Part Two, pp. 55-78.

Radzinowicz, L. (1957) *Sexual Offences* London, Macmillan.

Radzinowicz, L. (1961) *In Search of Crimonology* London, Heinemann.

Ringrose, C. A. D. (1975) 'Sociological, medical and legal aspects of rape' *Criminal Law Quarterly* no. 4.

Rock, P. (1973) *Deviant Behaviour* London, Hutchinson.

Rock, P. (1979) 'Another common-sense conception of deviancy' *Sociology,* 13, no. 1, pp. 75-88.

Rosen, I. (1979) *Sexual Deviation* Oxford, Oxford University Press.

Rosaldo, M. Z. and Lamphere, L. (1974) (eds) *Women, Culture and Society* Stanford, Calif., Stanford University Press.

Ross, S. (1909) 'Menstruation in relation to insanity' *Journal of Mental Science,* 60, April, pp. 278-80.

Routh, C. H. (1886) 'On the etiology and diagnosis, considered specially from a medico-legal point of view, of those cases of nymphomania which lead women to make false charges against their medical attendants' *British Gynaecological Journal* 8 December, pp. 485-511.

Routh, C. H. (1889) 'In a case of epileptoid seizure in which erotic symptoms were manifested to a marked degree' *British Gynaecological Journal* 10 April.

Rubin, G. (1975) 'The traffic in women: notes on the "political economy" of sex' in R. Reiter (ed.) *Toward an Anthropology of Women* New York and London, Monthly Review Press, pp. 157-210.

Saadawi, N. El. (1980) *The Hidden Face of Eve: Women in the Arab World* London, Zed Press.

Sachs, A. and Wilson J. Hoff (1978) *Sexism and the Law* Oxford, Martin Robertson.

Samuels, A. (1978) 'Sentencing the sex offender' *New Law Journal,* 1282.

Savage, G. H. (1884) *Insanity and Allied Neuroses* London.

Scully, D. and Bart, P. (1973) 'A funny thing happened on the way to the orifice: women in gynaecology textbooks' *American Journal of Sociology,* 78, no. 4, pp. 1045-9.

Schwendinger, J. & H. (1974) 'Rape myths in legal, theoretical, and everyday practice' *Crime and Social Justice, A Journal of Radical Criminology,* 1, Spring/Summer, pp. 18-26.

Senelick, T. (1979) 'Lady killers and ladykillers: recent popular Victoriana' *Victorian Studies,* 21, no. 4.

Shanin, T. (1972) 'Units of sociological analysis' *Sociology,* 6, pp. 351-64.

Skultans, V. (1975) *Madness and Morals: Ideas on Insanity in the Nineteenth Century* London, Routledge and Kegan Paul.

Smith, D. (1978) ' "K. is mentally ill": the anatomy of a factual account' *Sociology,* 12, pp. 23-53.

Smith, J. C. and Hogan, B. (1973) *Criminal Law: Cases and Materials* London, Butterworth.

Smith, J. G. (1824) *The Principles of Forensic Medicine* London, T. & G. Underwood.

Soothill, K., Gibbens T. C. N. and Jack, A. (1976) 'Rape: a 22 year cohort study' *Medicine, Science and Law,* 16, no. 1, p. 69.

Spratling, E. J. (1895) *Medical Record,* 48, p. 442.

Summers, R. (1978) 'The history of the police surgeon' *Police Surgeon* no. 14, pp. 46-58.

Sykes, G. M. and Matza, D. (1957) 'Techniques of neutralization: a theory of delinquency' *American Sociological Review,* 22, no. 2, p. 665.

Tait, R. L. (1877) *Diseases of Women* Birmingham.

Tait, R. L. (1883) *Diseases of the Ovaries* Birmingham.

Tait, R. L. (1889) *Diseases of Women and Abdominal Surgery* Leicester, Richardson.

Tait, R. L. (1894) 'An analysis of the evidence in seventy consecutive cases of charges made under the new Criminal Law Amendment Act' *Provincial Medical Journal,* 13, 1 May, pp. 226-33.

Tanner, T. H. (1864) *The Signs and Diseases of Pregnancy* London.

Taylor, A. S. (1865) *The Principles and Practice of Medical Jurisprudence* London, John Churchill.

Taylor, G. R. (1953) *Sex in History* London, Thames and Hudson.

Taylor, G. R. (1958) *The Angel Makers* London, Heinemann.

Taylor, L. (1972) 'The significance and interpretation of replies to motivational questions: the case of sex offenders' *Sociology,* 6, no. 1, pp. 23-39.

Thomas, K. V. (1959) 'The double standard' *Journal of the History of Ideas,* 20, no. 2, pp. 195-216.

Thompson, E. P. (1970) *The Making of the English Working Class* Harmondsworth, Penguin.

Tilt, E. J. (1850) *On the Diseases of Menstruation and Uterine Inflammation* London, J. & A. Churchill.

Tilt, E. J. (1851) *On the Preservation and Health of Women at the Critical Periods of Life* London, J. & A. Churchill.

Tilt, E. J. (1853) *Diseases of Women and Ovarian Inflammation* London.

Tilt, E. J. (1862) *On Uterine and Ovarian Inflammation* London, J. & A. Churchill.

Tilt, E. J. (1863) *A Handbook of Uterine Therapeutics* London, J. & A. Churchill.

Tilt, E. J. (1882) *The Change of Life in Health and Disease* London, J. & A. Churchill.

Traill, T. S. (1840) *Outline of a course of Lectures on Medical Jurisprudence* Edinburgh, Adam and Charles Black.

Trimmer, E. (1978) *Basic Sexual Medicine* London, Heinemann Pitman Press.

Tuke, D. H. (1892) *A Dictionary of Psychological Medicine.*

Walkowitz, J. (1977) 'The making of an outcast group: prostitutes and working women in nineteenth-century Plymouth and Southampton' in M. Vicinus (ed.) *A Widening Sphere. Changing Roles of Victorian Women* Bloomington, Indiana University Press.

West, C. (1856-8) *Lectures of the Diseases of Women* Pt. II, London.

Wigmore, J. H. (1940) *A Treatise on the Anglo-American System of Evidence in Trials at Common Law* (3rd edition) vol. III, Boxton, Little Brown.

Williams, G. L. (1955) *The Proof of Guilt* (1st edition) London, Stevens.

Williams, G. L. (1962) 'Corroboration — sexual cases' *Criminal Law Review* pp. 662-71.

Williams, G. L. (1963) *The Proof of Guilt* (3rd edition, revised) London, Stevens.

Williams, J. E., Hall, (1977) 'Serious heterosexual attack' *Medicine, Science and Law,* 17, no. 2, pp. 140-6.

Wood, A. D. (1973-74) 'The fashionable diseases: women's complaints and their treatment in nineteenth century America' *The Journal of Interdisciplinary History,* 4, no. 1, pp. 25-52.

Young, K. and Harris, O. (1976) 'The subordination of women in cross cultural perspective' in *Papers on Patriarchy* London, Women's Publishing Collective, pp. 38-52.

Index